Victory in
Tripoli

Victory in Tripoli

*How America's War with the Barbary
Pirates Established the U.S. Navy
and Built a Nation*

Joshua E. London

WILEY

John Wiley & Sons, Inc.

This book is printed on acid-free paper. ∞

Published by John Wiley & Sons, Inc., Hoboken, New Jersey
Published simultaneously in Canada

For general information about our other products and services, please contact our Customer Care Department within the United States at (800) 762-2974, outside the United States at (317) 572-3993 or fax (317) 572-4002.

Wiley also publishes its books in a variety of electronic formats. Some content that appears in print may not be available in electronic books. For more information about Wiley products, visit our web site at www.wiley.com.

Library of Congress Cataloging-in-Publication Data:

London, Joshua E.
    Victory in Tripoli : how America's war with the Barbary pirates established the U.S. navy and built a nation
        p.   cm.   / Joshua E. London.
    ISBN- 978-1-63026-037-8
    ISBN-10 0-471-44415-4 (cloth: alk. paper)
        1. United States—History—Tripolitan War, 1801–1805—Naval operations. 2. Eaton, William, 1764–1811. 3. Generals—United States—Biography. 4. Marines—United States—Biography. 5. Pirates—Africa, North—History—19th century.   I. Title.
    E335.L66   2005
    973.4'7—dc22   2005003025

Printed in the United States of America

10 9 8 7 6 5 4 3 2

To my wife, Anna Sarah, in recognition of the cheerful patience and fortitude of spirit with which she endured the terror of the Barbary pirates

To the United States, they believe they can dictate terms. Why should they not? Or why should they believe it will ever be otherwise? They have seen nothing in America to controvert the opinion. And all our talk of resistance and reprisal, they view as the swaggering of a braggadocio. . . . But whatever stratagem may be used to aid our measures, it is certain, that there is not access to the permanent friendship of these states, without paving the way with gold or cannon balls; and the proper question is, which method is preferable.

—William Eaton, U.S. consul to the
Regency of Tunis, 1799–1803

Contents

Photo section begins on page 133.

Acknowledgments

When I began this project, I had no idea just how much time and energy it would consume. Had I known in advance that the Barbary pirates would become a constant companion in my life for close to three years—permanently taking up several shelves of my library, engulfing my desk, overwhelming my filing cabinet, remaining an ever-present specter taunting and absorbing me for the first two and a half years of my marriage—I might not have bothered. Now that it is done, however, I am terribly pleased that I did.

I owe a very special and very deep debt of gratitude to Anna Sarah, my love, my friend, my wife, my researcher, my translator, my proofreader, and my best, and perhaps harshest, critic.

I have also been greatly encouraged by my parents: my mother, Bonne, who has never been critical of anything I have written, and my father, Martin, who has.

There are several people without whom this book would really never have been written. My friend and former boss, Josh Gilder, who got the ball rolling by passing my name along to the brilliant and indefatigable literary agent James C. Vines. Jimmy pushed and prodded me to come up with a good idea for a book. My initial efforts lacked inspiration, but within a couple of weeks my good friend and former colleague, the talented writer Mark Hemingway, suggested the idea that led to this book.

I would also like to thank my patient and focused editors at John Wiley & Sons, Thomas Miller and Teryn Johnson. It was Tom's decision to run with my book, and it was Teryn's task to make it readable. I hope Tom's decision proves as wise for both of us as Teryn's line editing proved for the manuscript. Thanks also to the many other hands on deck at Wiley, including senior production editor Devra K. Nelson.

My good friend the writer, author, speechwriter, and surfer Matthew Robinson gave me editorial and moral support from proposal writing to final draft. Without his wise counsel, fierce loyalty, and editorial brilliance, both I and this book would have suffered.

Throughout the course of this project I received assistance, guidance, and consultation from many different people around the world. While I couldn't possibly remember, much less thank, all of them, I did want to make special mention of those whose efforts were especially helpful: Professor Marshall J. Breger of Catholic University; Moncef Fakhfakh, the director general of the Tunisian National Archives; scholar and translator Asma Moalla; John Rhodehamel and Lita Garcia of the Huntington Library and Art Collection; Ambassador Richard Parker of the Middle East Institute; Professor Robert Allison of Suffolk University; Dr. Meyrav Wurmser of the Hudson Institute; Dr. Robert Book; Elizabeth Book; Seth M. Kronemer of the Howard University School of Law; Harris Vederman; Marc Radasky; and the obliging staffs of the Library of Congress, the Navy Historical Center, and the National Archives at College Park.

Introduction:
"Will Nothing Rouse My Country!"

A FRIGATE OF twenty-four guns sailed toward the harbor of Algiers, flying the American flag, at four o'clock in the afternoon of Wednesday, September 17, 1800. The Algerine captain of the port made his way out of the harbor to the ship in the bay, accompanied by U.S. consul general Richard O'Brien. They hailed her, boarded her, and identified her. She was the USS *George Washington*, commanded by Captain William Bainbridge—the first U.S. warship ever to enter the Mediterranean Sea.

But rather than bringing war to a known pirates' lair, Captain Bainbridge was delivering part of the long-overdue tribute promised to Dey Bobba Mustafa, the ruler of Algiers, as well as a consignment of commercial goods, including coffee, tea, sugar, and fish. Captain Bainbridge, like many in the nascent U.S. Navy, took a dim view of paying protection money to pirates; he considered the mission an avoidable blow to the honor of both his ship and his country. Nonetheless, he was pleased at the chance to strut American naval power in the region and eager to convey American vitality.

The diplomatic situation in North Africa at this time was complex and confused, and American prestige was running particularly low. To protect a vigorous maritime trade in the Mediterranean Sea, the United States had become ensnared in an established system of tribute and bribery to piratical Muslim overlords entrenched in their fortified seats thousands of miles from America's shores. Lacking in funds, behind in contracted obligations, caught up in European as well as domestic politics, seemingly impoverished of resolve, and obviously devoid of the means to project force in the region, America's diplomatic relations were uncertain. Longing for some exhibition of their nation's strength, resolve, and dignity, the U.S. government hoped the sight of the *George Washington* would help raise America's standing in Barbary and go some way toward persuading the various deys, beys, and pashas who ruled this region that the United States of America would not be mistreated with impunity.

The *George Washington* was a former merchantman that had been purchased by the U.S. government in 1798 and converted for war. This good, clean, powerful-looking warship had a well-trained, finely tuned, orderly complement under obviously capable command.

Captain William Bainbridge was a bright, six-foot-tall, dark-haired, twenty-six-year-old Princeton man, who had served with distinction in the merchant marine. He had been rewarded with responsibility very early in his seafaring career and had single-handedly quelled two mutinies. Despite having been too young to serve in the Continental Navy, Bainbridge had an easy time moving from the merchant marine to the U.S. Navy, entering as a lieutenant in 1798. Even though he had commanded the only U.S. warship compelled to surrender to the enemy during America's Quasi-War with France (1798–1801), his naval career was not retarded by the affair; upon release he was promoted to master commandant in 1799. He acquitted himself well, earning his captaincy in 1800. Bainbridge was eager to make a good showing of America's first naval presence in the Mediterranean, despite the nature of his mission.

The next morning, Consul O'Brien visited the ship and greeted Captain Bainbridge warmly. After taking stock of the diplomatic situation, however, O'Brien was not altogether impressed by his government's efforts. He later wrote to Secretary of State John Marshall that, as "we are upwards of 110 thousand dollars in debt to the [prominent Jewish money-lending house of] Bacris &

Bushnach of Algiers, we are nearly 2 years in arrears in our annuity to the regency," he was sorry to "find that few articles is sent on the annuities and no cash to pay our debts; we should be more punctual, if not we shall experience difficulties." Although greatly pleased at the arrival of Captain Bainbridge in a suitably impressive man-of-war, Consul General O'Brien had hoped his government would have taken his dispatches more seriously. "You had," he complained, "[a] full statement of our affairs in the last dispatches you received." He added that only one cargo to the regency of Tunis had been received to date, none to Tripoli, plus the pasha of Tripoli now "*demands* an extra present" that the government had still done nothing about. "Our Barbary affairs," he continued, "requires great attention, the[y] have been much neglected. I hope the other articles . . . will be attended to . . . with *speed*."

O'Brien was also disappointed and annoyed to find that despite several requests and appeals, his government had not seen fit to relieve him of duty. Like the other consuls, Richard O'Brien had become deeply depressed by the situation. "I am heartily tired of Barbary . . . I should think any employment in the U.S. should be preferred to our despised rank in Barbary," he wrote to William Eaton, the U.S. consul to Tunis.

In this humor, O'Brien and Bainbridge commiserated on their government's apparent misunderstanding and mishandling of the political and diplomatic situation in North Africa. Both men wished for a more active and energetic policy toward the Barbary pirates, O'Brien because of his experience in the region and Bainbridge because his sense of honor demanded it. At stake was the credibility and reputation of the United States of America and the protection of her maritime trade in the region. Neither man was prepared, however, for what was about to transpire.

On Friday, September 19, Consul O'Brien and Captain Bainbridge received a stirring surprise. Dey Bobba Mustafa informed them that as the United States was in arrears on its commitments to him, he would grant them the honor and opportunity to please him by performing a small service. Dey Mustafa required the use of the *George Washington* for the purpose of transporting an embassy to the Ottoman sultan in Constantinople, Turkey.

Consul General O'Brien declined without hesitation, citing the limitations of Captain Bainbridge's orders: America had no direct treaty or representation with the Ottoman Empire, and Bainbridge would not be able to properly protect the dey's cargo because the ship was permitted by their government to engage only with enemy French vessels, not Portuguese or Neapolitan—the current enemies of Algiers. The dey was furious. He could not understand why his request was being rebuffed; England, Spain, and France had all allowed their frigates to be used in this manner before. The matter was left unresolved, while O'Brien and Bainbridge commiserated.

The request sounded perfectly outrageous to Captain Bainbridge, and he pledged himself to get out of the dubious honor at all costs. He requested and was granted an audience with Dey Mustafa, during the course of which he endeavored through the dragoman to explain why the *George Washington* could not perform the dey's mission. Mustafa remained surprised by this curt refusal, and not a little annoyed, but acquiesced after the English consul volunteered an English warship that had that day entered Algiers.

After some days had passed, however, Dey Mustafa changed his mind. He rejected the English consul's offer and demanded that the American ship serve as his carrier. Besides his desire to repay the aggravation caused by the initial American refusal of this "honor," Mustafa did not entirely trust England with the money and treasure he planned to send. As he had recently made peace with France, Britain's archenemy, he supposed that an English ship might take this opportunity to punish him. Therefore, Dey Bobba Mustafa decided that he would simply impress the *George Washington* into service for his mission.

As the dey explained to Captain Bainbridge and Consul O'Brien, "You pay me tribute, by which you become my slaves. I have, therefore, a right to order you as I may think proper."

O'Brien and Bainbridge protested this proposed usurpation and emphatically refused to comply in any way. The thought of the USS *George Washington* being compelled into service by a shaggy, shabby, piratical Turk was just too much for them to bear. They adamantly refused the dey's "request" and objected and lobbied at length, trying again every argument and calling upon every resource at their disposal in their effort to prevent this hideous affront to the honor of the United States of America. They spent several days in intense and heated negotiations, but to no avail.

Finally, the dey issued an ultimatum: either they accept this duty or the ship would be blasted to bits and sunk where she rested. Although escape was feasible, the hazard was deemed too great and the likelihood of escape too small—besides the harbor guns, various ships from among the dey's corsair fleet had recently returned to port. Just to make sure O'Brien and Bainbridge understood the position they were in, Dey Bobba Mustafa matter-of-factly added that should they refuse his request, he would of course immediately declare war on U.S. commerce and enslave Bainbridge, O'Brien, and the ship's crew of 131 men, as well as any other Americans he might lay his hands on.

As Algiers was deemed the most powerful of the North African states, Dey Mustafa was indeed well positioned to threaten America's valuable trade in the Mediterranean. After all, the dey had already been given three magnificent American-built warships by the United States as part of their previous peace treaty/arms-for-hostage deal; these were the finest vessels in his pirate fleet. Further, Mustafa had been given no credible reason to suppose that the United States was likely to do anything by way of reproof or countermeasure.

Captain Bainbridge was mortified and enraged. As he later complained to Secretary of the Navy Benjamin Stoddert, if his countrymen had any idea of "the easy access of this barbarous coast called Barbary, the weakness of their garrisons, and the effeminacy of their people, I am sure they would not be long tributary to so pitiful a race of infidels." Despite such impotent seething, however, Bainbridge was forced to concede that the dey *was* essentially correct and that there was in fact nothing he nor O'Brien could do.

In the end, both O'Brien and Bainbridge agreed that their current predicament was unavoidable, part and parcel of the unfortunate and ill-considered policy the United States had chosen to adopt in dealing with the Barbary pirates. Bainbridge later reported his decision to the secretary of the navy:

> The unpleasant situation in which I am placed must convince you that I have no alternative left but compliance or a renewal of hostilities against our commerce. The loss of the frigate and the fear of slavery for myself and crew were the least circumstances to be apprehended; but I knew our valuable commerce in these seas would fall a sacrifice to the corsairs of this power, as we have no cruisers to protect it. Enclosed is the correspondence between Richard O'Brien, Esq., consul-general, and myself on the subject of the embassy; by which you will see that I had no choice in acting, but was governed by the tyrant within whose power I had fallen. I hope I may never again be sent to Algiers with *tribute*, unless I am authorized to deliver it from the mouth of our cannon. I trust that my conduct will be approved of by the President, for, with every desire to act right, it has caused me many unpleasant moments.

The outrage did not end there, however, as the dey further insisted that the *George Washington* sail to Constantinople under the red pennant of Algiers rather than the American Stars and Stripes.

Captain Bainbridge protested vehemently. O'Brien tried to explain that such a measure was entirely against protocol and would effectively and diplomatically take the ship out of legal commission of the United States Navy. A long discussion followed, precedents were examined at length, and it was pointed out to Bainbridge that France and Spain had both allowed the Algerine flag to be struck atop their mainmasts and that other nations had done so before as well. Bainbridge bristled under what seemed increasingly inevitable. At length, he announced

that as he was compelled to this endeavor anyway, he would cease
his objections.

As the ship's final preparations were still under way, however,
Bainbridge's sense of justice and patriotism kicked in. Once again
he refused to hoist the Algerine flag to the mainmast. At this
juncture, on Thursday, October 9, 1800, at around 2 P.M., a contingent of armed Algerine naval personnel boarded the *George
Washington* and proceeded—ignoring protocol and blind to the
protests of the American officers—to send one of their number
up the maintop with the red Algerine flag in hand. The American
flag was taken down and the Algerine flag was fixed in its place.
Satisfied with the deliberateness of their work, the boarding party
left the ship. The deed was done.

On October 19, the USS *George Washington* fired seven guns
in salute, the compliment was answered by the dey's harbor fortification, and the ship sailed out of the harbor. Many of the
American officers were demoralized and depressed; as Captain
Bainbridge reported in his log, "some tears fell at this instance of
national humility."

As the ship sailed out to sea, Consul General O'Brien feared
for the safety of American interests throughout Barbary.
Although he hoped Bainbridge's acquiescence would help save
the U.S.-Algerine peace, he recognized that he had just overseen
a diplomatic debacle for his country, a crushing blow to his
nation's honor, and the degradation of American prestige
throughout Europe. American affairs in Barbary were already in
shambles; this outrage merely demonstrated to the American
people how bad the situation truly was.

"Genius of My country!" wrote an outraged and despondent
William Eaton, the U.S. consul to the neighboring regency of
Tunis, to the secretary of state when he learned of the USS *George
Washington* affair. "How art thou prostrate! Hast thou not yet one
son whose soul revolts, whose nerves convulse, blood vessels
burst, and heart indignant swells at thoughts of such debase-
ment?" Eaton, heavy of hand and doubtless furrowed of brow,
continued:

Shade of Washington! Behold thy orphan'd sword hang on a slave—A voluntary slave, and serve a *pirate!* . . . Shall Tunis also lift his thievish arm, smite our scarred cheek, then bid us kiss the rod! *This is the price of peace!* But if we will have peace at such a price, recall me, and send a slave, accustomed to abasement, to represent the nation—And furnish ships of war, and funds and slaves to his support, and our immortal shame. History shall tell that the United States first volunteered a ship of war, equipped, a carrier for a pirate. . . . Frankly I own, I would have lost the peace, and been impaled myself rather than yielded this concession. Will nothing rouse my country!

Like his fellow consuls Richard O'Brien (consul to Algiers and consul general to the Barbary Coast) and James Leander Cathcart (consul to the regency of Tripoli), William Eaton disagreed profoundly with the policy of appeasement that the United States had adopted in its dealings with Barbary. He had come to despair of the lackadaisical manner in which his government seemed determined to continue its presence in the region. Although anxious to be rid of his consular duties and return home to his family, Eaton was eager to advance a scheme that would, he hoped, right the wrongs the national honor had been continually forced to suffer and set his country on a more dignified course with the Barbary pirates. His plan was to reverse the roles of diplomacy in the region by taking the fight directly to the piratical regimes. In this effort, the disgraceful affair of the USS *George Washington* would prove significant.

After Captain William Bainbridge completed Dey Mustafa's errand, he and the *George Washington* returned home, reaching Philadelphia on April 19, 1801. From there, he traveled to Washington, D.C., the new capital of the federal government, to report directly to the president.

Bainbridge returned to find the capital in heated activity. President John Adams of the Federalist Party had lost reelection by eight electoral votes to the anti-Federalist Thomas Jefferson of the Democratic-Republican Party. For the duration of the Adams administration, the Federalists had been working hard to maintain their position and protect their territory. Captain

Bainbridge's detailed report of his humiliation would outrage the nation and set in motion a flurry of furious goings-on in Washington. It would also set the stage for Thomas Jefferson's war against the terrorism of piracy in the Mediterranean Sea.

Although perhaps only half-remembered in the form of schoolboy adventure or folkloric historiography, the exploits of William Eaton on "the Shores of Tripoli" and Thomas Jefferson's war against the "Barbary pirates" form an unusual yet significant part of American history. The story of America's struggle against the terror of piracy in the Mediterranean stands as testament to the essential American attributes that have given rise to American exceptionalism: the problem-solving mind-set of the individual overcoming life's difficulties through brains and talent, faith and strength of purpose, and guts and perseverance. The United States of America, while still in national adolescence, embarked on a transoceanic adventure against a crafty and entrenched foe— an undertaking that proved one of the defining challenges of the young Republic.

After the thirteen colonies declared their independence in 1776, America was forced to grapple over the next forty years with the pirates of the Barbary States. While this period of American history is generally dominated by the story of America's independence, and by her direct struggles with England, France, and the politics of Europe, the Barbary dimension is, oddly, often ignored or considered peripheral. Yet America's fight against Barbary piracy was in many ways a direct extension and indeed another dimension of this same story.

As the western Mediterranean had over the centuries become the backwater frontier of the battles between crescent and cross, the rationalism, progress, and industry of the latter had in many respects outpaced and overshadowed that of the former. This was particularly so in North Africa, where the individual and collective history of the Maghrebi states clouded aspirations of peaceful commercial enterprise. The ravages of war and the exigencies of survival pushed the Muslim North Africans into permanent battle mode, and the glory of jihad was better known, and more devotedly sought, than the long-term benefits of a stable, liberal, and egalitarian regime. But the rulers of the Maghreb soon discovered the ease with which specific periodic interruptions in their ongoing war against Christendom could be used to improve their domestic standing—and fatten their treasuries. By establishing peace treaties, the Barbary potentates were able to extract large sums and substantial tribute from the great powers of Christian Europe.

The stronger powers of this Old World, such as England, France, and Spain, soon learned that appeasing the pirates with cash and bribes could serve them well, both commercially and politically. This unholy alliance in which the mightier nations of Europe specifically perpetuated this North African Islamic brigandage to control economic competition soon became an accepted geopolitical theater in its own right, replete with its own peculiar social norms and diplomatic protocol. By the time the American colonies rebelled from the sovereignty of the British Empire, the Mediterranean market had adjusted to the realities of Muslim piracy as Barbary diplomacy. Although wars were fought and battles were waged, the system of tribute, ransom, and bribery was entrenched and embraced. Naval force was but a tool for improving negotiations, rather than the means for changing the way the game was played.

Though the United States soon found its existence threatened and enfeebled by this Old World game, the nation was powerless, and so was forced to remain a lowly bit-player. From 1776 to 1784 the Americans resigned themselves to hide behind the skirts of their European forebears. When that eventually proved unworkable, the young nation came to realize, in 1785, that it would be necessary to follow the European path of establishing peace treaties with the Barbary States. The contours of this effort became complicated for everyone when the French

Revolution plunged Europe into another major war, one that would continue in hot or cold fashion until 1815. In time, however, the American people resolved to change the rules of this game and establish a new direction for their foreign policy.

In this fashion, the United States' confrontation with Barbary pirates would give birth to the U.S. Navy and the Marine Corps as well as raise serious questions about the president's right to wage undeclared wars, the need to balance defense spending against domestic appropriations, the use of foreign surrogates to fight our battles, and even whether or not it was a good idea to trade arms and money for the release of hostages.

Punctuated with accounts of stirring successes and humiliating failures, unbridled heroism and unfortunate cowardice, the American efforts in Barbary offer an examination of the effectiveness of cross-cultural diplomacy in times of both war and peace, and of diplomatic maneuvering both with and without the backing of force. American exploits in the region also offer an indepth account of naval might as an extension of public policy, and of the nature of military and diplomatic efforts divorced of regular communications or direct executive oversight. The United States resorted to naval blockades, covert operations and night raids, amphibious assaults, brute force, attempted regime change through coup d'état, employment of mercenary forces, and the secret betrayal of a trusted ally.

More fundamental, however, the nation was forced to confront, for the first time, the vital question of, as William Eaton put it, "whether our treasury shall be opened to buy oil of roses to perfume that pirate's beard or our gun batteries to chastise his temerity." Whether to give in to or actively fight against terrorism remains one of the most fundamental decisions of U.S. foreign policy to this day.

1

Barbary Piracy

PRIOR TO THE Revolutionary War, American merchant ships enjoyed British protection on the high seas. Under the terms of Britain's treaties with other nations, including the Barbary States, American ships were issued British-backed passes of safe conduct for the Mediterranean.

These maritime passes operated on a very simple yet effective system that declared the bearer immune from seizure. The pass would be cut in half along a serrated, lateral line, the top of which was issued to a ship's captain, while the bottom half was given to the Barbary regency and copied for distribution to the corsair captains. When a vessel was boarded by pirates, the ship's captain would produce his pass, and if the edges and words or images matched, it was usually accepted—although occasionally a palm or two would need greasing; the prize would be released and allowed to sail away unmolested. Although fraught with abuse and forgery, the system worked reasonably well.

This maritime protection allowed the thirteen American colonies to develop a hearty commerce that was important to long-term economic growth. Both sides of the Mediterranean, the European as well as the North African states, enjoyed American commercial activity in dried and pickled fish, wheat, flour, rice, onions, rum, lumber (oak, pine, and cedar), barrel staves, and beeswax. America's Mediterranean commerce—buying, selling, and shipping—involved close to a hundred American ships, manned by twelve hundred seamen, annually.

With the outbreak of the War of Independence, however, England withdrew this protection from America's merchant ships.

She issued new passes only to British merchants, and she informed the Barbary potentates that the old passes were not to be honored. Thus, American colonial shipping came to a halt—casting a doubtful shadow over the future of American commerce off Europe's western coast, as well as in the Mediterranean.

If American independence was achieved, it seemed highly unlikely that the young Republic would be in any financial or military position to initiate peace treaties in the traditional European fashion of bribery and tribute. Every effort would be made to obtain protection from friendly European powers, but the Europeans were in the habit of paying the pirates' extortion to gain entry to Mediterranean trade, and they were reluctant to extend assistance to a potential economic rival—no matter how friendly. Besides, this diplomatic agenda was being hampered as much at home as from abroad.

The new American states seemed allergic to the idea of vesting any authority in the Confederation, jealously defending every boundary of their own hard-won autonomy. Economically, the situation was no better; no uniform currency existed—and the various state currencies suffered rapid depreciation, both during and after the war. Agriculturally, supply far exceeded demand, and the farmer-debtors faced ruin and foreclosure. Commercially, the merchant class suffered from Old World mercantile exclusion, and the inconsistent tariffs between the states rendered some commercial efforts highly unprofitable.

Externally, this lack of domestic tranquillity made it doubly difficult for America to project permanence, strength, and unity of purpose abroad; this in turn affected the nation's credit, the appearance of commercial soundness, and prospects for diplomatic alliance. Not that domestic relief would have greatly lessened the diplomatic tasks facing the young Republic. Even if America projected political and economic strength, and immediately demonstrated to the world that a democratic republic could be made to work, the diplomatic arena would prove no more inviting. The Old World required more incentive than American commercial ideology or democratic political philosophy to substantiate interests of state.

Unfortunately, the United States found itself surrounded, if not overwhelmed, by the Old World. America's northern border faced Great Britain, while the king of Spain possessed the western lands across the Mississippi and the southern area from Florida to Patagonia. Further, the nations of Europe controlled the commerce of the Americas from Cape Horn in the Tierra del Fuego archipelago to the northern tip of the Hudson's Bay Company holdings.

But the Americans were determined to make their own way, to put their stamp on the world, and to serve as a beacon of liberty to those who labored under the oppression of kings and queens. Maritime trade and freedom of the seas was an essential component of the long-term viability of this independence, and America was determined to maintain it. Thus, the young Republic set out to renew its maritime commerce in the Mediterranean, home to the Barbary States.

From the Atlantic Ocean in the west to the sands of Egypt in the east, the Barbary States stretched for roughly 2,600 miles along the southern shore of the Mediterranean, with hinterlands reaching into the Sahara Desert. The lands of Barbary—modern-day Morocco, Algeria, Tunisia, and Libya—are known to the Arab world as the Maghreb ("Land of Sunset"), denoting Islam's territorial holdings west of Egypt, as opposed to the Mashriq ("Land of the Sunrise").

Historically, these North African territories were identified and defined more by their commercial coastal centers than by rigid geographic frontiers. The urban centers also generally served, at one time or another, as the capital cities. Thus, modern-day Libya used to be called Tripoli, the name of its capital city. Similarly, Algeria was formerly called Algiers, and Tunisia was known as Tunis. Even the kingdom of Morocco derives its name from the city of Marrakech, which has served as its capital at various times over the centuries.

The appellation "Barbary," a European term no longer in wide circulation, comes from uncertain roots, probably either the Greek *barbaros* or the Latin *barbarus*, meaning "barbarian," a term used by the Romans to describe people who spoke neither Latin nor Greek. The early people of this area, and still a significant ethnic minority, thus came to be known as Berbers—even by the Arabs, who derived from it the adjective *barbari* (meaning foreign and primitive).

Despite the ascendancy of the name Berber, these pastoralists always described themselves as *Imazighen*, meaning the noble or freeborn. Although they proved ferocious warriors throughout history, the Berbers have, ironically, been predominantly a conquered people ever since the arrival of the Phoenicians near the end of the second millennium B.C. Through the ages, the Berbers have been conquered, although never wholly subdued, by a variety of empires and nations—the Greeks, the Carthaginians, the Romans, the Vandals, the Byzantines, the Arabs, the Ottoman Turks, and most recently the French. The Arab conquest was the most substantial, however, and the Islamization of the Berbers was total. Through it the Maghreb was permanently entered into the Islamic world, and the people of Barbary became active religious partisans in the Mediterranean frontier.

For close to twelve centuries, the Mediterranean would be the general theater of an intermittent struggle—what the historian Fernand Braudel called a "perpetual brawl"—between the dominions of Islam and Christendom, each considering the other dangerous infidels. Over time, of course, both empires shifted, split, crumbled a bit, reconstituted themselves, suffered setbacks again, and so forth. Although Christendom and Islam continued to clash at regular bloody intervals, the Mediterranean slowly began to enjoy a modicum of commercial cordiality.

During the later Middle Ages, as the historian Bernard Lewis has pointed out, Muslims and Christians around the Mediterranean port cities traded in cloths, manufactured goods, slaves, horses, gold, ivory, ebony, animal skins, salted fish, salt, grain, olive oil, dates, vegetable dyes, and the like, and a variety of maritime rights developed. Europeans were generally allowed to obtain provisions and supplies, were granted local protection while at port, and were always granted shelter from sudden storms. A bureaucracy of customs and duty officials developed in the principal Maghrebi ports, leading to a relatively robust and orderly commercial interaction between Europe and North Africa. Much of this became formalized in various treaties between the Muslim and Christian people.

Throughout this period, religiously motivated piracy was common, and the victims of this intercourse were invariably enslaved, Christian and Muslim alike. Beyond the enslavement of the victims of piracy at sea, the various Barbary powers also conducted slave raids, often carrying away whole towns and villages. Besides the Maghrebi states, enormous slave-trading cultures developed in the Levant, from Cairo all the way to Constantinople, as well as in Christian Spain, France, Tuscany, and Malta.

By the fifteenth century, the relative order and calm of the Mediterranean and the high tide of Islamic success began to subside. Christendom had begun to contain the general threat of Islam and was faring better both culturally and militarily. The Christian age of exploration began in earnest, initially driven, at least in part, according to the historian Bernard Lewis, by the desire to outflank the Turks and discover alternate trade routes. Following and responding to internal European shifts, Portugal and Spain decided to purge the infidel from their lands and advance the Crusade into the North African coast.

Armed with the benefits of advances in military and naval technology as well as strategy, Spain pushed the frontier of battle into the Maghreb itself. In 1509, Spain began to establish presidios, or garrison posts, on strategic coastal points, both to keep the Muslim forces away from the Mediterranean and to enable Spanish commercial interests to have a stronger hand in the Saharan slave trade. In 1510, the Spaniards took a small island just off the coast of Algiers, enabling them to control the port; the island was later permanently connected to the mainland by a causeway.

By this time, however, the Ottoman Empire of Turkey was actively establishing itself as the dominant force in the Islamic world. Before the 1492 fall of Grenada, the last Muslim enclave in Spain, the besieged community of Moors had written to the Ottoman Turks begging for assistance against the Christian Reconquista of the Iberian Peninsula. Responding to this threat from Spain, the Ottomans established a naval presence in the Mediterranean—although they were too involved in their inter-Muslim war with the Safavids of Persia to intervene with significant military force.

The Mamluks of Egypt, a mighty warrior caste of former Ottoman slaves, became concerned with the Ottoman advance, and so established an alliance with the Safavids of Persia against the Ottomans. War quickly followed, resulting in the Ottoman occupation of Syria and Egypt. By 1517, the Ottoman Empire became a fixture of the Mediterranean frontier and the primary champion of Islam against the Christian infidel.

Within a few years, the famed pirate Khayr al-Din Barbarossa of Algiers would invite and establish the Ottoman presence in the Maghreb. Through this aegis, Barbary piracy would come into its own within the context of the Christian Spanish war with the Ottoman Empire.

By 1511, the Spanish dominated the Mediterranean Sea from their coastal fortifications. This infidel subjugation, coupled with the anger of the dispossessed Moors from Spain who had resettled in the Maghreb, initiated a religious fervor that prompted many Muslims to volunteer to fight the Spanish forces. The rulers of Tunis, in an effort to consolidate their authority while defending the faith, welcomed these volunteers.

The brothers Uruj and Khayr al-Din Barbarossa operated as pirates out of modern-day La Goulette, in Tunisia, under the nominal authority of Sultan Muhammad bin al-Hassan. From this base they defended Islam and reaped the material benefits of maritime plunder. The Barbarossa brothers developed a grand reputation for effectiveness, ferocity, and success in Spanish and Italian waters.

By 1515, Uruj Barbarossa, the elder brother, began to establish a personal pirate principality in Jijilli (modern-day Jijel, Algeria), on the eastern promontory of the Gulf of Bijaya (modern-day Bougie). Fearing the worst, the local rulers turned to Spain for protection. Uruj quickly established a new base for his piracy in Algiers and then continued the assault against other cities that had acquiesced to Spanish subjugation. By 1517 he held Algiers, Kabylia, Tanas, and Milyana, and in 1517 successfully invaded Tilimson. Uruj Barbarossa had harnessed the Islamic fervor to rout the infidel forces and was at the height of his greatness.

Spain dispatched troops from her presidio in Oran to put an end to his menace. Overestimating his powers, Uruj suddenly found himself besieged by Spanish forces in Tilimson and cut off from his lines of communication with Algiers. After six months, he fled. The Spanish went in hot pursuit, and in 1518 Uruj and his escort were killed.

Khayr al-Din Barbarossa succeeded his older brother as ruler of Algiers. Having learned from his sibling's mistakes, however, he approached the Ottoman Empire to consolidate his position.

In October or November 1519 Khayr al-Din embraced formal suzerainty of the Ottoman sultan and received two thousand Janissary troops (the loyal elite Turkish soldiery), as well as some artillery, in return. By 1525 he had consolidated and entrenched his position in Algiers.

Over the next eight years, Algiers became a significant naval base in the Christian-Ottoman conflict, and the Algerine pirates became the western division of the Ottoman sultan's naval forces. Khayr al-Din Barbarossa established much of the military organization that was to feature prominently in the Algerine regency and was to serve as the model for the later Ottoman regencies of Tunis and Tripoli. By February 1534, Khayr al-Din had moved to Istanbul and was made *kapudan pasha*, or admiral of the Ottoman fleet. He retired ten years later, in 1544, and died in 1546.

One of the chief accomplishments of Khayr al-Din's life was to turn Algiers into a massive, orderly principality and a strong component of the Ottoman's Mahgrebi empire. From Algiers, the Ottomans were able to repel later Spanish advances and establish an offensive line along much of the Mediterranean coast. The Ottoman Empire conquered Tripoli (in 1551) and then Tunis (in 1574). These three Ottoman regencies were initially treated primarily as strategic locations from which to base military operations against Christendom.

Since the Ottomans viewed their Maghrebi holdings in primarily military terms, Algiers, Tunis, and Tripoli remained engaged in Barbary piracy and official naval operations against Christians for several centuries. Piracy was deemed an acceptable and important component of the *al-jihad fi'l-bahr*, or the holy war at sea, and the *ta'ifa*, or community, of seamen became integral to the Muslim struggle with Christendom. Through piracy, the Ujaq, or Ottoman military forces in Algiers, attained religious prestige and, at times, prosperity. Piracy also provided the Maghreb with all its great military heroes—*ru'asa'* (singular *ra'is*)—or piratical captains, who distinguished themselves by seizing substantial prizes and attacking Christian ships.

Although originally an essential part of the Ujaq, the *ta'ifa* of seamen became a distinct group in their own right by the seventeenth century. This separation emerged because of the importance this *ta'ifa* held for the economy and the state revenues, as well as because of the heavy infiltration of foreigners—adventurers and pirates from all over the Mediterranean and even from parts of Europe. After converting to Islam, most of these foreigners were admitted into the *ta'ifa* of seamen because of their advanced knowledge and skills. These Ottoman regencies thus quickly developed into pirate republics governed by an Ottoman junta of soldiers and seamen.

Not satisfied with Turkish rule, the *ru'asa'* came to assert themselves such that, by 1660, it was they who chose the ruler of the regency. After the last *agha*, or commander in chief, who was made ruler of Algiers was butchered in 1659, the *ru'asa'* acquired the authority to select the officer who would serve as ruler; they gave him the title of *dey*, or "maternal uncle." The dey was theoretically answerable to the military council, but by the eighteenth century that council was stripped of its authority.

Istanbul still sent pashas to "govern" Algiers, but their role became little more than to communicate the Ottoman sultan's wishes to the deys who actually ruled. Although the sultan began in 1711 to bestow the title of pasha directly on the dey, his overlordship was less than absolute. Thus the government and significance of Algiers were very tightly bound with the notion and efficacy of its piratical status in the holy war at sea against the Christian infidel.

As in Algiers, the regency in Tunis was initially ruled by a pasha sent from Istanbul. By 1591, however, the deys of Tunis had rebelled, and eventually Tunis was brought under the virtual control of one of the deys, chosen by the other deys. This power center was soon dichotomized, however, by the office of the *bey*. Charged with control of the tribal communities and the collection of the taxes from the interior, the bey recruited local troops and began to accumulate power and prestige independent of the dey. The office of the bey thus became a rival power base to the dey, and eventually the primary ruler. As with the Algerine deys, the beys of Tunis also had the title of pasha conferred on them by the Ottoman sultan starting around 1704.

In contrast to Algiers, however, Tunis did not make a monopoly of piracy. Privateers were allowed to equip their own ships, run them like a business, and enjoy most of the booty themselves. Although Tunisian pirates were granted protection because of the religious nature of their enterprise, the beys were more interested in European trade and commerce because of the tariffs and customs they routinely charged. Piracy was also protected, and at times encouraged, because of the price the bey could exact for the treaties and truces piratical plunder tended to induce from European countries.

Before the Ottomans, Tripoli was simply a thoroughfare for pilgrims, merchants, and conquering hordes. Its government was essentially modeled after the Ottoman administration in Algiers, although Tripoli did not develop into a deylical or beylical regime as did Algiers and Tunis, respectively. Between 1551 and 1711, Tripoli was ruled directly by pashas appointed by the Ottoman sultan. Then Ahmad (or Hamid) Qaramanli, the chief of the cavalry, usurped power while the pasha was away in Istanbul.

Qaramanli was a fierce and wily man. In order to consolidate his power and prevent power plays and rivalries, he orchestrated the murder of three hundred leading officers in one night. The Ottoman sultan sent two expeditions to restore order but was unable to defeat Qaramanli. Recognizing the security of the Ottoman mantle, Qaramanli made his peace with the sultan, and in return he was appointed pasha in 1712. Ruthlessness with his enemies and the forceful suppression of all dissidents allowed him to secure his office with the locals, and his sponsorship of piracy earned him international prestige with foreign nationals and foreign powers. Except for one eighteen-month episode from July 1793 to January 1795, the Qaramanli dynasty controlled Tripoli until 1835.

Morocco suffered the least in terms of early invasion and occupation, and it had gained enough of a sense of national identity that it resisted Turkish invasion just when the other Barbary States

succumbed. Since the Arab conquest, Morocco had been dominated by a mix of *sharif* dynasties, or rulers who were direct
descendants of the Prophet, and tribal Berber dynasties. By the
fifteenth century, however, tribal dynastic rule had begun to fall
apart as Spain and Portugal successfully advanced into Moroccan
territory. Although Morocco finally pushed out the Portuguese
and began to flourish by the middle of the sixteenth century, the
ruling Sa'adiyan dynasty began to lose control toward the end of
that century due to familial infighting. By 1668, however, Sharif
Mawlay Rashid of the Alawite established his rule—the Alawite
dynasty continues to rule Morocco today—and unified the country with roughly its current borders.

Independence from the Ottoman Empire, however, meant
that Morocco was not forced into the Ottoman jihad, and so it
was free to enjoy a more complex relationship with Europe.
Indeed, even before the eighteenth-century reign of Sultan Sidi
Muhammad bin Abdullah (1757–90), Morocco had begun to use
its piracy as a tool of foreign and trade policies. Consequently, it
was to become the most tame and the least dangerous of the
Barbary pirate states.

In May 1786, Thomas Jefferson, then the U.S. ambassador to
France, and John Adams, then the U.S. ambassador to Britain,
met in London with Sidi Haji Abdul Rahman Adja, the resident
Tripolitan ambassador, to try to negotiate a peace treaty to protect the United States from the threat of Barbary piracy. These
future U.S. presidents questioned the ambassador as to why his
government was so hostile to the new American Republic even
though America had done nothing to provoke any animosity of
any sort. Ambassador Adja answered them, as they reported to
the Continental Congress, "that it was founded on the Laws of
their Prophet, that it was written in their Koran, that all nations
who should not have acknowledged their authority were sinners,

that it was their right and duty to make war upon them wherever they could be found, and to make slaves of all they could take as Prisoners, and that every Musselman who should be slain in Battle was sure to go to Paradise."

The candor of the ambassador from Tripoli was admirable. Although the piratical activities of Barbary had degenerated over the centuries from pure considerations of the glory of jihad to less grandiose visions of booty and state revenues, it is important to remember that the religious foundations of the institution of piracy remained central. Even after it became inordinately common for the pirate *ru'asa'* or even some of their crew to be renegade Europeans, it was still essential that these former Christians "turn Turk" and convert to Islam before they could be accorded any such honors as involvement in *al-jihad fi'l-bahr,* the holy war at sea.

Even after the Barbary rulers eventually began to allow nonreligious commitments to command their strategic use of piracy, the people of Barbary continued to consider the pirates holy warriors. The changes that the religious institution of piracy underwent were natural, if pathological. Just as the concept of jihad is invoked by Muslim terrorists today to legitimize and permit suicide bombings of noncombatants for political gain, so too *al-jihad fi'l-bahr* served as the cornerstone of the Barbary States' interaction with Christendom. The Islamic basis for piracy in the Mediterranean was an old and very well established doctrine.

To Muslims in the heyday of Barbary piracy, there were, at least in principle, only two forces at play in the world, the Dar al-Islam, or House of Islam, and the Dar al-Harb, or House of War. The House of Islam entailed Muslim governance and the unrivaled authority of the *shari'a*, the complex system of Holy Law. The House of War was simply everything that fell outside of the House of Islam—that area of the globe not under Muslim rule, where the infidel resides and rules. For the Muslim, these two houses were perpetually at war—at least until mankind should finally embrace Allah and his teachings as revealed through his Prophet, Muhammad.

The point of jihad is not to convert by force but to remove the obstacles to conversion for the infidels and the apostates, so that they shall either convert or become *dhimmis* (non-Muslims who accept Islamic dominion) and pay the *jizya*, the poll tax. The goal is to bring all of the *Dar al-Harb* into the peace of the *Dar al-Islam*, and to eradicate unbelief. The Qu'ran also promises those who fight in the jihad material rewards—booty and glory— in this world, and the delights of paradise in the next.

Another key aspect of the jihad for the Maghreb was the legitimate right of the Muslim to enslave non-Muslim prisoners of war. In Barbary's perpetual jihad, all captives were automatically deemed prisoners of war and were thus subject to enslavement. There were six basic outcomes for prisoners of war: death, ransom, exchange, taxation, release, and of course enslavement. In the Maghreb, enslavement was the favored option. As one fifteenth-century North African *fatwa*, or authoritative opinion on Islamic law, piously laid down: "[slavery is] a humiliation and a servitude caused by previous or current unbelief and having as its purpose to discourage unbelief." From such opinions the Barbary pirates were able to legitimize outright slave raids.

Strict *shari'a* doctrine does, however, allow interruptions in the perpetual struggle between the House of Islam and the House of War. These permitted interruptions took the form of temporary truces or peace treaties and often involved financial gifts. In practice, these peace treaties periodically suspended the jihad between Islam and the infidel for any variety of reasons, including, at times, alliance with the infidels in order to fight Muslim heretics or rival Muslim powers. The rulers of the Maghrebi states quickly learned how to raise revenue through such measures, and in 1662 Great Britain initiated direct treaties with the Barbary States in order to purchase outright immunity for its merchant shipping. By the end of the eighteenth century, however, the European powers were adept at appeasing the pirates with cash and bribes and had become well versed in manipulating the Barbary powers to stave off competition in Mediterranean trade—including competition from the Unites States of America.

As the British mercantilist John Baker-Holroyd, Lord Sheffield, famously pointed out in his 1783 pamphlet *Observations on the Commerce of the American States*, "It is not probable the American States will have a very free trade in the Mediterranean; it will not be the interest of any of the great maritime powers to protect them there from the Barbary States. If they know their interests, they will not encourage the Americans to be carriers— that the Barbary States are advantageous to the maritime powers is obvious. . . . The Americans cannot protect themselves from the latter; they cannot pretend to a navy."

2

Ensnared in Barbary

A S EARLY AS March 1783, American shipping had its first run-in with Barbary piracy. Two American ships, leaving the port at Marseille, almost fell to Algiers. The reports were uncertain, but it seems that "secret enemies" in Algiers—the British were suspected—had tipped off the dey of Algiers about these two unarmed American vessels traversing the Mediterranean. Nine pirate corsairs were dispatched to cruise for them. Although the Algerines apparently gave chase, the American ships were able to escape into Spanish-protected waters, through the Straits of Gibraltar. The Algerines had obviously decided that the young American Republic was fresh quarry, and it seemed likely that they or some other Barbary power would pick up the hunt with greater enthusiasm.

In the fall of the following year, the precariousness of the Americans' position suddenly became very clear. On October 11, 1784, pirate corsairs from Morocco seized the American brig *Betsey*. The merchant vessel from Philadelphia had set sail for Tenerife, but it was captured soon after it left the port of Cadiz. Captain James Erving and his crew, along with the ship and its cargo, were taken and detained as hostages.

News of the *Betsey*'s capture reached the United States by February 1785. The American press received and expressed grossly exaggerated accounts both of the *Betsey*'s capture and of the general situation in the Mediterranean. Reports of multiple captures by Morocco and Algiers were detailed in several newspapers, while leading papers in Pennsylvania and Virginia reported that an American captain had discovered from an Englishman that as many as six American ships had been seized by the Moors and their crews sold into captivity. By the summer of 1785, the media exaggerations subsided as hard facts emerged.

The situation was satisfactorily resolved with the friendly intervention of Spain's foreign minister, conde de Floridablanca. Besides spreading goodwill, the minister was eager to resolve the Mississippi question in North America and hoped that his intercession would help to maintain cordial relations with the United States—a potentially valuable regional ally against the British. On July 9, 1785, the emperor of Morocco liberally agreed to release the *Betsey*, including her crew and her cargo, in exchange for America's pledge to send a peace negotiator very soon to conclude a formal treaty. During the intervening months, the cargo and ship were lost, but Moroccan affability prevailed and restitution was made.

A mere three months after the *Betsey* was seized, however, a far greater disaster befell the United States in Barbary. Two American ships and their combined crew of twenty-one men were captured and enslaved by Algerine pirates. The Boston schooner *Maria* (or *Mary*), commanded by Captain Isaac Stevens, was seized off Cape Saint Vincent, at the southern tip of Portugal, on July 24, and the Philadelphia ship *Dauphin* (or *Dolphin*), commanded by Captain Richard O'Brien, was seized off Cadiz, Spain, on July 30, 1785. But this time, Spain would not come to the rescue.

After twenty years of heated warfare, Spain and Algiers had finally concluded a treaty in June 1785 that provided for the evacuation of the Spanish enclave of Oran, the exchange of some prisoners, and the ending of general hostilities. Unfortunately for the United States, this also meant that Spain would no longer block the Algerines from entering the Atlantic. Freed of this tether, Dey Muhammad Pasha bin Uthman of Algiers (1766–91) immediately set out his pirates in search of Portuguese ships bound for Lisbon; the cruise was successful, netting several ships from Portugal and Genoa as well as the two U.S. vessels. Pleased with his American seizures, Dey Muhammad Pasha declared war on the United States and sent his corsairs out to hunt for fresh prey.

News of the Algerine captures eventually reached America on October 13, 1785, and by the end of December Congress had received a letter from the American captains in Algiers detailing their ordeal. American prestige in Europe plummeted, insurance rates for merchant ships began to skyrocket, and the country now faced a substantial hostage crisis.

American maritime interests were in serious jeopardy, and the nation looked to resolve its problem diplomatically. Several months before the Algerine capture of the *Maria* and the *Dauphin*, on May 7, 1784, John Adams, the American minister to Great Britain, and Thomas Jefferson, the American minister to France, had been officially authorized by Congress to establish treaties of amity and commerce with the Barbary States. The ultimate goal of these negotiations was to secure the freedom of the seas and the opening of commercial markets for American shipping. Recognizing the enormity of the task, Adams and Jefferson asked Congress for greater direction and authority. Accordingly, in February 1785 Congress set a total budget of $80,000 for treaties with the four Barbary States, and on March 11, 1785, Adams and Jefferson were empowered to find and appoint agents to negotiate and formulate treaties with the Barbary potentates.

Thus, on October 5, 1785, almost six months after the *Betsey* and her crew were taken hostage, Adams and Jefferson finally appointed Thomas Barclay to conduct negotiations with the emperor of Morocco. Barclay, an American merchant living in Bordeaux, had been employed for some time by the U.S. government as a special commissioner to settle U.S. debts in France; he had been acting as U.S. consul. At the same time, the commissioners selected Captain John Lamb as agent to Algiers.

Barclay left Paris for Morocco on January 15, 1786; he reached Madrid in March and was well attended to at the Bourbon court.

On June 19, 1786, Barclay finally arrived in Marrakech and was warmly received. He was quickly granted an audience at court, the negotiations proceeded in earnest, and a liberal treaty was completed on June 23. The treaty was sent to the American Congress and was ratified one year later on July 8, 1787.

Unfortunately, John Lamb's mission to Algiers was a total disaster. Captain Lamb had earlier volunteered his services to Congress and apparently had some limited experience as a commercial agent buying mules and horses in Tangier. For want of another candidate, and as it was a time of crisis, Adams and Jefferson gave him the appointment.

Lamb was instructed to spend no more than $40,000 in securing a peace treaty with Algiers. By the time he had finally arrived in Paris to receive his commission, on September 19, 1785, the situation had changed, as Algiers had already declared war on the United States, captured two American ships, and enslaved their crews. Officially, Adams and Jefferson had not received congressional authority to direct Lamb to ransom the American hostages in Algiers. Nor did they have any way of obtaining it in a timely fashion. Rather than wait for Congress to consider the matter, render judgment, and then send their instructions across the Atlantic, Adams and Jefferson felt obliged to at least try to redeem their countrymen; they thought that a "moderate" price would surely be approved. Lamb was thus authorized to pay no more than $200 a man.

Lamb finally reached Algiers on March 25, 1786, but his mission was essentially doomed even before he landed, because Dey Muhammad Pasha of Algiers was not interested in establishing peace with America and so refused to permit Lamb on shore unless he limited his business to offering terms for the redemption of the American slaves.

Although a peace treaty seemed no longer open for discussion, Lamb thought he might still help his countrymen in bondage and so reluctantly accepted the diminution of his mission. He was granted an interview with Dey Muhammad Pasha on April 1, 1786.

Unfortunately, the dey's demands amounted to roughly $2,800 per hostage. Even allowing for vigorous negotiations, there was no satisfactory middle ground achievable, as the dey had no incentive at all to strike a bargain. The proceedings were little helped by Lamb's stunning incompetence as a diplomat.

The mission was a total failure and dramatically shook the confidence of the Americans suffering in Algiers. As Captain Richard O'Brien of the ship *Dauphin*—one of the American slaves Lamb was sent to free (he would later be appointed the U.S. consul general to Barbary in Algiers)—wrote to William Carmichael, the U.S. chargé d'affaires in Spain, "I am very confident that Mr. Adams and Mr. Jefferson acted for the best, but I take the liberty of mentioning to you that it was badly planned and worse executed."

The general ineffectiveness of the American efforts initiated an interesting policy debate between John Adams and Thomas Jefferson in the summer of 1786. The crux of this debate was whether it was better to resist and fight the pirates or to pay them the tribute they demanded in order to prevent them from molesting U.S. shipping, capturing U.S. vessels, and enslaving U.S. sailors.

Adams, who would later become famous as an early hawk in foreign affairs and one of the key figures pushing for the establishment of a United States navy, was led by his pragmatism, and his shrewd analysis of the situation at that time, to favor tribute and diplomacy over force. He thought tribute would prove cheaper than building and maintaining a naval force capable of effectively projecting his nation's power overseas. He doubted whether his countrymen could agree to build a navy for this purpose, and he was suspicious of Jefferson's pet idea of establishing an international naval coalition to suppress Barbary piracy. Jefferson, who would later lead the party most opposed to military and naval buildup and who strongly advocated using economics rather than military power to further foreign policy aims, was led by his idealism to favor war. He was convinced that the use of naval force would be at least as effective as paying tribute but that it ought to be preferred because it would probably be cheaper in the long run—and would certainly be more honorable.

Foreign Secretary John Jay weighed in on this debate. In a letter of December 14, 1786, he observed to Jefferson that "Congress cannot command money for that [ransoming of Algerine prisoners], nor indeed for other very important purposes; their requisitions produce little, and government (if it may be called a government) is so inadequate to its objects, that essential alterations or essential evils must take place." Jay, like Adams, would have preferred the luxury of Jefferson's militancy, but he found it an impossible policy to endorse given the realities of the government's financial situation. "If our government would draw forth the resources of our country, which would be abundant, I should," he wrote, "prefer war to tribute, and carry our Mediterranean trade in vessels armed and manned at the public expense." Meanwhile, the festering problem of American slaves in Algiers remained.

Unable to proceed with force of arms to redeem the Americans in Algiers, Jefferson turned again to diplomacy. In January 1787 he contacted the Mathurins, or Fathers of the Redemption, who had formed the Order of the Holy Trinity and Redemption of Captives in 1199, with headquarters in Paris. The members of this religious order had established their mission to redeem Christians enslaved in Barbary and to alleviate their suffering. They had founded missions and hospitals near the principal centers of slave trading and near slave prisons in the Barbary States. The Muslim authorities tolerated the active presence of the Mathurins because the priests proved useful in negotiating and securing funds from Christian nations.

Jefferson visited with the general of the order, Father François-Maurice Pichault, on January 10, 1787. Jefferson left the meeting elated, convinced that he had thereby initiated a plan that would ultimately release the Americans being held captive.

On July 18, Congress authorized him to use his own discretion in dealing with the Mathurins.

Jefferson's latest diplomatic efforts, however, served only to worsen the plight of the American slaves in Algiers. Father Pichault had cautioned Jefferson to keep U.S. involvement confidential; if Algiers should learn of U.S. backing, he argued, they would likely raise their asking price, and this inflation would probably bleed into all future Mathurin missions. Because of this concern, the Mathurins directed Jefferson to discontinue the allowance the United States had been issuing to the American captives, because it was deemed too obviously a government subsidy. Further, Father Pichault advised, the United States should do its best to convince the Algerines that they had officially abandoned the captives.

Dutifully, Jefferson tried to convince Algiers that the U.S. government was not particularly eager to ransom the American slaves. He also arranged for the suspension of the allowances being sent to the slaves in Algiers with the message that their government no longer wished them to have such aid and assistance.

This official indifference briefly caused a wave of political consternation in the United States. Those interested in the well-being of the slaves, as well as the slaves themselves, began sending impassioned pleas to their fellow countrymen in positions of influence. The plight of the American slaves in Algiers became a popular national cause.

Although Jefferson had formulated and executed this particular policy, Congress was not fully informed of the particulars, and the American public was kept entirely in the dark. Jefferson thought that by demonstrating indifference he could drive the price of redemption down and thereby render the prospect of future American slaves less attractive to the pirates. Unfortunately, the only audience to make note of this "indifference" were the Americans in Algiers, for whom this measure provoked demoralization and increased suffering.

Toward the end of 1788, the ransom money appropriated by Congress finally arrived. Jefferson quickly contacted the Mathurins with instructions to begin negotiations. Almost immediately, however, it became clear that the funds—amounting to about $555 per person—would once again be insufficient to the task.

In the end, the entire endeavor proved a waste of time. In the fall of 1789, the French Revolution effectively ended Mathurin involvement, as the Church was stripped of its lands and finances. By this time, domestic problems had eclipsed Barbary affairs, and the plight of the American slaves in Algiers was forgotten. No more American negotiators would go to Algiers until 1795.

Recognizing the need to revise the Articles of Confederation, the United States initiated a fundamental change to its system of government. State delegates convened a Federal Convention on May 14, 1787, in Philadelphia. A quorum of state delegates finally gathered, and a broad discussion and debate began. By mid-June the delegates clearly understood that the only satisfactory way to correct the Confederation was to draft an entirely new form of government rather than redraft the old one. This was done in closed sessions all through the summer of 1787.

The delegates worked hard to conceive and develop a constitution upon which to found a new central government that would be strong enough to tackle national problems yet still constrained so as not to threaten state sovereignty or individual liberty. On September 17, 1787, after many weeks of discussion and debate, those present unanimously agreed upon the new Constitution.

After a certain amount of fine-tuning and the addition of the Bill of Rights, the Constitution was finally adopted on June 21, 1788. The new government was set to begin on March 4, 1789, and the first presidential election was arranged. After an easy victory, George Washington was sworn into the office of president on April 30, 1789. John Adams became vice president, and Thomas Jefferson, who had just returned from his diplomatic stint in Paris, was appointed secretary of state.

While Congress and the executive branch were busy establishing themselves under the new Constitution, all Barbary affairs were essentially put on hold; Mediterranean trade remained closed.

Almost six months later, on Friday, May 14, 1790, Barbary affairs were finally taken up again as urgent matters of state. "A petition of sundry persons, citizens of the United States," the *Congressional Record* notes, "now in slavery in Algiers, was presented to the House and read, praying the interposition of Congress in their behalf, and that effectual measures may be adopted for liberating them from slavery, and restoring them to their country." The matter was referred to the secretary of state with "instruction to examine the same, and report his opinion thereupon to the House." Accordingly, on December 28, Secretary of State Jefferson wrote two reports, one for President Washington regarding the status of the nation's countrymen enslaved in Algiers, and one also to Congress regarding the United States' trade in the Mediterranean. Jefferson's report on Mediterranean trade was communicated to the House of Representatives on December 30 and to the Senate on January 3, 1791. President Washington, on December 30, 1790, sent Congress a message concerning the American prisoners in Algiers; he included Jefferson's first report along with some accompanying documents.

Jefferson was finally provided the opportunity to make his case for martial force. He proposed that it might be "better to repress force by force" and that the United States should raid Algerine shipping, capture their sailors, and hold them hostage until an exchange of prisoners might be worked out. He encouraged the Congress to consider "the liberation of our citizens" as having "an intimate connection with the liberation of our commerce in the Mediterranean," concluding that "the distresses of both proceed from the same cause, and the measures which shall be adopted for the relief of the one, may, very probably, involve the relief of the other."

Jefferson offered only three options to Congress: (1) ignore the threat and continue the status quo, by continuing to pay the high insurance premiums, risk the molestation of U.S. ships and shipping, then pay the exorbitant ransoms and tariffs, leading inevitably to the abandonment of the Mediterranean market; (2) "obtain peace by purchasing it," as was the practice of the nations of Europe; or (3) "repel force by force" and build a navy to fight the pirates.

Jefferson was confident that the only real option was to build a navy and go to war, though he pointedly raised doubts about the first two options just to be certain. He repeated his proposition for an international alliance to blockade the pirates, and he argued that they ought to be combated directly when necessary.

On January 3, 1791, Congress discussed these reports in closed session. On January 6, the Senate Committee on Mediterranean Trade agreed with Jefferson that "the trade of the United States to the Mediterranean cannot be protected but by a naval force." As there was no money in the Treasury, however, there was no immediate change in policy. The new government did very little, at this stage, to help the American slaves in Algiers or to secure U.S.-Mediterranean trade. As for Jefferson's pet scheme to build an international alliance, there is no indication that the proposal was ever taken very seriously by anyone.

On April 11, 1791, Sultan Sidi Muhammad of Morocco died, thereby presenting the United States with another pressing Barbary problem. As was customary in Barbary, when a ruler succeeded to the throne, "respectable presents" needed to be made to encourage him to recognize the existing treaty, although even with such bribes the likelihood of the successor altering the treaty at will was considerable. Sidi Muhammad's outcast son, al-Yazid (surnamed "the Bloodthirsty"), ascended immediately to the throne. Congress needed now to send someone to Morocco to maintain peaceful relations, and both President Washington and Secretary of State Jefferson urged it to take steps to restore the peace. On March 3, 1791, Congress appropriated $20,000, to be raised by duties on distilled spirits, to coax the new sultan into accepting his father's treaty with the United States.

To facilitate negotiations with al-Yazid, Jefferson appointed Thomas Barclay as first consul to Morocco on May 13, 1791. Barclay was instructed to spend not more than $10,000 for presents. Unfortunately, al-Yazid's ascension was hotly contested and civil war broke out, continuing even after al-Yazid was eventually slain. This protracted internal strife compelled Barclay to spend his time in Lisbon, Cadiz, and later Gibraltar, waiting for the country to settle down.

Meanwhile, the situation in Algiers had changed. On July 12, 1791, Dey Muhammad Pasha of Algiers died, and within thirty minutes, Sidi Hassan, the *vekil kharj*, or chief admiral, was selected to take his place.

The ease of Sidi Hassan's succession was assured through equal measures of bribery and treachery. First he bought the loyalty of the Turkish officers, and then he arrested, banished, or executed the principal officers of state who served the old regime, quickly replacing these losses with men whose loyalty was assured. Thus, Sidi Hassan became Dey Hassan Pasha—the title dey because the soldiers elected him, and the title pasha because the Ottoman sultan in Istanbul confirmed his election.

Dey Hassan Pasha let it be known among the American slaves that he was willing to ransom them home and that he would be less hardheaded about it than the previous dey. Captain Richard O'Brien, who had been routinely supplying information to Jefferson and others in the U.S. government—even despite lack of acknowledgment during the years of Mathurin involvement—thought that the United States might now be able to ransom himself and the other slaves fairly cheaply.

Unfortunately, Congress was preoccupied and so did not seize this opportunity. Neither peace nor ransom was attempted until the following year.

Finally, in early 1792, Congress took action.

On February 22, the Senate indicated that it would support a peace with Algiers, Tripoli, and Tunis for up to $100,000 annually and was willing to accept the ransoming of the American slaves in

Algiers for up to $40,000. On May 8, President Washington requested provision for a treaty with Algiers for up to $40,000 and up to $25,000 in annual tribute; the Senate expressed its willingness in the matter and resolved to accept an agreement of up to $40,000 for the ransom of the thirteen Americans still held in captivity in Algiers. That same day, Congress appropriated $50,000 to enable the dispatch of an envoy to Algiers.

Unfortunately, the task of appointing an envoy to negotiate peace and redeem the American slaves in Algiers proved unusually difficult. Besides all the normal delays and communications difficulties common to the period, Washington and Jefferson had a difficult enough time selecting someone who would live long enough to embrace the commission: John Paul Jones, the Continental Navy hero, was appointed on June 1, but he passed away on July 18, well before receiving his commission; the commission was to pass on to Thomas Barclay, who was still passively observing the civil war in Morocco from his perch in Gibraltar, but he took ill and died on January 19, 1793. Forced to select yet another agent, Jefferson finally settled on Colonel David Humphreys, the U.S. minister to Portugal.

Humphries was issued his instructions on March 21, 1793, but, owing to the speed of transatlantic communications, he did not receive his commission until September. Soon after he received his instructions, however, the situation with Algiers suddenly changed for the worse.

Portugal had for several years been engaged in a defensive blockade of the Straits of Gibraltar, preventing Barbary pirates from gaining access to the Atlantic. This blockade had had the happy side effect of protecting the shipping lanes of other nations, such as the United States.

Unfortunately, Portuguese success against Algerine piracy became problematic for Great Britain. If His Britannic Majesty's Government was to fight Napoleon, she would need the help of all her allies—which included *both* Portugal and, it was thought, Algiers. England had long ago convinced herself that friendly North African ports were needed to facilitate the Royal Navy's harassment of Spain, so it seemed only natural to assume that Algiers could play this role against French forces in the Mediterranean. Thus, England thought it wise to try and facilitate peace between Portugal and Algiers; such a move would also free up some of the Portuguese fleet for later cooperation against France.

Accordingly, in mid-September 1793, a twelve-month truce was agreed between Portugal and Algiers, guaranteed by England. As soon as the blockade was lifted, Dey Hassan Pasha unleashed his corsairs through the straits and into the Atlantic.

Between October and November 1793, the Algerine pirates captured eleven additional American merchant ships. Insurance rates for American ships increased from ten to thirty percent. The total number of American slaves in Algiers was now up to 119 souls. Before long, however, the truce between Portugal and Algiers evaporated, as the Portuguese were unwilling to meet the exorbitant demands the British had arranged. Although the Portuguese navy quickly resumed the blockade, the damage to the United States was already done.

As soon as Colonel David Humphreys learned of the fresh addition to the American slaves in Algiers, he tried, through the aegis of the Swedish consul, to gain permission to land at Algiers to negotiate with the dey. His continued requests were flatly refused. Outraged and indignant, Humphreys decided the matter was closed. He allotted $40,000 as a relief fund for the slaves and entrusted its direction to Robert Montgomery, U.S. consul at Alicante, Spain. Humphreys returned to Portugal and the duties of his station there.

Given the unfriendly climate abroad, and the ongoing troubles with the Creek, Cherokee, and other Indian tribes domestically, the American Republic had quickly to confront the realities and practicalities of provision for the national defense. On December 3, 1793, in his annual message to the second session of the Third

Congress of the United States, President George Washington issued a warning:

> I cannot recommend to your notice measures for the fulfillment of our duties to the rest of the world without again pressing upon you the necessity of placing ourselves in a condition of complete defense. . . . The United States ought not to indulge a persuasion, that, contrary to the order of human events, they will forever keep at a distance those painful appeals to arms with which the history of every other nation abounds. . . . If we desire to avoid insult, we must be able to repel it; if we desire to secure peace . . . it must be known that we are at all times ready for war.

A few days later, Washington's warning was underscored by world events when he learned of the truce between Portugal and Algiers and the threat it posed to U.S. merchant ships. On December 16, President Washington turned back to Congress and presented an updated account of the Barbary issue. A lively congressional debate ensued.

The Federalists, under the general leadership of Secretary of the Treasury Alexander Hamilton, mostly favored a strong central government and were more or less calibrated to the commercial interests of the northern and eastern seaboard states. The Democratic-Republicans, under the general guidance of Secretary of State Thomas Jefferson, exhibited an active sympathy to states' rights and southern agricultural interests. Thus, two factions emerged in one of the earliest and most consequential political debates in American history, which naval historian Craig Symonds famously categorized as the great divide between the navalists and antinavalists.

The ensuing congressional debate quickly developed along geographical lines. Representatives of the southern states were mostly Democratic-Republican and antinavalist and so opposed the plan, while congressmen from the northern states were Federalist and navalist and so endorsed it. The philosophical divide was a mixture of pragmatism and idealism. The Democratic-Republicans/antinavalists thought the nation's future was to be pursued through westward expansion and thought a navy not only a waste of resources but likely to draw the nation into energy-draining foreign adventurism. To Federalists/navalists, a navy was the most practical means of castigating the pirates, protecting U.S. commerce and foreign interests, and providing a means to secure respect and influence in Europe.

On March 10, 1794, the House of Representatives finally passed a bill providing for naval armament, which was ratified by the Senate on March 19 and signed into law on March 27. Thus, the terror of the Barbary pirates gave direct genesis to the United States Navy. Indeed, as the legislation clearly states, "Whereas, the depredations committed by the Algerine corsairs on the commerce of the United States, render it necessary that a naval force should be provided for its protection . . . "

Unfortunately, the birth of the U.S. Navy was no more exempt from the laws of politics than are mortals from the laws of physics. Rather than concentrate the naval construction in one or two shipyards so as to simplify logistics and increase quality control, the government was prevailed upon by special interests. The six ships of the U.S. Navy were to be built in six different states— thus establishing the pork-barrel nature of U.S. naval construction. Four forty-four-gun frigates, the USS *United States*, the USS *Constitution*, the USS *President*, and the USS *Chesapeake* were to be built in Philadelphia, New York, Boston, and Norfolk, respectively. The three thirty-six-gun frigates, the USS *Chesapeake*, the USS *Congress*, and the USS *Constellation*, were to be built in Norfolk, Portsmouth, and Baltimore, respectively.

Congress, meanwhile, wished the diplomatic effort in Algiers to continue. On July 19, 1794, it authorized Colonel David Humphreys to spend up to $800,000 to redeem the American slaves and purchase a peace treaty. Humphreys was told to give special priority to ransoming the slaves and was permitted to spend up to $3,000 per man. The plight of the slaves was getting worse, and between January and August 1794, fourteen American captives in Algiers perished—eleven from plague, three from smallpox.

It is not entirely clear, however, that Humphreys actually received the July 19 communiqué. He suddenly decided to return to the United States and abandon his peace efforts, leaving Lisbon in November 1794 and reaching Newport, Rhode Island, in February 1795.

Although he had no desire to persist in his diplomatic mission to Algiers, Humphreys was persuaded to continue his service. He was issued supplementary instructions to employ a Mr. Joseph Donaldson Jr. as the U.S. agent to Algiers and then go to France to secure French assistance in the negotiations.

In April 1795, Humphreys and Donaldson set sail, reaching Gibraltar on May 17. By July, Humphreys and James Monroe, the U.S. minister to France, secured the promise of French assistance and obtained the services of Joel Barlow, a distinguished American expatriate with influence in Paris, to aid the negotiations, while Donaldson sent letters to the American captives. Humphreys planned to establish his base of operations for Barbary in Portugal and Spain, leaving the field direction to Barlow and the actual negotiations to Donaldson.

Dey Hassan Pasha granted Donaldson permission to enter Algiers on September 3, 1795. The next morning, September 4, the negotiations for peace between the United States and Algiers and the ransom of the American slaves was initiated. Donaldson relied heavily on the advice of the American slaves James Leander Cathcart, who had risen to prominence as a trusted Christian slave-secretary to the dey (he would later be appointed U.S. consul to Tripoli), and Captain Richard O'Brien, who had been feeding intelligence to his government throughout most of his captivity.

The negotiations were heated at times, but they were ultimately productive. In very little time, a settlement was made and a treaty agreed to. The United States was to pay $642,500 in cash up front, followed by annual tribute of 12,000 Algerine sequins in naval stores (roughly equivalent to $21,600 worth of materials—powder, shot, oak planking, pine masts, etc.). Donaldson agreed, and the dey consented to this arrangement—"more to pique the

British" (as he was still angry with them for the dissolution of the "truce" with Portugal), he later told Cathcart, "than in consideration of the sum, which I esteem no more than a pinch of snuff." Donaldson was generally pleased, and he thought the additional demands unavoidable. Thus, on September 5, 1795, peace was proclaimed by the dey and the American flag was given a twenty-one-gun salute.

To the United States, however, the sum was no trifle: once the cost of the naval stores was properly factored in and the other assorted bribes, gifts, and payoffs were accounted for, the U.S. Treasury later estimated the true cost of this peace with Algiers to be $992,463.25, or equivalent to about $14,274,865 in today's terms (at that time the entire federal budget for fiscal year 1796 was $5.7 million).

Now all that was needed to free the American slaves in Algiers and secure the peace was to deliver the cash; Donaldson turned his attention from securing the peace to financing it. To Dey Hassan Pasha, however, such distinctions were meaningless; without ransom and tribute, "peace" would quickly turn into war.

Delivering the cash was, unfortunately, to prove a far more difficult task for the United States than the negotiations themselves. Finalizing the peace became, thus, a fairly complex affair.

To the dey, international finance was something of an enigma. One either had hard cash or one did not claim to have funds and did not incur financial obligations or debts. To do otherwise was simply a form of fraud. As the time passed without any word of impending payment from the United States, the dey became convinced that he had been deceived. Every week and every month that passed without arrival of the funds in Algiers made matters worse with Dey Hassan Pasha.

Before too long, Joel Barlow landed in Algiers to take an active role in pacifying the dey while he and Donaldson awaited the money. As the months passed, so did the dey's patience. Barlow spent many thousands in bribes trying to curry favor in the dey's court and buy time; eventually he and Donaldson offered the "gift" of a new American-made frigate of thirty-six guns (later valued at a total expense of $98,377.09) in exchange for another three months of the dey's forbearance. Before long, Barlow found himself in the unenviable position of having to lie, dissemble, cheat, bribe, and otherwise keep the peace while he awaited the arrival of the American treaty funds.

Captain Richard O'Brien, who had been freed to carry the treaty to Humphreys for approval, had since been sent off to try and collect the necessary cash on American credit in London and then Hamburg. When none proved available, Captain O'Brien sailed back home. Soon thereafter, on June 18, 1796, he was employed by the secretary of state to return to Algiers, as captain of the brig *Sophia*, to help Donaldson and Barlow or otherwise make himself useful. He reached Lisbon by late July and commiserated with David Humphreys, who had managed to secure $200,000 in gold.

Joseph Donaldson Jr. meanwhile had left Algiers in April 1796 for Leghorn—the port city on the Ligurian Sea at the western edge of Tuscany—in hopes of obtaining gold bullion. He managed to obtain $100,000 in gold specie (at unfavorable interest rates) by July 1796, but he was not able to send it back to Algiers for many months due to a British blockade of the port. Donaldson would be unable to send his shipment to Algiers until January 10, 1797.

On October 1, 1796, Captain Richard O'Brien sailed the *Sophia* into the harbor at Algiers with $200,000 in gold bullion in his hold. After one year and twenty-five days of waiting, Dey Hassan Pasha would finally receive his cash. Captain O'Brien had been delayed because Tripolitan pirates had captured the *Sophia*; O'Brien had talked Pasha Yusuf Qaramanli of Tripoli into releasing the ship and its gold by pointing out that the gold was intended for the dey of Algiers, so its seizure would surely start a war.

At the conclusion of the peace transaction, the dey magnanimously asked Barlow to request a favor. Seizing this opportunity, Barlow asked the dey for his assistance in securing peace treaties with Tunis and Tripoli. He said he planned to send O'Brien on the *Sophia* to negotiate on these terms and hoped the dey would be willing to write letters to both of these regencies urging them to accept the American offer. Dey Hassa Pasha agreed to Barlow's request, adding that the United States could look to Algiers to guarantee the peace with both Tunis and Tripoli; he suggested that O'Brien approach Tripoli with cash in hand, since that regency was relatively poor, and he even offered to provide O'Brien with the necessary funds.

With such grand assurances in hand, Joel Barlow and Captain Richard O'Brien readied themselves to pursue their peace negotiations with the remaining regencies of the Barbary Coast. After just over eleven years of aggression against the United States, the American-Algerine relationship seemed now to be on a firm, peaceful footing, and the Americans held captive in Algiers were given their freedom.

Eighty-two American sailors—those who had survived the hard labor, brutality, and languor of enslavement, as well as the outbreaks of plague—arrived safely back in Philadelphia on February 9, 1797. A crowd of interested spectators gathered to witness the return of the captives. The former slaves were then taken to a local tavern, where presumably, they were entertained. Nothing further was done. Those among them who could still earn a living proceeded to do so, while those who could not turned to private charity—no government funds were made available. Still, these men were now free to pursue their own destinies.

In establishing the peace treaty with Algiers, America freed its enslaved citizens, protected its commerce from Algerine piracy, and spurred the growth of its own navy. However, this peace had a steep price—and not just a financial one. American peace in Algiers was now dependent on the eminently purchasable honor of a pirate thug. As Captain Richard O'Brien was fond of saying, "Give a Turk money with one hand and you may take his eyes out with the other."

The U.S. government and its representatives on the ground were thus forced to deal respectfully with pirates and slave traders, treating them as superiors while attempting to pacify their whims and meet their exorbitant demands for ransom. The American diplomats had caved in to extortion, perpetrated deceptions, actively engaged in bribery, turned a blind eye to larceny, and essentially agreed to trade military arms—naval stores, a thirty-six gun frigate—for hostages. Another of Captain O'Brien's favorite sayings: "Money is the God of Algiers, and Mohamed their prophet."

Although the United States would successfully sign peace treaties with the four Barbary States, the Mediterranean Sea was not at peace. Throughout this period, the region was awash with blood. Almost all of the major European powers had been in and out of war since the 1789 revolution in France, and England and France went to war against each other in 1793, with the Mediterranean Sea playing host to many battles.

The Anglo-French war exacerbated the divide between the Federalists and the Democratic-Republicans in American politics, further hampering the growth of the U.S. Navy. After the outbreak of the European conflict, President George Washington proclaimed the United States to be a neutral nation and denied the use of American ports to the principal combatant nations. As Britain had naval superiority at that time, the French thought this "neutrality" favored the British and protested that denying access to U.S. ports violated the terms of the 1778 Treaty of Alliance between France and America—which the French understood to specifically command future American assistance to France in case of her going to war with England as an exchange for French aid in the American struggle for independence from England. The Democratic-Republicans took up the French protests and decided the matter was a Federalist scheme to help England at the expense of France—the nation they considered the world's beacon of liberty and human rights. To the Democratic-Republicans, the creation of a navy was simply a devious endeavor to drag the United States into war with France, and thus they considered such a naval force detrimental to the liberty of the United States. The Federalists, however, were just as avowedly pro-Britain as the Democratic-Republicans were pro-France. They looked to Britain as the paragon of social and economic stability, and they were greatly troubled by the forces unleashed in the French Revolution and worried over the outcome of the European war.

In 1794, after much debate, a bill was passed in Congress calling for the building of a naval force subject to peace with Algiers—no thought was given to the other Barbary regencies. Once peace with Algiers was proclaimed, however, President Washington had to work hard in March 1796 to convince Congress to complete at least part of the navy. The delays in naval construction and the tremendous sums being spent—far in excess of initial stipulations or expectations—only served to embolden the Democratic-Republican opposition. Further, the peace treaty made with Algiers in September 1795 was extremely expensive, made more so by the delays in concluding it and the endeavors to stave off dissolution of its terms. Indeed, the expense proved so great that the European nations grew apprehensive and complained that the American peace might have established a precedent and be used by the Barbary regencies as the base for all future negotiations—particularly with the richer nations of Europe. The Democratic-Republicans thus equipped made Washington's success at continuing naval construction a bitter, hard-fought one. Just before President Washington left office, peace was declared with Tripoli in January 1797, and by that point peace with Tunis seemed imminent, since America was being aided by Algiers—peace was eventually declared in August 1797.

John Adams took up the office of president in March 1797. Although there were no presidential term limits at this time, Washington had opted out of running again. Despite the aversion to political factions by America's Founding Fathers, by this time two distinct parties had emerged in institutional form: the Federalists and the Democratic-Republicans. The Federalists nominated John Adams as president and Thomas Pinckney as vice president, while the Democratic-Republicans put up Thomas Jefferson and Aaron Burr. Because the Constitution did not take institutional parties into consideration, the election returns produced a split victory: John Adams became president while Thomas Jefferson became his vice president.

By the time Adams became president, all substantive issues relating to Barbary affairs were subject to the peace treaties and agreements made under President Washington. There was little Adams could do beyond trying to make good on the U.S. commitments to the Barbary regencies. Not that much could have been done differently anyway, as there was still no finished American navy—thanks largely to the Democratic-Republicans in Congress. Without a naval force, the nation had no strength or leverage with which to bargain, either in Barbary or anywhere else.

American commerce prospered because of U.S. neutrality during the European conflict, which added much-needed wealth to the American economy and helped considerably to strengthen the new constitutional government. Indeed, American merchant shipping became the preferred neutral maritime carrier of the Old World, even though U.S. vessels sailed without protection or even the threat of force. Unfortunately, complications and insecurities arose because both England and France desired to employ American shipping but refused to allow each other to do so profitably—effectively harassing American trade. The situation was made more precarious by the fact that the primary borders of the United States were with territory held by the main European combatant nations. Adding to these difficulties yet further, President Adams had to balance out the pro-British sentiments of the Federalists—his own party—with the pro-French sentiments of the Democratic-Republicans. As historian William M. Fowler Jr. eloquently put it, "Caught between the tiger—France, powerful on land—and the shark—Great Britain, powerful at sea—the

United States found itself in the uncomfortable position of being a neutral carrier, harassed by both sides." In this effort, President Adams focused more of his attention on Europe than on Barbary.

Following the unsatisfactory Jay Treaty of 1794, Franco-American relations were near dissolution. The French considered the treaty an American betrayal and a violation of American neutrality, and they retaliated by refusing to receive an American ambassador and by seizing American ships. The situation had grown steadily worse by the time Adams became president in March 1797. On May 16, the new president addressed Congress, informing it of French misconduct and urging it to recognize the importance of military and naval preparedness. In June, Timothy Pickering, the secretary of state, presented a report of the complete record of foreign violations of American neutrality since October 1796: out of 319 incidents, one was blamed on Spain, two on England, and all the rest on France. This report added a sense of urgency to President Adams's message to Congress.

In order to stave off potential disaster, Adams sent three envoys to Paris during the summer of 1797 empowered to negotiate an amicable settlement with the French government. The envoys failed, however, and the situation worsened. In his annual message to Congress on November 22, 1797, Adams criticized the French and urged Congress "to place our country in a suitable posture of defense." By March 1798, he began to contemplate asking for a declaration of war—though he abandoned this option when he realized there was no support in Congress. On March 19, he reported to Congress, "I perceive no ground of expectation that the objects of their [his three envoys in Paris] mission can be accomplished on terms compatible with the safety, honor, or the essential interests of the nation." He alluded to certain dispatches he had received from his envoys in Paris, which directly informed his perception. The House of Representatives responded on April 2, 1798, by requesting to see the dispatches— although the House promised to keep the records confidential so as not to alarm the public. Adams sent these documents to Congress the following day.

The dispatches revealed that certain agents of the French government—referred to simply as X, Y, and Z—had approached the American envoys and told them that relations would only be restored by a public apology from President Adams and a large Barbary-style bribe from the U.S. Treasury. Despite a pledge of confidentiality, the House voted to reverse itself and make the dispatches public knowledge. The Democratic-Republicans protested this decision, sensing it would have a prejudicial effect on American opinion, but the Federalists controlled both the House and the Senate. The public and congressional response was predictable: anger and offense.

Prompted by the clarion call of newspaper editorials and popular opinion, Congress enacted a law on April 17, 1798, "to provide an additional armament for the further protection of the trade of the United States; and for other purposes." Congress also appropriated $950,000 for the president to build, purchase, or hire "a number of vessels, not exceeding twelve, nor carrying more than twenty-two guns each to be armed, fitted out, and manned under his direction." In order to prevent administrative disaster, the Federalists pushed the Congress to establish, on April 30, 1798, a Department of the Navy directed by a secretary of full cabinet rank—the secretary of war would not be able to handle the additional burden, plus the Federalists did not wish their precious navy to play second fiddle to the army. While Adams appointed Benjamin Stoddert, a Maryland merchant operating in Georgetown, as secretary of the navy, the Congress authorized the president to direct the navy to retake American vessels seized by the French and to actively "seize, take, and bring into any port of the United States" any armed vessels found lingering around the American coast. Thus started a Quasi-War with France, as well as some practical training for an infant naval force.

This Quasi-War between the United States and France had consequences for Barbary. After France invaded Egypt and then the Levant, Turkey declared war on France and formed an alliance with Russia and England in that effort. Thus Algiers, Tunis, and Tripoli—countries with a semi-tributary connection to the Turkish sultan—were drawn into declaring war on France and all her European allies. The Mediterranean Sea thus became problematic to all, Muslim and Christian alike, yet it remained profitable to any who could safely traverse her waters, because of the relative scarcities the war created. Consequently, the Barbary powers wished to increase their naval strength and embraced the necessity of finding a neutral carrier for their commerce—for all concerned, the United States proved the ideal neutral carrier to be pressed into service.

One other consequence of the deteriorating Franco-American relations was a shift in the diplomatic climate of the Barbary regencies. The French consuls at the Barbary States generally had undue influence with the various Barbary regal retinues as a result of commercial interests and healthy bribes to key government ministers. Further, these connections were often kept secret—sometimes even from the local Barbary ruler. The American consular representatives thus had to navigate through and around such palace intrigue and machinations.

3

Eaton Enters Barbary

PRESIDENT JOHN ADAMS, in a June 23, 1797, message to both houses of Congress, brought two issues to their attention: an early arms deal with the dey of Algiers, and the necessity of appointing consular agents to the Barbary States.

Adams informed Congress that the dey of Algiers had commissioned the construction of two vessels to be equipped as cruisers, under the direction of Captain Richard O'Brien, and then delivered in Algiers to the dey. "A compliance with the Dey's request appears to me to be of serious importance," the president said. He highlighted that these vessels would be treated as a straightforward sale of arms—"He [the dey] will repay the whole expense of building and equipping the two vessels." Adams also reminded Congress that the United States was "under peculiar obligations to provide this accommodation" and needed to keep the dey pacified: "He has advanced the price of our peace with Tripoli, and become pledged for that of Tunis." Adams then called upon Congress to establish consular services in Barbary under the direction of a consul general in Algiers. The various diplomats serving the United States had long been advocating the use of resident diplomatic agents in Algiers to maintain peace and oversee and protect American affairs in Barbary.

Congress agreed on both issues. Thus, the U.S. government decided to comply with Dey Hassan Pasha's request to purchase two American-made warships; $45,000 was appropriated. As to the consular issue, on July 6, 1797, Congress passed an "Act in addition to the law of the United States concerning Consuls and Vice Consuls." On December 25, Captain Richard O'Brien was appointed the United States consul general to the Barbary Coast with supervisory authority over the other U.S. consular agents in Barbary, as well as the resident consul to Algiers.

Captain Richard O'Brien was a natural choice, having had both firsthand contact with the Algerines as a slave, where he was widely regarded as a leader and representative of the Americans held captive, and experience serving as an ad hoc U.S. agent in the matter of obtaining funds in Europe to conclude the peace in Algiers, and then as a peace negotiator with Tunis and Tripoli. Further, he had very early in his captivity volunteered not only in assisting, without remuneration, the American community of slaves in Algiers but also in amassing facts and intelligence for the U.S. secretary of state. His appointment was undoubtedly helped by the October 18, 1796, unsolicited endorsement Joel Barlow wrote to the secretary of state: "I beg you to remark the superior sagacity and talents displayed by Captain O'Brien . . . a more suitable person than he cannot probably be found to be placed here as Consul for the United States. . . . He has a singular talent in which is called Algerine management."

On July 7, 1797, Adams selected two unlikely candidates to round out his consular appointments: William Eaton as consul to Tunis and James Leander Cathcart as consul to Tripoli. Cathcart, like O'Brien, had firsthand experience in Barbary as a former slave, and in certain respects had higher qualifications than O'Brien. He had worked himself up through the ranks of Christian slaves to become Dey Hassan Pasha's primary Christian secretary, making him a central figure in the dey's court. However, unlike O'Brien, Cathcart had the rare ability to alienate everyone around him—a fact dutifully noted for the U.S. government by, among others, Joseph Donaldson Jr., Richard O'Brien, and Joel Barlow.

Indeed, when Barlow had earlier learned that Cathcart sought the consulate in Algiers, he had specifically written to the secretary of state to advise against such appointment. As Barlow wrote: "I am told that Mr. Cathcart has hopes of obtaining the Consulate at this place. He has neither the talents or the dignity of character necessary for that purpose; though I sincerely wish that he might be employed in the business of the peace presents and the tribute, in which I think his intelligence and industry would enable him to render essential service."

William Eaton was an unusual choice for the U.S. consul resident to the Ottoman regency of Tunis: he had no naval background; had never been overseas, let alone to a Muslim country or North Africa; and had no formal diplomatic training of any sort.

Born in Woodstock, Connecticut, on February 23, 1764, Eaton was an intelligent and precocious young man. At age sixteen he ran away from home and then lied about his age to join General Washington's Continental Army; by the time the War of Independence ended, he was a sergeant. He went on in 1792 to serve the U.S. Army as a captain fighting Indians in the Ohio territories and negotiating with the Creeks and Cherokees on the Georgia frontier; in this service he attracted the attention—and soon thereafter the friendship and political protection—of Timothy Pickering, the U.S. secretary of war.

Captain Eaton left the army, after about eight years of active service, under slightly opaque circumstances due to allegations of financial improprieties made against him by a superior officer; he was officially cleared of all charges by a court-martial review board. Eaton possessed an independent mind and an often intemperate tongue; he had also developed an unfortunate habit of making powerful enemies. He quickly salvaged his career, however, with a brief, successful stint under Timothy Pickering as a secret agent in an espionage/treason investigation. He proved his worth to the influential secretary of war and so was again selected for special service when Pickering became secretary of state. Instead of being assigned to covert counterespionage fieldwork, however, Eaton was chosen by Secretary Pickering to serve as consul in the recently created office of the U.S. consul resident to Tunis.

President John Adams submitted William Eaton's nomination to Congress, and Eaton was duly given his appointment on July 7, 1797. While waiting for the ship that would take him and

James Cathcart (newly appointed U.S. consul to Tripoli) to their posts in North Africa, he spent his time courting useful friendships with congressmen and other politicians, as well as trying to learn about the Barbary region. He and Cathcart finally set sail from Philadelphia on December 22, 1798, aboard the *Sophia*, a converted merchantman mounting twelve cannon, commanded by Captain Henry Geddes.

They sailed in company with four ships—the *Hero*, carrying stores for the Barbary regencies as stipulated by the peace treaties, and three armed vessels to be delivered directly to the dey of Algiers: these ships were the brig *Hassan Pasha* and the schooners *Skjoldebrand* and *Lelah Eisha*.

The *Sophia*'s voyage to Algiers was not smooth. The trip lasted thirty-six days, most of which were stormy and uncomfortable. One of the ships in the *Sophia*'s consort, the *Hero*, was separated from the company during a severe gale on the third night out and then sprung a leak and was forced to turn back. "It is sad to reflect," William Eaton noted in his journal, "that our beloved nation could sink so low in her self-esteem [as to pay such lavish tribute to pirates]. I pray that I will have an opportunity to cause the rulers of Barbary to think more highly of us in years to come."

Unfortunately, the entire trip aboard the *Sophia* was made all the more volatile and disagreeable by James Leander Cathcart.

It was only with great reluctance that James Cathcart had even accepted his consular office. He had been greatly angered that he was not offered the senior "consul general" posting in Algiers, as he considered himself more fit than anyone for that position, given his experience in the dey's court. It was not simply that Cathcart did not get the preferred posting, of course, but that Richard O'Brien got it in his stead. Cathcart considered this fact a personal betrayal by O'Brien. Indeed, Cathcart had come through the course of his brooding to convince himself that Richard O'Brien owed his entire Barbary career to him.

Along the way, Cathcart also managed to offend Captain Geddes with his egoistic and overbearing manner by offering for no particular reason to run the ship. Before long, most of the people aboard the *Sophia* were revolted by Cathcart's "repulsive manners" and "sour, forbidding, self-centered" personality.

The worst storm of the voyage, however, and the one that would have the most lasting consequences for Barbary diplomacy, was Cathcart's decision to bring Jane, his pregnant, fifteen-year-old wife of six months, and his wife's newly employed English servant girl, twenty-year-old Elizabeth Robeson. Not surprisingly, this happy domestic party quickly soured. Miss Robeson took an active dislike to the Cathcarts during the course of the trip and soon refused to continue in their service.

Miss Robeson had left England principally to join her brother in Philadelphia, but she discovered he had since sailed away to Asia. Once her money ran out, she sought employment, accepting work for the Cathcarts as a servant to Jane. It is not clear whether James Cathcart tried to take liberties with her or whether he simply treated her poorly, as a mere servant rather than a lady. In any event, she made her displeasure with the Cathcarts very clear and very public. In the close and cramped quarters of the *Sophia*, this little dispute turned into full-blown drama.

As William Eaton reported the affair in his journal, Miss Robeson was openly expressing her disappointment with Cathcart's manners by the time the *Sophia* reached the Straits of Gibraltar. "I once heard her remark that the rank Mr. C. held under the appointment of the President of the United States had deluded her into a persuasion that his family and manners must have been at least civilized if not refined." She considered him a tyrant and made no efforts to conceal her contempt. Cathcart, in turn, cursed her and impugned her character and integrity. As Eaton put it, "a storm arose accompanied with thunder and smut . . . many choice names selected from the catalogue of infamies."

Despite Cathcart's heated report of her character, Eaton indicated that he observed nothing that "would justify an impeachment of her honor." To Eaton, who had left his wife and stepson back in the United States, the matter was fairly straightforward: "She is a woman" and therefore ill suited for keeping company "among barbarians."

On February 9, 1799, the *Sophia* entered the harbor at Algiers. Elizabeth Robeson immediately announced that she would not travel further in the company or the employ of James Cathcart, demanded passage back to the United States, and sought the protection of Consul General Richard O'Brien.

O'Brien's heart evidently bled for Miss Robeson, as he took her under his protection in the American consulate. The meeting would prove quite propitious, as they would marry roughly six weeks later, on March 25. Unfortunately, the bonds of this wedlock created a permanent aperture in the working relationship between James Cathcart and Richard O'Brien. Cathcart considered the marriage further proof of O'Brien's betrayal. He insisted that O'Brien had "seduced his maid from him"; that O'Brien "took every means to entice her from the service of a young creature [Jane Cathcart] in a barbarous community, when it was impossible to procure another female attendant." Cathcart also wrote to Secretary of State Pickering to impugn both O'Brien and his new wife.

Making matters even worse, O'Brien's marriage conferred rapid social promotion on Elizabeth Robeson, the Cathcarts' former servant girl. Instead of being a "humble companion" to Mrs. Cathcart, the former Miss Robeson was now the wife of the consul general to Algiers and thus a superior in the social and diplomatic protocol—a change James and Jane Cathcart never learned to forgive or make their peace with.

When Richard O'Brien arrived in Algiers to take up his new consular duties on January 26, 1798, he was granted an immediate audience with the dey. He learned to his dismay that there were serious problems with the American naval stores that had been delivered to Algiers thus far. Virtually all of them were in some measure unacceptable to the dey.

Only three American shipments of military and naval stores had previously been delivered to the dey, the first not having arrived until October 1797. A fourth, on board the schooner *Hamdullah*, had embarked for Algiers in December 1797 but had been held up in Gibraltar, where it eventually joined that of the *Crescent* and so was only now being received. Moreover, not all of the shipments arrived complete—at least one ship, the *Newport*, had hit a terrible gale, forcing the captain to throw substantial amounts of the cargo overboard. There were also some serious problems with the quality of some of the stores, while others had suffered from bad weather and were rendered unusable.

On top of these problems, O'Brien discovered that the United States was also due to give its biennial "presents of friendship" to the regency, and the dey was annoyed that these obligatory consular gifts had not been furnished. Fortunately, Hassan Pasha's mood softened considerably when O'Brien delivered the *Crescent* to him as a gift and then gave him the schooner *Hamdullah* as a replacement of a portion of the military and naval supplies. The quality of both vessels was very great, far better than most that Algiers had at her disposal. In order to make sure the dey's mood stayed positive, O'Brien also made good on the consular and "friendship" presents by immediately procuring these articles from the Bakris (the local Jewish merchant bankers), at a cost of roughly $40,000.

A couple of weeks later, however, on May 15, 1798, a little shy of seven years after succeeding to power, Dey Hassan Pasha passed away of natural causes. His age was not recorded with certainty. Almost immediately, Dey Bobba Mustafa, formerly the *khaznaji*, or treasurer, tranquilly succeeded him; the changeover of new officers transpired peacefully as well. Mustafa, who was also Hassan's nephew, had begun as a common soldier but had risen through the ranks via Hassan Pasha's influence.

Consul General Richard O'Brien now had to bring consular presents to the new dey and his new ministers, and, more importantly, had to secure ratification of all of the previous dey's agreements with the United States. In order to effect this, however, O'Brien needed to borrow more money, about $5,500, from the Bakris—his own funds were already spread too thin. Fortunately,

Dey Mustafa accepted everything rather well for the time being. The United States was still in arrears, however, in terms of the stipulated naval stores as well as the warships the late dey had commissioned. O'Brien was able to cool the situation somewhat with another $8,000 in cash.

Matters with Algiers became complicated again, though, when on January 23, 1799, the *Lelah Eisha* finally arrived. Although it had been previously arranged that the ship would substitute for some of the requisite military and naval stores, Dey Hassan Pasha had been dead for roughly eight months. Dey Bobba Mustafa considered the schooner a fine vessel and demanded her as a gift.

O'Brien refused, explaining that he was not empowered to give such a gift. Dey Mustafa did not care about O'Brien's authorization. Either the ship is given gratis to Algiers, or there would be trouble, the dey threatened. O'Brien refused to budge. In a matter of days the impasse escalated, and O'Brien feared that the dey might simply seize the vessel and declare war.

On Monday, February 4, 1799, the U.S. schooner *Skjoldebrand* entered Algiers. Four days later, the *Hassan Pasha* arrived as well. "The whole maritime class of the Algerines," O'Brien wrote, "were captivated with those vessels." Suitably impressed with the condition of the ships, the regularity of the crew, and the quality of the craftsmanship, Dey Mustafa switched his desire from the *Lelah Eisha* to the *Hassan Pasha*. He became adamant that he would have that brig at any cost.

After a discussion of this matter with the *vekil kharj*, or chief admiral, who served as both the officer in charge of maritime affairs and as the foreign minister, O'Brien quickly realized that the exact terms of the Algerine treaty with the United States were not known to the new dey, to the *vekil kharj*, or to any of the other new ministers and officers at court. "Then I was determined," O'Brien proudly reported, "to see how far I could work on him."

O'Brien pushed his advantage and used the opportunity to clear his government's debt to Algiers as far as possible. He solicited the expensive help of Bakri and Bushnaq (or Bujnach;

another prominent Jewish banking firm that the Americans came to rely heavily on for assistance), both of whom knew the actual terms of the treaty—the price was the whole of the *Sophia's* cargo.

O'Brien inflated the value of the American-built ships and convinced the dey to accept the two schooners—the *Lelah Eisha* and the *Skjoldebrand*—in full payment of American tribute for more than two years. He gave the dey the *Hassan Pasha* as a gift, an expression of friendliness to further guarantee acceptance of this arrangement, and he asked for a written receipt and an acknowledgment of Dey Bobba Mustafa's acceptance of terms. As he was later able to report, "The whole of our stipulation for naval and military stores I have entirely done away and paid our stipulated annual tribute with this regency up to two years and one half from the date of the treaty."

When William Eaton reached Algiers on Saturday, February 9, 1799, he had no real idea of what awaited him. Unlike O'Brien and Cathcart, he had no experience with Muslims or with North Africa. In fact, until the *Sophia* Eaton had hardly any experience at all of being on a boat, much less traveling overseas. Although he had studied maps, pored over reports, and read Volney's *Travels through Egypt and Syria in the Years 1783, 1784, & 1785*, he knew little of what to expect.

The first major task Eaton would grapple with once he reached Tunis would be the renegotiation of the Treaty of Amity and Commerce with Tunis. This treaty contained three articles— articles XI, XII, and XIV—that had met with serious objections in Congress, but on March 6, 1798, the Senate had nevertheless ratified the treaty, subject to revision. On December 18, 1798, O'Brien, Cathcart, and Eaton were officially tasked—either together or in any combination of two—with this renegotiation effort.

Along with these instructions, however, Secretary of State Timothy Pickering also gave Eaton additional, confidential instructions for his consular post in Tunis. Pickering and Eaton were old friends, Pickering having early on solicited Eaton's loyalty with political patronage and protection.

The secretary of state, a staunch Federalist, believed that part of his duties lay in furthering American commercial and trade interests. The Mediterranean had proved itself a worthwhile and highly remunerative market, marred only by the attitude of the Barbary regencies. Pickering believed Tunis might enjoy a more stable government than her Barbary neighbors, so he considered her trade potential worthy of cultivation. Eaton was thus instructed to consider trying to convince the bey and his court of the relative value of pursuing commerce with America over plundering her shipping. As Pickering noted in his instructions:

> It may be thought chimerical to entertain an idea that these Barbary powers are ever to cease from their predatory wars; and while some of the Christian nations would rather encourage than repress them, and it is the general practice of mankind to seek favors by flattering the predominant passions of men possessing power, it may appear like a piece of knight errantry to attempt to reclaim them. Nevertheless, the idea is not to be rejected nor forgotten. The great commerce of Tunis, where too it is stated that the government is hereditary, offers the best encouragement to the attempt, should a distant prospect of success present.

Eaton was instructed to gather information on Tunisian trade, the products and manufactures of the country, the imports and exports, the trends and fluctuations of market prices and the rates of exchange, and the accepted standards and practices of conducting business within her domain. Pickering believed that American entrepreneurs would leap at the chance to enter the Tunisian market and press their comparative advantage. "If ever," he wrote Eaton, "the states of Barbary lay aside their practice of depredating on the commerce of Christian nations, it will probably be owing to an extension of their own commerce." Such a realization, Pickering thought, "may convince them where their true interest lies by the greater advantage derived from trade."

William Eaton's first sampling of Barbary diplomacy would prove, however, a more authoritative guide than any of Pickering's instructions. On February 22, 1799, he, James Cathcart, and the captains of the *Sophia*, the *Hassan Pasha*, the *Lelah Eisha*, and the *Skjoldebrand* were granted the opportunity to meet Dey Bobba Mustafa of Algiers, who was eager to have his recent and hard-fought deal with O'Brien given its due appreciation. This meeting was entirely typical of all such diplomatic meetings in Barbary, and it quickly established William Eaton's distaste for his new career. As he recorded in his consular journal later that day:

> Consuls O'Brien, Cathcart and myself, Captains Geddes, Smith, Penrose, Maley, proceeded from the American house to the courtyard of the palace, uncovered our heads, entered the area of the hall, ascended a winding maze of five flights of stairs, to a narrow, dark entry, leading to a contracted apartment of about twelve by eight feet, the private audience room. Here we took off our shoes and entering the cave (for so it seemed), with small apertures of light with iron gates, we were shown to a huge, shaggy beast, sitting on his rump upon a low bench covered with a cushion of embroidered velvet, with his hind legs gathered up like a tailor, or a bear. On our approach to him, he reached out his forepaw as if to receive something to eat. Our guide exclaimed, "Kiss the Dey's hand!" The consul general bowed *very elegantly*, and kissed it, and we followed his example in succession. The animal seemed at that moment to be in a harmless mode; he grinned several times, but made very little noise. Having performed this ceremony, and standing a few moments in silent agony, we had leave to take our shoes and other property, and leave the den without any other injury than the humility of being obliged in this involuntary manner, to violate the second commandment of God and offend common decency. Can any man believe that this elevated brute has seven kings of Europe, two republics, and a continent tributary to him when his whole naval force is not equal to two line-of-battle ships? It is so.

The stark contrasts that life in Barbary presented were both moving and difficult for William Eaton. He felt these states had tremendous potential. "The country on the sea coast of this kingdom [Tunis] is naturally luxuriant and beautiful beyond description," he noted in one of his earliest dispatches. "Were it in the possession of an enlightened and enterprising people," he added, "I know not why it might not vie with the opposite continent in every thing useful, rich and elegant." Eaton was a keenly observant analyst of human affairs in Barbary, but unlike modern State Department mandarins, he was willing to render judgments and eager to voice them. Before long, he came to feel that their civil society and religious institutional arrangements militated against the entrepreneurial spirit. As he noted in another dispatch, "Considered as a nation, they are deplorably wretched, because they have no property in the soil to inspire an ambition to cultivate it. They are abject slaves to the despotism of their government, and they are humiliated by tyranny, the worst of all tyrannies, the despotism of priestcraft. They live in more solemn fear of the frowns of a bigot who has been dead and rotten above a thousand years, than of the living despot whose frown would cost them their lives."

The more time Eaton spent in the region, the more he came to consider the people of Barbary pathetically behind the Christian West. In his opinion, Algiers suffered because "her spirit of enterprise is relaxed," and "her subjects have neither relish nor stimulus to ambition—Her religious system favors indolence by inspiring a reliance [on the will of Allah]." He began to suspect that Islam, at least as practiced in Barbary, closed the Arab mind "to the gift of reason." Indeed, he thought Islam essentially damned a person to a stupid, backward existence: "The ignorance, superstitious tradition and civil and religious tyranny, which depress the human mind here, exclude improvement of every kind; consequently the same habits, customs and manners which were observed in the East three thousand years ago, are still prevalent here. Everything is done to the greatest possible disadvantage."

Yet not all of Eaton's comparative ruminations reflected so poorly on Barbary. "Barbary is hell," he wrote in his journal. "So, alas, is all of America south of Pennsylvania; for oppression, and slavery, and misery, are there—!" Indeed, Barbary slavery led

Eaton to serious soul-searching. As he wrote to his wife, "remorse seizes my whole soul when I reflect that this is indeed but a copy of the very barbarity which my eyes have seen in my own country. And yet we boast of liberty and national justice." How often "in the southern states of my own country," he continued, "have I seen weeping mothers leading the guiltless infant to the sales, with as deep anguish as if they led them to the slaughter." Even worse, he admitted, his "bosom" had remained "tranquil in the view of these transgressions upon defenseless humanity." Indeed, Eaton asserted, "truth and justice demand from me the confession that the Christian slaves among the barbarians of Africa are treated with more humanity than the African slaves among the professing Christians of civilized America; and yet here sensibility bleeds at every pore for the wretches whom fate has doomed to slavery."

Eaton's primary thoughts and observations, however, came back to his military training and his sense of duty. Almost immediately following his arrival in Barbary, he began contemplating ways for his nation to rid itself of the blight of Barbary piracy or at least to lighten the hassle of Barbary diplomacy. Thus, when after a reconnaissance he was not impressed with the military capability of Algiers, he was quick to suggest offensive strategies:

> All the batteries of Algiers are in a ruined condition: the gun carriages almost uniformly rotten; and garrisoned by undisciplined, half-starved Turks, who devote much more time to their pipes and prayers than to their arms and police . . . there is not stand of arms among the citizens nor other defensive weapon, and they could be forced on board [American] vessels before the least succor could be given from any quarter. These hostages in America would give the command of terms; for being principally Moors it would produce general insurrection in the country if they should not be redeemed. Eight regular battalions could effect this enterprise. . . . We have heard much of the irresistible intrepidity of the Turkish military here. It is all hyperbola. Here is nothing like an organized military. The camp, as their force is termed, is an awkward squad of insolent Turks, whose only feats of valor consist in swaggering once a year into the country among the wretched, defenseless Moors to gather taxes. They have neither tactics nor discipline. There is not a bayonet in Barbary.

Not much should be feared nor expected from a people whose principal ministers, principal merchants, and principal generals consume day after day in the same company smoking tobacco and playing at chess—While the citizens and soldiers are sauntering in rags, sleeping under walls, or praying away there lives under the shrines of departed saints—Such is the military, and such the industry of Barbary—Yet to the shame of humanity they dictate terms to powerful nations!!!

Tunis did not fare much better under Eaton's observations. "The military force of Tunis is rather imaginary than real," he wrote to Pickering, "and they have less discipline than the rudest troops I have ever seen in America; and I have seen our militia from Boston in Massachusetts to Lexington in Kentucky, and from the north boundaries of Vermont to the south boundaries of Georgia." He went on to describe their army, infantry, and even their horses as inferior in every respect to American forces. He considered them "totally undisciplined. . . . On their march they drive on helter skelter, as void of tactics as the tigers of their desert, and their encampments are as irregular as their exercise. Such are all the soldiery whom I have seen, and I have reason to believe such are all whom the kingdom can produce." He likened them to the Native American Indians "in their complexion and habits . . . and . . . manners," but he found the natives of Barbary wanting in that they lacked "that wild magnanimity, that air of independence, which animate those freeborn sons of our forests."

On March 2, 1799, William Eaton and James Cathcart sailed out of Algiers for Tunis aboard the *Sophia*. Eaton was to begin his career as resident U.S. consul there, while James Cathcart accompanied him to assist in renegotiating the three articles of the 1796 U.S.-Tunisian peace treaty before continuing on to his consular posting in Tripoli.

4

The Trials and Tribulations of a U.S. Consul

ON MARCH 12, 1799, after ten days' journey, the *Sophia* anchored in the Bay of Tunis. Eaton and Cathcart obtained permission to land two days later and made their way to the city. Having no Consular House established, they proceeded to the home of Joseph Famin, the U.S. chargé d'affaires, who welcomed them warmly. The duration of the afternoon was spent "in the formality of receiving visits" from the various European consuls in Tunis.

That evening, Eaton and Cathcart dined with Major Perkins Magra, the British consul. Magra warned them not to trust Famin, adding that "he was a dangerous man" to U.S. interests in Tunis. He also warned Eaton "that snares were set" for him "on many sides and that the utmost vigilance might not save" him "from falling into some of them." In this, Magra's warning comported well with the suspicions of U.S. Secretary of State Timothy Pickering: that Famin was an agent of France, or that he was in league with the bey (or a member of his court), or that he, being a merchant, was simply placing his commercial interests above those of the United States.

Joseph Etienne Famin, a French merchant in Tunis, had been engaged in 1796, on the advice of Louis-Alexandre d'Allois d'Herculais, the French consul in Algiers, to help negotiate the U.S. peace treaty with Tunis. He obtained a six-month truce between the two nations on June 15, 1796, and then negotiated a treaty on August 1, 1797.

Eaton soon learned, however, that the American suspicions of Famin were wholly justified. Famin had strong commercial ties to Bey Hammuda Pasha's closest and most influential adviser, the *sahib al-tabi'* (Keeper of the Seal), a renegade known as Yusuf Khoja (Joseph the Clerk), who was heavily involved in Tunisian commerce. According to Eaton, the close relationship between the *sahib al-tabi'* and the bey was the sort that "would excite a blush in the countenance of the most depraved of nature's children, and however singularly unnatural, his favorite minister [*sahib al-tabi'*], a lusty Turk of about thirty-three, is the first object of his passion."

During the 1797 peace negotiations, Famin had incorporated the three aforementioned objectionable articles into the treaty, one of which was specifically designed, at the expense of the United States, to improve the commercial interests of himself and the *sahib al-tabi'*. These were immediately spotted and rejected when the treaty was first submitted to Congress for approval, and its final ratification depended entirely upon their excision or revision.

As Eaton and Cathcart did not trust Famin, they tapped into the network of Barbary Jews for alternative support on the ground in Tunis. The Americans were put in contact with Solomon Azulai, a Jewish banker. Azulai had some measure of influence at court and in Tunisian commercial circles, and for a fee, he agreed to represent Eaton's interests in Tunis, also establishing a line of credit for him.

On March 15, 1799, Eaton, Cathcart, Azulai, and Famin entered the Bardo, the bey's palace. They were granted an audience with Bey Hammuda Pasha and were introduced by Famin. (Eaton's detailed and lengthy account of these negotiations is considered a classic example of the problems American negotiators have routinely encountered in the Middle East and the Maghreb over the years.)

The bey was not in a terribly receptive mood for the Americans:

"Is your vessel a vessel of war?" he asked.

"Yes," they replied.

"Why was I not duly informed of it, that you might have been saluted, as is customary?"

"We were unacquainted with the customs," they assured him.

"[The] true cause," Eaton noted in his journal, "[was that] we did not choose to demand a salute which would have cost the United States eight hundred dollars."

"Had you not an agent here who could have informed you?" asked the bey. "And have not I ministers," he added icily, "who could have introduced your concerns to me, without the agency of a *Jew*?"

"True," they responded, "we had an agent here, but we were uninformed of the mode of making communications." Eaton noted in his journal that they "had been advised at Algiers, not to employ M. Famin" and so made their "arrangements accordingly."

"It is now more than a year since I expected the regalia of maritime and military stores, stipulated by treaty," the bey complained. "What impeded the fulfillment of the stipulation?"

Eaton and Cathcart responded with a handful of excuses, including the lengthy and inevitable delays in transatlantic communications and the Quasi-War with France. "Besides [all of this]," they explained, "when the treaty was laid before the government for ratification, it was found exceptionable. We are come forward empowered to agree on the necessary alterations." Once the problematic articles of the treaty were satisfactorily renegotiated or expunged, "the Government of the United States will cause every exertion to be made for the fulfillment of the obligation on their part." Further, once the bey agreed to the requested changes, they were prepared to pay him the equivalent value of the stipulated naval stores in hard cash—they explained that they thought cash might be preferable, as the stipulated naval stores would be near impossible to ship due to the open European hostilities.

The bey was neither convinced nor amused. "I am not a pauper," he said. "I have cash to spare. The stores are at this moment more than ever peculiarly necessary in consequence of the war with France [and the difficulty in procuring these items in Europe]." He began to shift the proceedings toward his fresh demands. "You have found no difficulty," he said, "in fulfilling your engagements with Algiers and Tripoli; and to the former have very liberally made presents of frigates and other armed vessels."

Eaton and Cathcart tried to explain that the bey was misinformed and that the dey of Algiers had paid for his frigates. Again, the bey remained skeptical. "I shall," he said after some discussion, "expect an armed vessel from you gratuitously, after the business is settled, as you have given Algiers." Eaton and Cathcart calmly refused, explaining that such a gift was entirely out of the question and would not be granted by their government.

Through the course of extensive and relatively complicated negotiations over the next ten days, Eaton and Cathcart eventually succeeded in amending the three offending treaty articles. The effort was not painless, however, and Eaton did not respond well to Bey Hammuda's threats and bullying. "It is hard to negotiate," he ranted in one of his early State Department dispatches, "where the terms are wholly *EX PARTE*." The Barbary regencies were, he continued:

> indulged in the habits of dictating their own terms of negotiation. Even the English, as the Consul himself informed me, on his arrival and reception here, had furnished him [the bey] a present in cash and other articles valued, in England, at seventeen thousand pounds sterling. But Tunis trembles at the voice of England. This then must be a political intrigue of England to embarrass the other mercantile Christian nations, and it has the effect. To the United States, they believe they can dictate terms. Why should they not? Or why should they believe it will ever be otherwise? They have seen nothing in America to controvert this opinion. . . . But whatever stratagem may be used to aid our measures, it is certain, there is no access to the permanent friendship of these states, without paving the way with gold or cannon balls, and the proper question is, which method is preferable.
>
> So long as they hold their own terms, no estimate can be made of the expense of maintaining a peace. They are under no restraints of honor nor honesty. There is not a scoundrel among them, from the prince to the muleteer, who will not beg and steal. . . .
>
> The United States have set out wrongly, and have proceeded so. Too many concessions have been made to Algiers. There is but one

language which can be held to these people, and this is *terror*. If my own feelings were to dictate the answer to the demands submitted, it would be a solemn one. But whether good policy would dictate this is the question. We should get little and might lose much. At all events we should have to buy a peace at last, and redeem our captives, unless we could effect the entire destruction of the Regency, or convince them of our ability to do it.

The negotiations were a taxing, tedious, and needlessly complicated affair. Besides Eaton and Cathcart, they also involved Famin, Azulai, the Algerian ambassador to Tunis, the *sahib al-tabi'*, and various court ministers and advisers. Adding to the general discomfort of the situation, the bey refused to allow Eaton to establish a consular residence until the negotiations were settled.

As the haggling became more heated, Eaton found the institutional corruption and avarice appalling, and thought the rigors of court etiquette—all the removing of shoes, the bowing before the bey, the kissing of the bey's hand, the drinking of coffee, and so forth—repugnant and oppressive. He was greatly relieved when the proceedings were completed on March 26, 1799, and the Senate eventually ratified the treaty on January 10, 1800. Success in hand, William Eaton established his consular residence in Tunis, while James Cathcart departed for Tripoli.

Following well-established custom, Eaton turned his energies toward distributing cash and trinkets (about $6,000 worth) as goodwill "presents" to the bey, the members of his family, his ministers, friends of the court, and what seemed like a multitude of other associated Tunisians. As with the peace negotiations, however, disbursing the presents proved a thoroughly deflationary activity for Eaton's sense of honor, both personal and national.

The process was made all the more demeaning when the haggling continued even at this stage: the *khaznaji* complained that his present was not as valuable as the present Eaton had given to the *sahib al-tabi'*, the *vekil kharj* demanded more jewelry and cloth, the bey's secretaries demanded gifts, the secretaries to the secretaries demanded gifts, even the bey's household servants demanded gifts. Eaton had little choice but to comply. "Thus," he wrote to O'Brien, "I have finished my first chapter of accidents in this land of rapine and sodomy."

While Eaton was prepared to discipline himself to cope with the Tunisians, he could not persuade himself to tolerate Joseph Famin. Nor did Famin try to make it easy for Eaton to tolerate him. Eaton's arrival formally brought an end to Famin's representative authority for the United States and thus diminished the Frenchman's standing at a time when Tunis and France were at war with each other. On top of this, Eaton's successful revision of the peace treaty set back Famin's commercial advantage and reduced his usefulness to the *sahib al-tabi'*.

By June 1800, Eaton had made some real progress in neutralizing Famin's influence at court. He then learned that Famin was directly responsible for the bey's "extraordinary demand for jewels" and that the Frenchman was actively, and currently, trying to convince Bey Hammuda that the United States had "no serious intentions of fulfilling their engagements with Tunis." Immediately, Eaton took action: he accosted Famin at the marine gate, accused him, again, of duplicity, and then savagely horsewhipped him in front of a crowd of nearly a hundred onlookers.

A tribunal was called, and Eaton was brought before the bey to answer for his behavior. Although Bey Hammuda Pasha's sympathy was with Famin, Eaton seized the chance to finally rid himself of the Frenchman by repeating all his suspicions and providing corroborating evidence—the most damning of which was a document wherein Famin referred to the prime minister and his commercial agents as "thieves and robbers." The evidence was deemed overwhelming, and the bey's mind was changed. Famin was found the guilty party, and Eaton was vindicated—the Bey Hammuda Pasha even gave Eaton's hand a "cordial squeeze." Concluding the tribunal, the bey proclaimed, "I have always found him [Eaton] a very candid man, and his concern for his fellow citizens is not a crime."

Nevertheless, keeping the peace in Barbary was an exasperating affair. The bey's demands seemingly knew no limits. Eaton had no choice but to agree, and he informed his government to make provision. As per usual, despite the manifest urgency of the matter, the U.S. government was not quick to dispatch the promised military and naval stores or procure the additional presents and trinkets needed to purchase the goodwill and cooperation of the bey and his court. As the weeks and months passed without any sign of the promised American "regalia" arriving in Tunis, the bey grew increasingly petulant. While Eaton stalled and equivocated, the bey's demands grew larger and more fervent and were expressed with increased frequency and with greater vituperation and bullying. Eaton grumbled to the State Department that

> [t]he game of the Mediterranean Christians [has been] wrested from them [the Tunisians] by the more mighty hunters of the North and East; what have they for one hundred and twenty bloodhounds, which now lie kenneled in their ports, to be employed about? They must be let loose upon somebody. They already scent our merchantmen. And finding the least plausible pretext, they will be loosed to the chase. If then our stipulations be not punctually observed, where is the guarantee of our safety? Shall we rely on treaty compact? Treaties are dead languages with these regencies. . . . We cannot place any reliance in their *good faith*. Can humanity move them? Why should we expect from inveterate pirates, virtues seldom practiced among civilized and Christian nations? Have we the vanity to believe they are afraid of us? What should have produced this impulse? They have seen nothing here to excite terror but the little Miss *Sophia* disguised in men's clothes. The poor thing excited pity rather than alarm.
>
> When I observed to the Bey at one of our interviews that we had whipped the English, he shrewdly asked whether *we* did it or whether the *French* did it *for us*? As I have before said, nothing will prevent us from being blood-sucked by this daughter of the horseleech except formidable force, faithful fulfillment of our stipulations or further sacrifices.

American commercial activity seemed to grow exponentially due to America's neutrality during the prolonged European conflicts at the end of the eighteenth century, the bloody wars of the French Revolution (1789–99) that gave way to the even bloodier Napoleonic Wars (1799–1815). The resurgence of an entirely unprotected American merchant presence in Barbary—roughly eighty American merchant vessels ventured through the Mediterranean in the spring of 1799 alone—merely agitated an already restless bey, particularly as he was running out of "enemies" upon whom to unleash his pirates. Eaton had been warning of the precariousness of this situation for some time, and he grew increasingly concerned:

> Europe will see a rival accumulating wealth and power in the west by this monopoly [of being a neutral carrier during the European wars]. Jealousy and envy will conspire with national interest to procure the sentence against us, *Delenda est Carthago!* ["Carthage must be utterly destroyed!"] But this must be done by intrigue, by assassination. These pirates present themselves as suitable instruments of this policy. They are suffered in existence for no other purpose but to be thus used. Peace and war with them are articles of commerce; and they may be set on or bought off by the highest bidder.

By July, the insecurity of this situation seemed hopeless to William Eaton. He considered it a foregone conclusion that the U.S. government would not fulfill the treaty obligations in the time remaining. He tried repeatedly but unsuccessfully to convince the bey to accept a cash settlement in lieu of the stipulated military and naval stores and in place of the jewels demanded by the bey as his "present." Eaton continuously wrote to the secretary of state and others of influence urging the need for the United States to make good on her commitments and to send a warship of some sort—even a small one would do—to ensure that the treaty would be kept and that the United States would be respected. Otherwise, he feared, avarice would trump diplomacy, and the United States would soon be compelled to redeem slaves and forgo her Mediterranean commerce.

Eaton's fears were partially substantiated by a spectacle he witnessed on June 28, 1799, at a dinner party hosted by the *sahib al-tabi'*. Earlier that day, the *sahib al-tabi'* had, on the bey's behalf, once again declined Eaton's offers of cash in lieu of promised goods. He explained to Eaton that the bey was greatly annoyed with the United States because Tunis was desperately in need of the military and naval stores, particularly as these items were almost impossible to procure in Europe because of the war. "[W]hile we were at dinner," Eaton reported, "a body of Turks came armed to the garden, and even into the courtyard, and demanded money, alleging *that the government having made peace with everybody had reduced them to famine; but they were resolved not to starve!* This circumstance confirms that opinion heretofore advanced that they must be let loose upon somebody."

Eaton thought war even more likely when he learned that the Portuguese and Sicilian ambassadors had successfully concluded peace agreements with the bey. There was now no one to block the pirates of Tunis from entering the Atlantic through the Straits of Gibraltar. When he tried again, on July 4, 1799, to push his "project of a cash payment," the bey showed no interest. As Eaton reported, "He laconically answered 'No sum whatever; you need not think more of it.'" Hammuda Pasha explained that he no longer wished Eaton to mention this matter again, either to himself or to any of his ministers. Time was running out for the United States to satisfactorily meet her treaty obligations.

By the end of 1799, all three consuls—O'Brien in Algiers, Cathcart in Tripoli, and Eaton in Tunis—were profoundly downhearted. War seemed always on the verge of outbreak, their personal safety at times uncertain, and their government constantly out of touch. As William Eaton wrote to Richard O'Brien, "It seems that our government either do not understand our communications, or do not believe them, or are indifferent to them (a thing impossible)." The situation was apparently doomed. What, after all, was the point of their struggles if the government they represented neglected its treaty obligations and refused to protect its interests in the region?

Consul General Richard O'Brien wrote to the secretary of state with more disconcerting news on March 12, 1800.

Following the outbreak of a short-lived war between France and Algiers, the French consul had been clapped in irons, and all the Frenchmen in Algiers had been rounded up and enslaved. This action was taken despite treaty stipulations that specifically provided time for retreat following the declaration of war. (Before long, however, the dey made peace with France—thereby angering the Ottoman sultan.) Watching Algiers flout her treaty with France made O'Brien more than a little uneasy. Similarly, the Spanish consul had been put in chains upon his government's failure to pay her tribute on time.

When Dey Mustafa grew tired of haggling over Danish tribute, he threatened to enslave the Danish consul and declare war against Denmark. The Danish consul immediately fled Algiers when the news reached him; and when the Swedish consul informed the dey of the Dane's flight, he was very nearly beheaded—the dey pulled out a scimitar and took a swipe at the consul's head; the Swedish consul ducked, fled the castle, and then Algiers. Richard O'Brien began to view the security of his position very suspiciously.

Meanwhile in Tunis, the *Sophia* returned from the United States on March 24, 1800. Among the dispatches was a letter from President John Adams to "Hammuda Pasha, Bey of Tunis, the well guarded city and abode of felicity." The president gave the usual excuses for American tardiness in paying up: "four [months] had elapsed when your letter . . . arrived," "pestilence raging in some of our principal cities," "inhabitants to flee into the country," "delays unavoidable," etc. President Adams then assured the bey that the United States would fulfill her obligations as stipulated in the peace treaty between their two friendly nations. The letter was dated January 15, 1800.

Bey Hammuda Pasha was suitably pleased, but he showed concern that the president failed to mention the jewels. Eaton explained that the items he desired were being made especially for him in London.

On April 12, 1800, the *Hero* finally arrived, carrying part of the long-awaited naval stores. The ship had experienced countless delays in trying to reach Barbary and had to return to port several times for repairs and the replacement of stores and supplies. Although the freshly delivered naval supplies were of fine quality, the ship was small and rotten, definitely not the sort of vessel anyone had expected from a young upstart nation whose consuls had been trying hard to portray her as a mighty force to reckon with. Immediately, American prestige sank even lower. After reading through the newly arrived dispatches, Eaton attempted to lessen the blow to American prestige by assuring the bey that "the stores now preparing to ship at New York, will sail with a squadron."

Also among the new dispatches was a letter from Secretary of State Timothy Pickering. Despite the urgency and importance Eaton had expressed in the matter of obtaining jewels for the bey, Pickering suggested that Eaton should haggle with Hammuda Pasha in order to buy time and save money. "Perhaps," the letter read, the bey's demands "may yet be parried; or at least reduced to one half the amount. . . . I hope he will be softened; and that you will either do away this claim, or reduce it to a small value." After a few more lines of worthless advice, the secretary of state added, "It will not do to *lose* our *peace* with Tunis for the value of this present."

The situation in Tripoli, meanwhile, was little better. The perfidious Pasha Yusuf Qaramanli had decided on April 18, 1800, that he was not being treated as an equal to Tunis and Algiers. Cathcart's efforts to spread goodwill were not as effective as those of his colleagues in Algiers and Tunis.

The pasha complained that the United States had lately given him little more than compliments, promises, and other immaterial gifts—and he assured Cathcart that he put no value in such words. He pointed out that "the heads of the Barbary States knew their friends by the value of the presents they received from them." Warming to his theme, he told Cathcart that he would have an easier time believing that American pledges of friendship were genuine if they would give him a cruiser or a brigantine of war, as they had done with Algiers.

Cathcart tried in vain to dissuade the pasha from this view and from making this demand. Although it was essentially of no real utility to James Cathcart, the U.S. treaty with Tripoli expressly provided that any disputes between the United States and Tripoli, such as this one, were to be submitted for arbitration to the dey of Algiers.

Pasha Yusuf Qaramanli's displeasure increased dramatically when he learned, a month later, that Bey Hammuda Pasha of Tunis had received better presents from the United States. Cathcart tried again to calm the pasha and assure him that the United States held him in very high esteem. As usual, however, his efforts had no effect upon the regency.

Qaramanli instructed him to write to his government, to "acquaint the President of the United States that he is exceedingly pleased with his proffers of friendship; . . . that had his protestations been accompanied with a frigate or brig-of-war, such as we had given the Algerines, he would be still more inclined to believe them genuine." He complained bitterly of the "indifference" Tripoli was being shown. Cathcart wrote that the pasha intended to remain aggravated at least "until he received some further marks of the President's esteem more substantial than mere compliments."

Indeed, Pasha Qaramanli was so irritated that on May 25, 1800, he wrote a letter directly to President John Adams. Although he acknowledged the general profession of amity and goodwill that President Adams had conveyed through Consul James Cathcart, Qaramanli pressed his case:

> But, our sincere friend, we could wish that these, your expressions, were followed by deeds, and not by empty words. You will therefore endeavor to satisfy us by a good manner of proceeding. We on our part will correspond with you, with equal friendship, as well in words as deeds. But if only flattering words are meant without performance, every one will act as he finds convenient. We beg a speedy answer without neglect of time, as a delay on your part cannot but be prejudicial to your interests.

To emphasize his meaning, Pasha Qaramanli elucidated to Cathcart that if the United States did not endeavor to satisfy Tripoli, he would "declare war, in form, against the United

States." Yusuf Qaramanli expected and was accustomed to compliance. "Let them know," he told the consul, "that the French, English, and Spaniards, have always sent me presents to preserve their peace," and if the government of the United States of America "do not do the same, I will order my cruisers to bring their vessels in whenever they can find them."

Cathcart wrote his superiors to inform them of this conversation and to assure them that Pasha Qaramanli had every intention of following through on these threats. He thought that compliance would pacify the pasha for only about a year or so, but not much longer than that. "I therefore can see no alternative," he wrote the secretary of state, "but to station some of our frigates in the Mediterranean, otherwise we will be continually subject to the same insults . . . and will still continue to suffer."

Although O'Brien, Eaton, and Cathcart did not always see eye to eye on matters of policy or diplomacy, they all agreed that the United States was in an absurdly precarious situation—one that could be easily bettered through some mixture of compliance and force. Pay what was owed, they argued, but respond to fresh demands with brawn and gumption. "If the United States persists in resignation and passive obedience," Eaton warned, "they will find that *Qui se fait brebis le loup le mange*. He who makes himself a sheep must expect to be devoured by the wolf." Any warship would do, they thought, to stave off the attention of the Barbary bullies and teach them that America would protect its honor and its commerce.

5

America Declares War

WHEN JOHN ADAMS entered the office of president in March 1797 to take up the duties of that exalted station, the United States had already established official diplomatic relationships with Morocco, Algiers, Tunis, and Tripoli. Under the previous administration of President George Washington, several costly peace treaties with the Barbary States had been negotiated, signed, and ratified. A variety of very expensive extracontractual payments and agreements had also been entered into and solemnly promised. Thus it fell to Adams to carry out these stipulations and obligations. By this time, however, the political parties were sharply divided over foreign and domestic issues, even on as simple a matter as whether or not the United States could or should maintain a strong navy to project her national will and protect her national interests. Consequently, the matter of improving the United States' relationship with the Barbary regencies was fundamentally crippled.

The European conflict complicated matters even further. As the premier neutral maritime commercial carrier, America found itself trying to steer a course between France and England, with both nations eager to force America's hand to their own side, and to the exclusion of their rival. Navigating this path was no simple task, and it fell to President Adams to maintain diplomatic impartiality and nonalignment with the quarrels of the Old World.

Throughout, President Adams had to produce and propound policy in the context of the vicious rivalry between his own party, the Federalists, who insisted America take the side of England, and the Democratic-Republicans, who insisted the United States should throw its lot in with France. The government was thus preoccupied in its foreign affairs and other pressing matters that threatened the country far more directly than the petty demands of Barbary pirate warlords, whose dominions were many thousands of miles away. Embarrassingly, there were also inevitable yet considerable delays and communications foul-ups when, in the fall of 1800, the nation moved its capital from Philadelphia to Washington, D.C.

Despite the grumbling of O'Brien, Cathcart, and Eaton, however, the Adams administration was not indifferent to or obtuse about the Barbary situation. The fact that Secretary of State Pickering ordered William Eaton to conduct some intelligence-gathering as to the naval and military capabilities of some of the Barbary States is evidence of the administration's intentions to enter that theater in a more forceful fashion at an appropriate juncture. Indeed, there was at least one concerted attempt by the administration to send naval cruisers into the region, although this effort faltered because of more pressing matters and the natural limits of such an endeavor in the greater context of the European war. President Adams was, unfortunately, not adept enough at party politics to stay the course, so little was ever actually done.

Before long, internal administration differences led to a dramatic political upheaval for Adams. Angered by his efforts to seek a diplomatic solution to the Quasi-War with France, elements of the Federalist Party turned against him. He, in turn, felt compelled to defend himself by attacking back. Adams also suspected that members of his cabinet were conspiring against him, and in May 1800 he forced James McHenry, his secretary of war, and Timothy Pickering, his secretary of state, to resign. They were, he decided, more loyal to Alexander Hamilton, leader of the opposition within the party.

This was, however, an election year. Federalist dissension in the ranks crippled the party's ability to perform for the collective good. Adams lost the support of the majority of the Federalists and soon faced as much opposition from within his own party as from Thomas Jefferson's. Jefferson's Democratic-Republicans knew a good thing when they saw one and effectively went after the divided Federalists hard. They employed every political strat-egy they could think of, including outright slander. The cam-paign was bitter and fierce.

John Adams lost by eight electoral votes, while Jefferson tied Aaron Burr, his own vice presidential running mate, with seventy-three votes. The final decision fell to the House of Representa-tives. After four days and thirty-five different ballots, Thomas Jefferson finally gained a majority and was elected president of the United States; Burr became his vice president.

Before leaving power, the Federalists were determined to cor-don off as much political territory as they could and maintain their grasp on the mantle of power. On February 13, 1801, they pushed through a judiciary reform bill that, among other things, eliminated one Supreme Court justice (lowering the number from six to five) and created sixteen new judicial offices by dividing the Union into sixteen districts, organized into six circuits. Adams nominated the bulk of these judges on February 20, 1801, and the rest had their names submitted for nomination on February 24.

That same day Congress finally passed legislation organizing a proper government seat for Washington, D.C., the new federal city; President Adams had to appoint not only a few more judges but also many other officers. This activity, coupled with the appointment of John Marshall, Adam's second secretary of state, as the new chief justice of the Supreme Court, prompted Thomas Jefferson to con-demn Adams for these last-minute "midnight appointments." Adams left for home on the day of Jefferson's inauguration.

In these final days of the Adams administration, as his party desperately maneuvered to retain some grasp on the reins of gov-ernment, the pro-navy Federalists ironically came to decide that they needed to reduce the size of the U.S. Navy before the anti-navalist forces of Jefferson took control. As the war with France had ended and the antinavalist Democratic-Republicans had won the presidential election, it seemed inevitable that the navy would take a big hit. So, eager to see it done right and by them rather than by the antinavalists, the Federalists decided to head Jefferson's party off at the pass by pushing their own bill through, reducing the navy on their own terms. The measure euphemistically "providing for a naval peace establishment" went through on March 3, 1801, the day before Adams vacated his office.

The bill enabled the navalists to unburden themselves of the converted merchantmen and lighter-draft ships, most of which were unfit for serious battle or faraway patrols. What the navy needed was frigates, not converted merchant vessels. This measure protected the first-class frigates and authorized the president to sell off every other ship in the fleet. At the extreme, this provision would command the retention of thirteen frigates, six of which would be kept in active service, although the crew would be reduced by one-third, while the remaining seven frigates would be laid up. The president was also authorized to excuse, at his discretion, a majority of officers and personnel, requiring the retention of only 9 captains (out of 28), 36 lieutenants (out of 110), and 150 midshipmen (out of 344). Thus any number of worthless, unfit, or overaged seamen and officers could be safely and gracefully retired.

Not surprisingly, Jefferson's administration put this law into action by actively reducing the size of the U.S. Navy. Secretary of the Treasury Albert Gallatin, the Swiss-born Pennsylvania congressman, was tireless and thorough in his efforts to reduce the national debt and balance the federal budget. The largest departmental budget was the navy, so that was high on the list of reductions. Retirements were forced, ships were sold off, frigates were laid up, and economies were made.

The scene was now set for Captain William Bainbridge as unwilling courier for Dey Bobba Mustafa of Algiers.

Captain Bainbridge's mission had originally been to deliver tributary payments and give a much-needed booster shot to American honor and prestige in the region. Now he and his ship had been impressed into the service of the dey of Algiers, by force, to courier an Algerine embassy to Constantinople—sailing under the Algerine flag. The humiliation Bainbridge endured reflected terribly on the United States. The USS *George Washington* was not simply an American vessel, but a U.S. national ship of war—the first ever to enter the Mediterranean Sea.

In neighboring Tunis, U.S. consul William Eaton was nearly overcome with anger and indignation. "I never thought to find a corner of this slanderous world where 'baseness' and 'American' were wedded," he wrote in his journal, "but here we are the byword of derision, quoted as precedents of baseness, even by Danes!" The catastrophe weighed heavily on Eaton's mind. "History shall tell," he noted, "that the United States first volunteered a ship of war, equipped, a carrier for a pirate. It is written. Nothing but blood can blot the impression out. . . . Will nothing rouse my country!"

As the *George Washington* sailed out of the harbor of Algiers on her new mission, she fired seven guns in salute, compliment was answered by the harbor fortification, and the ship sailed out to sea. As soon as they were at sea, Bainbridge lowered the Algerine pennant and raised the American flag to a dominant position.

The three-week journey from Algiers to Constantinople was uncomfortable. The weather was mostly disagreeable, the winds were bad, and the ship was horribly overcrowded—with a 131-man crew, the Algerine ambassador, a hundred of his attendants, a hundred slaves, and close to two hundred assorted animals. Further, every day, five times a day, at sunrise, midmorning, afternoon, sundown, and evening, the Muslims had to perform the *salat*, or the daily set ritual of prayer. To do so they required enough silence and space to achieve a state of ritual purity, they needed to be in a ritually clean location, and they had to face the direction of Mecca, the birthplace of the Prophet Muhammad, throughout the prayer. So five times a day the Muslims congregated on the main deck, getting in the way of the sailors. As they were at sea in unfavorable winds, however, the ship needed to tack frequently, which meant that the worshipers had just as frequently to shift during their devotions in order to continue facing Mecca. Although this display was at first amusing to the Christian contingent, it quickly lost some of its entertainment value. Further, the Muslims became increasingly frustrated by the situation, annoyed at the audience, and angry with Captain Bainbridge. Eventually the Algerine ambassador posted a man in the binnacle to observe the compass and signal direction during the *salat*.

In this spirit, the ship continued her course until very early Sunday morning, November 9, 1800, when it neared the Dardanelles, the western section of the strait dividing Europe from Asia. The weather had improved, the wind was fair, and the USS *George Washington* was having an easy time of it.

The channel along the Dardanelles averages about three miles wide, although at the narrowest section it contracts to less than three-quarters of a mile across, and the sides are almost within shouting distance apart. At this position, the gateway to the Turkish kingdom, stand two castles, one on either side of the strait, nearly directly opposite each other: the Sedil Bahr on the European shore and the Kum Kaleh on the Asian.

According to custom, ships were commanded to anchor and present their passports before being granted permission to continue through the channel and on to Constantinople. The batteries of the castles were, however, stationary heavy cannons, and so were effective only so long as the target had not passed them.

Captain Bainbridge had no passport to produce, and he was not interested in being detained while the Algerine ambassador tried to smooth things over. He was in entirely foreign territory now, and he did not trust either the Algerines or the Turks. So as he neared the castles, he ordered the crew to run across the decks and act as if he were going to take in sail, heave to, and anchor so as to present the ship, as was customary. He fired a salute of eight guns using double charges, which was promptly returned by the batteries of both castles with a salute of six guns each. As the scene was now enveloped in clouds of white smoke and the castles' vision was impaired, Bainbridge directed his crew to rapidly make sail; they took on canvas and sailed swiftly onward. The *George Washington* bore speedily off and safely out of range of the castles' guns.

The following day, they passed the island of Marmara and caught their first glimpse of "the Spires of Constantinople." Captain Bainbridge recorded in his log that "the City [is] beautifully situated on the sides of 7 Hills gently ascending from the sea making a most Beautiful appearance from the Sea."

On Tuesday, November 11, the *George Washington* sailed into the Haliç, or Golden Horn—the horn-shaped estuary that provides Constantinople's main harbor. The ship was approached cautiously by a dispatch boat from the harbor, for no other ship had ever made it past the gateway castles and entered the Golden Horn without having been first invited by the sultan. Aboard the dispatch boat, an officer hailed Captain Bainbridge and asked him to identify under what flag the ship sailed. Captain Bainbridge answered that he sailed under the colors of the United States of America; the officer hurried back to the harbor to report.

Before long the boat returned, and the captain of the harbor presented himself to Bainbridge. Aboard the *George Washington*, the harbor captain reported, in excellent French, that no one had ever heard of the United States of America, and that a more thorough explanation was required for identification.

William Bainbridge explained that the United States of America was part of the New World that had been discovered by Christopher Columbus. The harbor captain accepted this, and the *George Washington* was allowed to anchor in the outer harbor off the Yedikule battlements. A throng of curious onlookers and soldiers crowded the castle and fortifications behind the harbor.

Some hours later the harbor captain returned in a larger boat, accompanied by the master of the port. They boarded the *George Washington* as official representatives of the Ottoman sultan.

The USS *George Washington* was thus recognized as a friendly vessel, and on the sultan's behalf the master of the port presented Captain Bainbridge with a lamb as a token of peace, and many bunches of flowers as an expression of welcome. Per instructions from the sultan, the harbor captain conducted the frigate into the inner harbor of Constantinople, where she anchored opposite "the Grand Signors Barracks." The *George Washington* fired a twenty-one-gun salute as she passed the sultan's palace.

Within the hour, Captain Bainbridge received an invitation for an audience with the Ottoman sultan, Selim III. Although Sultan Selim exhibited an intelligent curiosity about the United States of America, his ignorance of the New World was too substantial to allow for any significant or meaningful exchange of views in the allotted time. Curiously, the sultan took note of the stars on the American flag and commented that as his flag also had one of the "heavenly bodies," there must be some sort of similarity between the religion, laws, and customs of America and those of Turkey. To his mind, America was not a Christian nation, and thus was not like the nations of Europe.

Over the course of his stay in Constantinople, Captain Bainbridge befriended Kucuk Husayn Pasha, the *kapudan pasha* (the chief admiral of the Ottoman navy), who was also the brother-in-law of the sultan, and a close adviser. The two got along famously. During one of their meetings in the *kapudan pasha*'s palace, Bainbridge was questioned on how he managed to pass through the Dardanelles without being detained. It quickly emerged that the governor of the castle at the gateway had been sentenced to death for his negligence and was to be beheaded in two days' time. Captain Bainbridge immediately explained his ruse and insisted that the governor of the castle was not to be faulted and that the blame rested entirely on his shoulders. If anyone was to be punished, Bainbridge declared, it was he. The *kapudan pasha*'s admiration for Bainbridge grew tenfold by this display, and the governor of the castle was pardoned.

Besides laying the groundwork for future peace negotiations between the United States and Turkey, Bainbridge also learned what had become of the Algerine ambassador whom he had been compelled to take to Istanbul. The sultan, it seems, took great offense at Dey Bobba Mustafa's peace with France and his active hostility toward nations at peace with Turkey (owing in no small measure to Bainbridge's conversations with the Kucuk Husayn Pasha). Selim III refused to receive the dey's presents, treated the ambassador very shabbily, and ordered him to convey the message that the dey was ordered to declare war against France and send a million piastres back to Constantinople within sixty days. Although the Algerine ambassador immediately decided to remain in Constantinople and stay with the dey's gifts, he asked Bainbridge to return to Algiers and convey the sultan's written message.

Captain Bainbridge decided it was indeed time to return and made preparations to depart. Since he had made a very favorable impression in Turkey, the *kapudan pasha* gave him a *firman* from the sultan that guaranteed his ship respect and protection in all Turkish ports and ordered that the USS *George Washington* be given a full salute as it passed the fortification at Tapana, an honor that would normally never be granted to anyone but the *kapudan pasha* himself.

On January 21, 1801, the *George Washington* returned to Algiers, where Dey Bobba Mustafa had fresh demands for the ship to return to Constantinople, but his leverage was exhausted. Bainbridge and Consul General Richard O'Brien refused, declaring that they would rather risk war than submit to such a humiliation again. Dey Mustafa became belligerent, until Bainbridge produced the Sultan's *firman* guaranteeing respect and protection. At the sight of this document, Bobba Mustafa changed immediately from an angry and ferocious pirate to a humble and obsequious servant. He apologized, professed his friendship with the United States, and immediately set in motion total compliance with the sultan's orders. For although Algiers was only nominally under the suzerainty of the Ottoman sultan, Dey Mustafa could not afford to cross so powerful and legitimate an authority. Algiers declared war on France the very next day and released four hundred slaves who had been taken while under the protection of British passports. Bainbridge then, in an effort to deny the dey some vengeance, used his newfound influence to secure a forty-eight-hour window for all the Frenchmen in Algiers to escape, and then agreed to take them all to Alicante aboard the *George Washington*.

Only later did Bainbridge learn that the United States and France were, by this time, no longer engaged in their undeclared quasi-war with each other. Needless to say, he received Napoleon Bonaparte's thanks and appreciation for this service.

On April 19, 1801, the USS *George Washington* reached Philadelphia. Feeling humiliated by the Algerine impressment and frustrated by his government's policies, Captain William Bainbridge hastened to Washington, D.C., to brief the new president on the situation. President Jefferson salved Bainbridge's ego by commending him for the "judicious and skillful manner in which he had discharged his duties while under the pressure of such embarrassing circumstances." In repayment for his conduct, Jefferson retained Bainbridge's captaincy even though he was second to last on the list.

Bainbridge's report rocked the nation. The shame and indignity of the affair was overwhelming and pushed the nation toward an active belligerence to the nations of Barbary. Suddenly, the many U.S. consular dispatches from Barbary were thrown into sharper focus. Richard O'Brien, William Eaton, and James Cathcart had long been urging their nation to take decisive action. Eaton, in particular, considered it wholly preposterous that the first U.S. warship to enter the Mediterranean, bearing the name of the nation's greatest hero and first president, should humbly submit to being impressed under a pirate flag. "Are we then," Eaton asked, "reduced to the humility of bartering our national glory for the forbearance of a Barbary pirate!" After so humiliating a defeat of the national will, how could the United States ever hope to command respect in Barbary and prevent future abuse? "When has a tyrant ever been known to lift his foot from the neck of a voluntary slave?" demanded an incredulous Eaton of the secretary of state in one of his dispatches. The picture he painted was not particularly pleasant:

"Do you not give money to Algiers?" says the Organ of a nation to an American envoy! "Are you not tributary to the pitiful sandbank of Tripoli?" say the world—and the answer is affirmative without a blush! Habit reconciles mankind to everything, even humiliation, and custom veils disgrace. But what would the world say if Rhode Island should arm two old merchantmen, put an Irish renegade in one and a Methodist preacher in the other, and send them to demand a tribute of the Grand Signor [the Ottoman sultan]? The idea is ridiculous, but only so because novel. It is exactly as consistent that Tripoli should say to the American nation, "Give me tribute, or tremble under the chastisement of my navy?" One old clump from Boston [the Tripolitan flagship *Meshuda*, formerly the *Betsey* of Boston], and a polacre or two from some complaisant Christian capitals, and that my Yankee adventurers should succeed, would not be more unaccountable than that these wretched hordes of sea robbers should have so gotten the ascendancy of the enterprising world!

Thomas Jefferson was no stranger to the U.S.-Barbary relationship, and Bainbridge's experience was reason enough to galvanize the country behind a more robust Barbary policy. Indeed, almost everyone was dissatisfied with the situation in the region, not only by the countless humiliations and depredations of the present, but also by the treatment of Americans in the not so distant past. For, only two years before Bainbridge's account of his mistreatment, America had zealously caught the anti-Muslim-pirate bug from the popular publication of the *Journal of the Captivity and Sufferings of John Foss*. Foss's *Journal* initiated a cottage industry of captivity narratives, plays, fiction, and other forms of popular entertainment. The nation was tired of kowtowing to the pirates, and Jefferson was eager to settle the matter with force.

With six frigates remaining on active duty, President Jefferson set his mind to the Barbary problem. On March 9, 1801, he convened his cabinet to consider sending a naval squadron into the Mediterranean "to guard against exigencies or by a demonstration of our power to reduce the capricious Sovereigns of Barbary to a sense of justice thro' the medium of their fears." Jefferson was tired of paying tribute—he called it "money thrown away"—and deemed the principle for this form of diplomacy unsound. "There is no end to the demand of these powers," he said, "nor any security in their promises." Writing to his friend James Madison, the new secretary of state, he said, "I know that nothing will stop the eternal increase of demands from these pirates but the presence of an armed force." He also remarked that he felt sure that such a force would be cheaper, on top of being more honorable.

During the March 9, 1801, cabinet meeting, the U.S. attorney general, Levi Lincoln of Massachusetts, instructed President Jefferson against going to war with the Barbary pirates. The president, said Lincoln, could not order American warships to attack any foreign vessel without the approval and authorization of Congress—in other words, a congressional declaration of war. Secretary of State James Madison and Henry Dearborn, the new secretary of war, suggested that a squadron be sent with standing orders allowing them to engage any enemy that threatened American commerce. Although the item was tabled and the cabinet pressed on with other items, the matter was not forgotten, and the impulse toward war did not abate.

A few days later, on March 13, Madison began to receive dispatches from U.S. consul James Cathcart regarding the situation in Tripoli. Thus the issue of Barbary belligerence cropped up afresh, particularly as some of these dispatches were close to six months old. Madison learned that on September 25, 1800, another U.S. ship had been taken by Tripoli. The *Catherine*, an American brigantine from New York under the command of Captain James Carpenter, was on its way to Leghorn with close to $50,000 worth of cargo when she was captured by a Tripolitan xebec (a two- or three-masted, lateen-sail Mediterranean vessel similar in size to a navy brigantine); the ship was taken to port, the crew was robbed, and the cargo was plundered.

The *Catherine* languished for nearly a month before Cathcart obtained her release. The pasha said it had been taken by mistake and that the captain who took her had been punished. Apart from this concession, however, the pasha remained belligerent and obstinate.

Pasha Qaramanli openly threatened to declare war against the United States if his latest set of demands for more cash were not met within six months. As Cathcart reported from his October 16 interview with the pasha, Qaramanli was merely toying with him, happy either to have his demands met or to go to war with the United States:

> The Pasha then commenced thus: "Consul there is no Nation I wish more to be at Peace with than yours, but all Nations pay me & so must the Americans." I answered "we have already paid you all we owe you & are nothing in arrears." He answered that for the Peace we had paid him it was true, but to maintain the Peace we had given him nothing. I observed that the terms of our Treaty were to pay him the stipulated stores [and the] cash and in full of all demands forever. . . . The Pasha then observed that we had given a great deal to Algiers and Tunis. . . . Why do they [the U.S. government] neglect me in their donations, let them give me a stipulated sum annually, and I will be reasonable as to the amount. . . . He then [expressed] . . . that he hoped the United States would neglect him as six or eight vessels of the value of his would amount to a much larger sum than ever he expected to get from the United States for remaining at Peace.

Cathcart toiled hard at changing the pasha's mind, but to no avail. The United States was given not more than six months to change the treaty to Qaramanli's liking, or else the Tripolitan pirate navy would make war on U.S. commerce in the Mediterranean. In April, Madison received another dispatch from Cathcart reporting that the pasha's resolve had strengthened and that war would be forthcoming unless the United States attempted to pacify him. Cathcart decided that the situation was irreparable and notified all U.S. consuls in the Mediterranean region to warn American ships from those waters due to the Tripolitan threat.

Indeed, at this point Cathcart had truly exhausted his abilities and was not prepared to cope any further. As he wrote in his January 4, 1801, dispatch to Madison, "I am under the necessity of observing that my situation is peculiarly disagreeable." He complained of having been neglected by his government: "unsupported by government, not having received but one letter from the Department of State in two years . . . add to this that my instructions are merely answers to some questions which I asked before my departure and are couched in such terms as will not authorize my taking one decisive measure unless first approved by [Richard O'Brien]." Cathcart then attacked O'Brien as a knave, a liar, a miscreant, and a tool of the Jews of Algiers. He pleaded in his dispatch either for the secretary of state to convince the government to listen, "or that otherwise the President will please appoint some person more adequate to the task imposed upon me than I am; for I find that I cannot under existing circumstances remain longer here."

Madison understood from these dispatches that the situation was dire and critical. It seemed inevitable now that the United States would strike back. As William Eaton had written in his consular dispatch, "It is devoutly to be hoped that the United States may have the honor (very easily obtained) of setting the first example among the tributaries of chastising the insolence of their lords." Armed with Cathcart's reports of Tripolitan agitation, Jefferson was determined to force his cabinet to make a decision.

On May 15, the cabinet was reconvened and the Barbary question was once again brought forward. The primary issue President Jefferson put before them was simple: Should the United States send a squadron to the Mediterranean, and if so, what should the mission be? Once again it was suggested that a Mediterranean cruise was an excellent idea, and once again it was suggested that the president not declare war but, rather, simply authorize the use of retaliatory force. This time, however, the cabinet united and urged immediate action. The president agreed, and the decision was taken to dispatch a naval squadron of four vessels.

On May 20, 1801, Commodore Richard Dale was given command of this squadron, which consisted of three frigates and a schooner—the flagship USS *President* (a frigate of forty-four guns); the USS *Philadelphia* (a frigate of forty-four guns), commanded by Captain Samuel Barron; the USS *Essex* (a frigate of thirty-two guns), commanded by Captain William Bainbridge; and the USS *Enterprize* (a schooner of twelve guns), under the command of Lieutenant Andrew Sterrett. Commodore Dale was instructed to observe and assess the situation and respond as needed. He received dispatches and instructions from the secretary of state for O'Brien, Cathcart, and Eaton and was loaded with cash and other prizes for the U.S. consuls to use to pacify the Barbary regencies.

In case any of the Barbary States had declared war on the United States, Dale was instructed to blockade the enemies' ports and to use his force "so as best to protect our commerce and chastise their insolence—by sinking, burning, or destroying their vessels wherever you shall find them." Additionally, Secretary of State Madison made clear to Dale that this mission was expected to both protect U.S. interests in the region and allow for a suitable testing ground for the U.S. Navy and Marine Corps. It was assumed that American affairs would be in disarray and in grave danger in Barbary, but it was hoped that the situation was not out of control and that Dale's squadron would prove sufficient to the task.

On June 2, 1801, Commodore Richard Dale's squadron disembarked from Hampton Roads, Virginia. Although the mission was peace, the vehicle was war.

Unbeknownst to the Jefferson administration, however, was that just a couple of weeks earlier, Pasha Yusuf Qaramanli of Tripoli had beaten him to the punch. On Thursday, May 14, 1801, after protracted and unsatisfactory diplomacy between James Cathcart and the regency of Tripoli, Qaramanli sent word to the American consulate that he was sending men over to chop down the American flagpole—the traditional method of declaring war in Tripoli. Cathcart made a final, pitiful attempt to stave off this inevitable event by promising $10,000 in cash. This gesture failed.

The pasha's men arrived that afternoon to chop down the flagpole; the whole affair took little more than an hour. The pasha took no other action at this time. Cathcart spent the next ten days packing up his belongings, securing the American consulate, and readying his wife and daughter to leave. He was expected to sail for Tunis, but instead he headed for Leghorn to try to make a few dollars in commerce.

"Thus ends the first act of this tragedy," James Leander Cathcart wrote to the secretary of state in his report of the incident. "I hope the catastrophe may yet be happy."

6

American Might, Frustrated

RICHARD DALE, a native of Norfolk County, Virginia, had been at sea since age twelve and had early on displayed an uncommon ability to handle a vessel. Before age twenty he had already commanded several merchant vessels. Early in the American Revolution, Dale had served in the Virginia state navy, was captured by the British, and switched sides to join the Loyalist forces until an American Continental Navy brigantine captured him. Dale switched back to the American side and served from mid-1776 as an officer in the Continental Navy until the British took the ship on September 19, 1777, and Dale was imprisoned in England. He soon escaped, was recaptured, and then escaped again, making his way safely to France. He returned to America and served with distinction as a lieutenant on board the Continental warship *Bonhomme Richard*.

Dale's naval reputation was solidified for the ages on September 23, 1779, when he performed valiantly during the *Bonhomme*'s desperate battle with the HMS *Serapis*. After the war, Dale returned to the merchant marine, and in 1794 he was one of the first six men to be made a captain in the new United States Navy.

On May 22, 1801, Captain Dale took command of the squadron and became the commodore. The four-ship squadron set sail for Gibraltar out of Virginia early in the morning on June 2. During the first ten days of the journey, it experienced mostly foul weather—heavy rains with strong easterly winds. After four days, Dale permitted Lieutenant Andrew Sterrett of the lighter and faster-sailing sloop-of-war *Enterprize* to break company and make her own way for Gibraltar; the ship had difficulties keeping up with the squadron in rough seas but had the capacity to far outpace the frigates once the weather cleared. The *Enterprize* reached the port of Gibraltar, which was under British control at this time, on June 26, five days ahead of the rest of the squadron.

Upon his arrival, Commodore Dale set out to make contact with John Gavino, the U.S. consul in Gibraltar, and try to obtain permission from the British forces to use Gibraltar as a supply base for his squadron. With a secure base in Gibraltar, the United States would be able to safely send supply ships, rendezvous with Dale in protected waters, and securely resupply his squadron on station; the procedure had proven successful during the Quasi-War with France. Fortunately, the British agreed to the arrangement.

Dale found that the port was virtually empty. Most of the Royal Navy ships had been deployed to blockade the French and Spanish forces at Cadiz. Even more surprising was the presence of Tripoli's two largest pirate ships, the twenty-six-gun *Meshuda* (it was originally the captured Boston brig *Betsey*), the flagship of Ra'is Murad, the Tripolitan Admiral of the Marine, with a complement of 260 men, and a sixteen-gun brig with a 160-man crew. Pasha Yusuf Qaramanli had sent Ra'is Murad out to Gibraltar specifically so that he might cruise the Atlantic in search of American ships, and the British had quarantined the Tripolitan vessels at port for fear of the North African plague.

In Gibraltar, Commodore Dale quickly discovered that Tripoli had declared war against the United States. He also learned of the woeful state of American-Barbary relations. As he wrote to the secretary of the navy on July 2, "I am very sorry to say our Barbary Affairs look very gloomy." He went on to lament that the United States "Government has not paid more attention to the information that has been received from that quarter, I am fearful it will cost the United States many thousand dollars before things are put to rights." He also discovered the American merchantman *Grand Turk* at port; she was laden with tribute for the bey of Tunis but had been quietly moored there for seven weeks because she was afraid to venture out into the Mediterranean. Also tethered to the port was another American vessel, the brig

Hope of Baltimore, which had been laid up for about six weeks for fear of capture. Evidently, Dale discovered, there were "upwards of twenty [or seventy?] sail of Americans" laying at Barcelona and other ports, all afraid of venturing out because of Barbary piracy.

Ra'is Murad was quick to deny any warlike intentions toward the United States, but Commodore Dale did not believe him and was determined to prevent him from leaving Gibraltar. Because the British port was neutral territory, however, Dale could not attack or otherwise assault the pirate captain and his ships while they were safely moored under British protection. So Dale ordered Captain Samuel Barron to lay the *Philadelphia* off Gibraltar and take the Tripolitan ships the moment they tried to leave. Ra'is Murad chose to stay put and avoid a conflict with the superior forty-four-gun American frigate; Tripoli was thus denied her two largest ships, as well as the admiral of her fleet. The rest of the American squadron continued with orders as originally planned.

Captain William Bainbridge's *Essex* sailed with the *Grand Turk* and the Baltimore vessel to provide protection and, it was hoped, some inspiring intimidation; the *Essex* would then continue to Marseille, Barcelona, and Alicante and attempt to convoy other American merchantmen. Commodore Dale sailed his flagship, the *President*, to Algiers, accompanied by Sterrett's sloop-of-war, *Enterprize*. Both ships reached Algiers on July 9, 1801.

U.S. consul general Richard O'Brien met with Commodore Dale and informed him of the situation in Algiers. O'Brien was very pleased to see the American warships and hoped they would have a quieting effect upon the dey. Dale gave O'Brien a letter from him to the dey expressing American friendship and esteem, but he gathered from O'Brien's reports that Algiers was not yet ready to appreciate his visit in any diplomatically meaningful way, so he decided to leave. Even before finishing his inspection of American-Barbary affairs, however, Commodore Dale had already determined for himself the state of America's relationship with the Barbary potentates, as he wrote to the secretary of the navy on July 19, 1801: "I think they must be a damned set, the whole tribe, Algerines, Tunisians, and Tripolitans. There is nothing that will keep their avaricious minds in any degree of order, and prevent them from committing depredations on our commerce whenever they may think proper, but for the United States to keep constantly four or six frigates in the Mediterranean, without that, there is never any security for our commerce."

The *President* weighed anchor and sailed for Tunis on July 11 but experienced harsh weather. Early that morning, at 6 A.M., the winds snapped a mast and tore the mainsail and four of the top-sails—"the ship," Dale wrote, "is very bad off for topsails." Indeed, once he was finally out to sea he decided the area was as bad as the regency: "The bay of Algiers is a bad place for ships to anchor in; I don't think I shall let an anchor go there again."

The two ships of the U.S. Navy's Mediterranean squadron then proceeded to Tunis, arriving on July 17. The *Essex* and the *Grand Turk* arrived the following day. Dale met with William Eaton, gave him fresh dispatches from the State Department, and had Eaton convey the latest updates on the diplomatic situation there. Like O'Brien, Eaton was overjoyed to see the American warships enter the port; as he rather optimistically entered atop the day's entry in his journal, "Here commences a new era in the annals of the United States and Barbary."

Fortunately, these visits had the desired effect upon the regency—a particularly welcome respite for Eaton, as the bey's demands had begun to spiral out of control in mid-April: forty twenty-four-pounder cannons, forty pieces of additional assorted artillery, ten thousand stands of arms, and so forth. Dale quickly formed a positive opinion of William Eaton—"he appears to be a very proper person for a Consul at such a place; he seems to feel for the honor of his country." Taking on fresh water at Tunis, Dale proceeded to Tripoli accompanied by the *Enterprize*; the *Essex* meanwhile continued on its mission of providing safe conduct to merchant ships.

Dale's mission was now to blockade Tripoli, cruise her waters, and intercept her pirate ships, whether going or coming. The *President* and the *Enterprize* reached the waters of Tripoli by July 24, 1801, and immediately began to patrol the area. As his orders proscribed direct assault against the city or the harbor fortifications, Dale simply secured a perimeter and dispatched a message to Pasha Yusuf. His letter was clear and direct:

> Having the honor to Command an American Squadron, sent into the Mediterranean Sea by the President of the United States to protect its commerce, I was sorry to hear on my arrival at Gibraltar, Algiers, and Tunis from the American Consuls there . . . that Your Excellency had declared war against the United States . . . the Squadron under my command will do everything in their power to take and destroy the corsairs and other vessels belonging to your excellency. . . . If your Excellency has any disposition, in a just and honorable way, to make peace with the United States, you will please to let me know by sending a boat off.

Pasha Yusuf Qaramanli was unmoved by this and sent word back that his declaration of war was wholly justified. He claimed that America had broken the treaty first and that the United States had provoked him into his current action. Dale responded that the treaty expressly required any disagreements between the United States and Tripoli to be arbitrated by the dey of Algiers and that by bypassing this stipulation and declaring war, the pasha had broken the treaty in an unjust fashion.

Dale pointed out that he was not authorized to negotiate a new treaty, but that he was prepared to negotiate the pasha's surrender. He also contacted the Danish consul, Nicholas C. Nissen, whom Cathcart had deputized to handle American affairs in Tripoli, to try to further the negotiations. These proceedings continued for roughly two weeks to no particular effect.

All the while, the blockade was strictly enforced but had little success, though it did manage to pin down and obstruct Tripoli's warships and trading vessels. The drafts of both U.S. warships were too deep, however, to block the shallow-draft Tripolitan feluccas from zipping along the coastal shoals.

Meanwhile, Qaramanli continued to play his usual delaying tactics. Naval blockades were a tedious and exhausting affair, and Qaramanli hoped to force Dale's squadron into running out of fresh water and, perhaps, food. As the July heat picked up, the fresh water did indeed begin to disappear rather quickly. Before very long, the hot, tedious, and wearying days of stalled negotiations and constant blockade patrols were taking their toll, and the *President* and the *Enterprize* had nearly exhausted their supplies of essential provisions. The nearest source for resupply was the island of Malta, under British control, and a relatively short voyage away.

On July 30, Commodore Dale ordered Lieutenant Andrew Sterrett to sail the *Enterprize* to Malta "to take in as much water as you can possibly bring back," adding, "you will please to make every exertion to join me again as soon as possible." In case the *Enterprize* should run into an enemy vessel that she could confidently handle, Sterrett was to engage the enemy, "heave all his guns over board, cut away his masts, & leave him in a situation that he can just make out to get into some port." The most important thing, however, was to bring back fresh water, not take on Tripolitan cruisers.

Sterrett broke away for Malta as ordered. The next day, on August 1, he ran across a fourteen-gun Tripolitan pirate ship called the *Tripoli*, commanded by Ra'is Muhammad Rous, with a complement of eighty men. Sterrett struck up British colors as a *ruse de guerre* and hailed the cruiser. Having no quarrel with the English, Ra'is Muhammad Rous allowed the *Enterprize* to come alongside his ship. Lieutenant Sterrett briefly interrogated him as to the purpose of his voyage, and Ra'is Muhammad Rous replied honestly that as his nation was at war with the United States of America, his mission was to take American ships; he lamented that he had not yet encountered any to take. Sterrett responded by lowering the British flag, raising the American colors, and firing a volley of musketry into the *Tripoli*. Ra'is Muhammad Rous returned with a partial broadside.

This melee raged over the next three hours, as the two ships valiantly assaulted each other. Ra'is Muhammad Rous tried to ram the *Enterprize*, but Sterrett outmaneuvered the *Tripoli* while maintaining continuous fire. The *Tripoli*'s guns fired sporadically, the *Enterprize*'s in concentrated, timed, rapid, disciplined broadsides. Unable to outgun or outmaneuver the American ship, the

Tripoli tried to swing alongside and board, the traditional Barbary pirate tactic. The pirates made at least three attempts to board the American vessel, but each time they were repulsed as Sterrett's marines swept the *Tripoli*'s deck with musket fire, mowing down the Tripolitans and cutting away their grappling hooks.

The *Enterprize*'s marines were able to keep the pirates off her decks, while her guns pounded the *Tripoli*. The Tripolitan pirates made several attempts to strike her colors in mock surrender in an effort to fool Lieutenant Sterrett into lowering his guard, but each time the ruse failed. Finally, after the third such attempt, Sterrett decided to play for keeps and sink the *Tripoli*. He mercilessly and repeatedly fired broadsides into her, raking her deck, smashing her masts, and pounding through her hull at the waterline.

The precision training of the American crew provided that all six guns would discharge in unison. Seemingly without pause, Sterrett's gunnery crew would load, fire, clean, prep, reload, and fire, again and again, and each time a broadside of six powerful, concentrated blasts would smash into the *Tripoli*. Quickly, the enemy ship became enveloped in smoke, debris, splintering wood, shrapnel, flying limbs, blood, tears, confusion, and fear. All the while Sterrett's marines unleashed and maintained a steady barrage of killing force against any who stood upon the *Tripoli*'s decks. Armed with various weapons, Sterrett's marines provided covering fire in offense and concentrated fury in defense.

Although she fought brave and hard, at noon the *Tripoli* struck her colors again, but this time it was plain that the surrender was genuine. A shaken and bleeding Ra'is Muhammad Rous stooped over the tattered railing of his wrecked ship and threw the Tripolitan flag into the sea, begging for mercy. Lieutenant Sterrett's boarding party found the *Tripoli* a bloody, broken mess—out of a crew of eighty men, thirty were dead, and thirty were wounded—including Ra'is Muhammad Rous and his second in command.

The *Enterprize* suffered no casualties and no injuries and was none the worse for wear.

The encounter was at once a testament to American ability and skill and to the poor training and undisciplined capabilities of the Tripolitan pirate navy. Sterrett and his crew would later be favorably cited for their gallantry by Congress; the lieutenant would be given a commemorative sword, and his crew would be awarded one month's additional pay. More importantly, however, Sterrett's victory proved a useful point of reference to President Thomas Jefferson in his explanations and justifications of his Barbary policies to Congress.

Following Commodore Dale's strict orders, Lieutenant Sterrett had the *Tripoli*'s guns, powder, small arms, sabers, swords and pikes thrown over the side. What remained of her masts was chopped down. Since the *Tripoli*'s surgeon had been killed during the battle, Sterrett sent the *Enterprize*'s surgeon and surgeon's mates over to tend to the Tripolitan crew. Entirely without means of attack, or defense, but still afloat, the *Tripoli* was left drifting amid the debris.

While Sterrett continued on to Malta to fetch water, Ra'is Muhammad Rous eventually sailed the *Tripoli* back to its home port, where a furious Pasha Yusuf Qaramanli awaited. Muhammad Rous was stripped of his command, publicly ridiculed and humiliated, and then given five hundred bastinadoes (blows across the soles of the feet with a cane).

Meanwhile, U.S. consul William Eaton wrote Commodore Dale to inform him of his activities in Tunis. Eaton had taken it upon himself sometime earlier to declare the blockade of Tripoli well before it had begun. He issued warnings, denied passports, and otherwise confused and scared the marine administrative apparatus in Tunis. As Eaton wrote, "I kept the enemy three months in a state of blockade when we had not a ship of war within three hundred leagues from this port; his chief commerce and whole supplies of provisions depending on Tunis, and my passports being still withheld." Commodore Dale heartily approved of Eaton's measures and encouraged him to continue his efforts.

When the *Enterprize* finally returned to the squadron, she came with insufficient water to provide for the *President*. Dale was forced to take his flagship off to Malta for provisions. With the

Philadelphia keeping watch at Gibraltar and the *Essex* still employed in convoying American merchant ships, the sloop-of-war *Enterprize* was—alone—supposed to maintain the blockade. The American naval squadron seemed strapped for resources, with more duties than ships to handle them.

Commodore Dale returned to the blockade at the end of August, picking up twenty-one Tripolitan prisoners off a Greek vessel while en route. He maintained steady communications with Pasha Qaramanli through the Danish consul Nicholas Nissen's offices, but to little effect, as no treaty negotiations could be made. Pasha Qaramanli had little interest in his subjects being held prisoner aboard the *President*, and Dale was obliged to let them all go rather than entertain the burden of so many captives. Little was accomplished through diplomatic channels.

Before long, Commodore Dale's men began to fall ill for want of fresh provisions, and by September the *President* had 152 men of her crew listed as seriously ill. On September 3, 1801, Dale had little choice but to leave Tripoli; U.S. consul William Eaton, who had been busily trying to maintain the blockade on paper, was ordered to continue the fiction for as long as possible. Tired, unhappy, and frustrated, the commodore set a course for Gibraltar, where the American resupply ship *American Packet* had been expected. The *Enterprize* was sent off to collect dispatches and meet up with the flagship before heading back home to the United States.

Soon after the *President* reached Gibraltar, Commodore Dale discovered that Spanish forces had blockaded the port and that Ra'is Murad and the crews of both of his vessels had been allowed to escape, although the ships had been abandoned. The Tripolitan admiral had bribed some locals to ferry himself and his 366 men across the strait to the coast of Morocco. Once they reached the safety of the Maghreb, they marched overland to Tripoli. With no more prey at port, Commodore Dale ordered Captain Bainbridge to take the *Philadelphia* to Tripoli to observe the harbor, and then to proceed to Syracuse, on the island of Sicily, for the winter. The *Essex* was ordered to winter near the Straits of Gibraltar. Unfortunately, the Spanish had detained the *American Packet* at port for over ten days, and most of her provisions had rotted.

Dale intended to keep only two frigates in the region during the winter months. Bainbridge was ordered to periodically cruise Tripoli out of Syracuse, hopefully showing just enough muscle to calm the pasha, while Barron was to maintain an American show of force from Gibraltar, providing safe passage for American merchantmen. On October 3, Commodore Dale ordered Lieutenant Andrew Sterrett to sail the *Enterprize* back to the United States.

Dale then returned to Algiers in the hope of calming the regency and obtaining diplomatic assistance in the war against Tripoli. He and Richard O'Brien met with the dey of Algiers. Little was accomplished beyond empty pledges of assistance, but the dey did agree to accept cash in lieu of stipulated tribute. Dale gave O'Brien $30,000 in hard cash that he had brought for this purpose. Before the commodore disembarked, the American merchantman *Peace and Plenty* carrying U.S. tribute for Tunis arrived under the protection of the USS *George Washington*, Lieutenant John Shaw commanding. Commodore Dale ordered Shaw to continue on to Tunis and then to sweep the Mediterranean ports to convoy American shipping.

Dale sailed on to Port Mahon, Minorca, to investigate rumors of possible Minorcan assistance to Tripoli's war effort, which he soon discovered were unfounded. On November 30, 1801, therefore, he decided to make his way back to the United States. Unfortunately, the local harbor pilot ran the *President* aground while taking her out of the port, and though she did not suffer any major damage, a transatlantic voyage without repairs would have been unwise and irresponsible. Therefore, Dale took his flagship to the French port of Toulon for repairs, where he was required to sit in quarantine for fifteen days before the *President* was allowed to dock. Dale was to remain at Toulon for several months.

On January 10, 1802, the USS *Boston* (thirty-two guns), commanded by Captain Daniel McNeill, arrived in Toulon to deliver the new U.S. minister to France, Robert R. Livingston. Captain McNeill also had orders to make contact with Commodore Dale and put his ship at the Mediterranean squadron's disposal. Dale ordered him to join Captain Barron in patrolling off Tripoli. The squadron now had one more ship with which to try to force Pasha Qaramanli to stand down.

Although Dale continued to command the Mediterranean squadron from Toulon, the entire campaign had faltered. Little had been accomplished in Barbary, and Tripoli remained a belligerent thorn in the side of American national honor and American interests in the region. Further, Dale was ready for home, his supplies were depleted, and the enlistment period for his crew, which Congress had designated at no more than one year, had ended.

On February 10, 1802, Commodore Dale finally left Toulon and sailed for Gibraltar. He entered the port and found, to his surprise, that Morocco had begun to take part in the protests against the U.S. blockade of Tripoli. The emperor of Morocco, Mawlay Souleïman, had announced that he demanded a passport for a Tripolitan cruiser that was to sail from Tangier to Tripoli laden with wheat to alleviate the famine that he understood to be rampant there and that was supposedly exacerbated by the American blockade. He also called for the release of the *Meshuda*. Although Dale refused with as much deference as he could muster, he instructed the U.S. consul at Tangier, James Simpson, to try to placate Souleïman and prevent future displays of Islamic solidarity with Tripoli.

Commodore Richard Dale left the Mediterranean on March 9, 1802, arriving at Hampton Roads, Virginia, on April 14, 1802. Glad to be rid of the burden of Barbary, he resigned his commission shortly afterward and retired to Philadelphia.

On February 6, 1802, Congress finally recognized that Tripoli had declared war against the United States, and so passed "an act for the protection of the commerce and the seamen of the United States against Tripolitan cruisers." With this action, Congress gave the president complete discretion to use the U.S. Navy and even empowered him to commission privateers. Congress did not make financial provision for additional naval vessels and did not allow for an open war as such, but President Jefferson had been given enough of a green light to proceed. The president instructed his naval officers "to subdue, seize and make prize of all vessels, goods, and effects, belonging to the Dey of Tripoli" and to proceed with whatever measure "the state of war will justify."

Jefferson intended to send another naval squadron to the Mediterranean, of roughly the same size, to continue where Dale had left off. Since the next available officer, and Jefferson's preferred commander, was unwilling to lead the squadron, the appointment fell to Captain Richard Valentine Morris, the next officer in line. Morris was a politically well-connected man: his father, Lewis, had signed the Declaration of Independence; his uncle, Governor Morris, had helped finance the Revolution and was a member of the Constitutional Convention; his brother was Robert Lewis Morris, a representative from Vermont who had allowed his state to go to Jefferson instead of Burr in the last congressional ballot to determine the president. Unfortunately, as President Jefferson would soon learn, Morris was a very poor naval commander.

This second Mediterranean squadron, under the command of Commodore Richard Morris, consisted of the flagship USS *Chesapeake* (a frigate of thirty-six guns); the frigate USS *Adams* (twenty-eight guns), commanded by Captain Hugh Campbell; and the frigate USS *Constellation* (thirty-six guns), commanded by Alexander Murray; as well as the sloop-of-war USS *Enterprize*, still under the command of Andrew Sterrett.

Although Secretary of the Navy Robert Smith did not give Commodore Morris too many specific instructions, it was clear that he wished Morris to be active and forceful and to get results for the president. Morris was told to use his "best exertions to keep the enemy's vessels in port, to blockade the places out of which they issue, and prevent as far as possible their coming out or going in." He was also instructed to bring aid and relief to American merchant ships and to convoy them safely, and he was given discretion to split up his forces, if necessary, to best effect these various objectives. On February 18, 1802, through a special presidential commission, Richard Morris was "authorized and directed to subdue, seize and make prize of all" Tripolitan ships and goods "and to bring or send the same into port, to be proceeded against and distributed according to law."

In order to make haste, Secretary Smith ordered that the ships of the new squadron be dispatched to Barbary as they became ready, rather than wait around so that the entire squadron might leave as one unit.

On March 14, 1802, Captain Alexander Murray left New York aboard the *Constellation*, arriving at Gibraltar on April 28. Commodore Morris did not leave Hampton Roads until April 27, so the *Chesapeake* arrived in Gibraltar on May 25, while the *Adams* was delayed at port and did not reach Gibraltar until July 21.

Opting away from quick action, Commodore Morris decided to wait nearly two months for the arrival of the *Adams* before carrying out any of his orders. Dithering idly in Gibraltar, he enjoyed the hospitality of the British garrison and spent time relaxing with his family. Morris had, indeed, brought his family who soon became known to many as "the Commodores—his wife," his young son Gerard, and Sal, his black maid." Commodore Morris also carried on board the former U.S. consul to Tripoli, James Leander Cathcart, who had been dispatched to reinitiate negotiations with Pasha Qaramanli, should such an opportunity present itself.

"Who, except an American," William Eaton scoffed when word of the squadron's activities reached him in Tunis, "would ever propose to himself to bring a wife to war against the ferocious savages of Barbary?" Eaton was concerned that the Barbary potentates were finding it difficult to believe that the American squadron was willing to take any serious action. "At the commencement of this war," he wrote in his State Department dispatch, "much was expected by Europeans from the enterprise of Americans. On the appearance of our squadron, something was dreaded by these regencies. But our operations have disappointed the expectations of the one and removed the apprehensions of the other. One year ago Tunis would not have dared the affront exhibited with these dispatches."

Not one ship of Morris's new squadron even so much as approached Tripoli until June 1802. When the *Constellation* finally reached those troubled waters, Captain Murray was entirely unable to maintain a blockade.

Murray found that the *Boston*, commanded by Captain McNeill, as well as four Swedish ships, was already in place before Tripoli. The blockade was not going terribly well, however. Although the *Boston* had recently engaged three Tripolitan corsairs, she managed to sink only one. The other two hid beneath the gun batteries of the Tripolitan harbor fortress. The Swedish ships were large and cumbersome and had great difficulty chasing down the Tripolitan corsairs. Before long, the *Boston* disengaged from the blockade altogether, ostensibly to procure provisions in Malta, but the erratic Captain McNeill decided not to return to the blockade but to sail home instead. Meanwhile, captain Murray sent the *Enterprize* off to Gibraltar with a convoy. Before long, the Swedish ships left as well in search of provisions, and Captain Murray found himself alone in trying to maintain the blockade.

The *Constellation* spent most of the next two months attempting to blockade Tripoli by herself. The effort was not going well. For one thing, the ship's draft was too deep for the shallow waters. On top of this was the poor decision-making of Captain Murray, who insisted on keeping the *Constellation* so far off the harbor as to be over the horizon—practically guaranteeing that he wouldn't spot any blockade runners and couldn't hope to catch up with any that might be unlucky enough to actually get spotted.

Indeed, Ra'is Murad and his navy had no difficulty running the blockade to obtain supplies or, even more embarrassingly for the United States, to threaten American shipping. In June 1802 three Tripolitan pirate ships ventured out, one of which quickly captured an American merchantman, the *Franklin* of Philadelphia, en route to Marseille from the West Indies. Although the ship's captain, Andrew Morris, had been assured that the American blockade was in place and effective, he discovered that the Mediterranean was far from secured. As he wrote to James Cathcart, "I cannot pass over the disappointment I experienced in not falling in with some of our vessels of war during one months captivity on board the [Tripolitan] corsair." This was especially so, lamented Captain Morris, off the coast of Cape Bon, in Tunis, just across from Sicily, "a place," he noted, "that the necessity of strictly guarding must appear to every naval commander at war with Tripoli." Even more embarrassing, however, was that Captain Andrew Morris found himself being brought back to Tripoli in full daylight:

> [W]hen [on, roughly, July 19] we had arrived within about five leagues of the port [of Tripoli], the corsair with our flag reversed began according their custom to salute, and so continued at intervals for more than five hours until we anchored in the harbor; and strange to relate, all this was done in view of a Swedish and American frigate, who never made the least effort to obstruct our progress when it was certainly in their power to capture or run the Pirate on shore before it was possible for them to be protected from their [harbor gun] batteries . . . this transaction was in open day in sight of thousands amongst which the consuls of different nations can testify.

The American frigate that Captain Andrew Morris spotted was none other than the very placid USS *Constellation*. Morris and his eight-man crew were later taken to shore and paraded through the streets as evidence of America's impotence in the face of Tripolitan prowess. Morris and the four American members of his crew were ransomed for $6,500, which the U.S. government paid. Captain Murray did absolutely nothing about it. As William Eaton commented in a letter to Secretary of State Madison, "[The] government may as well send out Quaker meeting houses to float about this sea as frigates with Murrays in command. The friendly salutes he may receive at Gibraltar produce nothing at

Tripoli." It is possible, however, that Captain Murray was simply following his superior's lead in doing nothing.

Indeed, Commodore Richard Morris had not yet even left Gibraltar. Initially, the *Chesapeake* sat at her mooring in Gibraltar's harbor waiting for the *Adams* to arrive; she was also undergoing repairs that Morris insisted were needed because of faulty naval inspections prior to the mission. He then claimed that his presence was needed to stand watch over the *Meshuda*, Ra'is Murad's abandoned flagship that had been pinned down in Gibraltar by Captain Bainbridge the year before.

Surprisingly, Emperor Mawlay Souleïman of Morocco was once again asserting his demands for the release of the *Meshuda* and/or the issuance of ship passports so that he could send a cargo of wheat to Tripoli. Souleïman's naval force was too small to be of any immediate concern, but he was actively fitting out new ships and had big plans and great hopes. The U.S. consul to Tangiers, James Simpson, was growing anxious and uncertain and appealed to Commodore Morris. Prudently, the commodore refused to consent to issuing Morocco with passports, which would have enabled the emperor to show solidarity with Tripoli by sending supplies.

In response, Emperor Souleïman declared war against the United States on June 25, 1802. Fortunately, this "war" would not advance beyond a mere declaration, and Simpson would soon enough mollify the emperor and reestablish peace without a single shot being fired.

Lieutenant Sterrett arrived in Gibraltar with the *Enterprize* in mid-July, and then on July 21, 1802, the squadron was finally complete with the arrival of the USS *Adams*. The *Adams* brought fresh orders, dated April 20, instructing Commodore Morris to send the entire squadron to Tripoli along with James Cathcart, who was empowered to negotiate with Qaramanli.

On August 17, Commodore Richard Morris finally accepted that he had to venture forth into the Mediterranean as part of his Barbary mission. He sailed the *Chesapeake* along the north shore of the Mediterranean, heading for Leghorn, accompanied by the *Enterprize*. They joined a convoy of ships heading to various ports; Morris opted for a leisurely voyage, taking time to enjoy nearly every port of call along the way before finally reaching Leghorn on October 12. To his surprise, he found Captain Murray's *Constellation* moored in the harbor.

In early August, Captain Alexander Murray had begun to run out of provisions. His supply of fresh water was nearly depleted, and the *Constellation* was in need of some general maintenance. Uncertain of when, or whether, any U.S. relief ships might venture toward Tripoli to assist in the blockade, he decided to head to British-controlled Malta for some temporary supplies. Before long he decided to go to Leghorn for additional provisions. The American blockade was thus lifted, and since Sweden soon made peace with Pasha Qaramanli, the city and regency of Tripoli remained completely unencumbered by U.S. intervention for the duration of 1802.

Commodore Morris, unbothered by the lifting of the naval blockade of Tripoli, ordered the *Constellation* to head to Toulon for maintenance and repairs, and then to Gibraltar to obtain provisions for the rest of the squadron. Morris also reversed his earlier decision to refuse the emperor of Morocco his demands, and authorized Captain Murray to instruct James Simpson, the U.S. consul in Tangiers, "to grant passports to vessels bound to Tripoli laden with wheat." The commodore was concerned over Morocco's previous threats, and anyway he understood from Murray that Tripoli suffered no famine and so had no particular need for Emperor Souleïman's wheat. After Leghorn, the *Chesapeake* sailed to Malta, then Palermo, and then Syracuse, and finally back again to Malta.

Since Pasha Yusuf Qaramanli of Tripoli had declared war against the United States of America, President Thomas Jefferson had dispatched two successive squadrons under two different commodores. The United States had been claiming for years that one day it would send its warships into the Mediterranean and teach the Barbary pirates a lesson they would not soon forget. Unfortunately, the lesson appears to have been that the United States was unable to stand up to the Barbary regencies, and it was indeed very well learned.

After two years of Mediterranean operations, the American frigates had left and Tripoli remained—a fact not lost on the dey of Algiers or the bey of Tunis, and much celebrated by the pasha of Tripoli. America had failed to further the cause of bringing Tripoli to terms or the cause of humbling the pretensions of the pirate regencies. Indeed, all reports from Tripoli indicated that Pasha Qaramanli now fully expected to succeed against his American foes.

Richard O'Brien, William Eaton, and James Cathcart were particularly frustrated and angry. For years they had fought diplomatically to salvage their nation's honor and interests, only to see it sullied and jeopardized through indolence and languor. By August 1802, Eaton was convinced that America's Mediterranean operations had produced little more than "additional enemies and national contempt." While O'Brien could not understand how American naval power could appear so lame and lazy against Tripoli, "the most insignificant of powers," Cathcart was convinced that American prestige would be forever lost in Barbary if his country did not take some direct offensive action immediately. On this the three men could agree.

The situation demanded direct action but instead received naval officers who preferred to drink at every port, travel the European Mediterranean coast, and engage in duels and other foolish behavior.

"What have they done," William Eaton asked in angry disappointment, "but dance and wench?"

7

Slouching toward Failure

WHILE COMMODORE MORRIS embarrassed the United States with his ineffectual Mediterranean cruise, the diplomatic situation in Barbary began to deteriorate rapidly.

Soon after declaring war against the United States, Pasha Yusuf Qaramanli had sent an emissary to Tunis, Algiers, and Morocco to try to foment solidarity and elicit assistance. Qaramanli had explained to them that he was merely striving to assert his independence, consolidate the authority of his regime, and rebuild his regency. His war against the Americans was, he argued, just and proper. American tactics, in contrast, were injudicious and dishonorable, as their blockade sought to prevent all commerce, not just piracy, and so punished everyone; besides, regional commercial interdependence meant that the American blockade would probably adversely affect all of Barbary commercial interests, not just Tripoli's. Further, the American belligerence was at its foundation just a manifestation of the struggle between *Dar al-Islam* (the House of Islam) and *Dar al-Harb* (the House of War).

The other Barbary States agreed and pledged their assistance. The American war against Tripoli was understood in the light of the infidel's encroachment against the *Dar al-Islam*. The fact that Tripoli seemed to be winning only spurred the Barbary regencies into greater enthusiasm for their efforts.

The Barbary regencies sent arms, ammunition, food, and other provisions, sometimes by running the blockade and sometimes by creating a defensive cover for Tripolitan corsair movement.

They frequently allowed Tripoli's ships to use their own flags
to provide further cover for blockade running. Tunis even tried
a more pacific route by offering to mediate between Tripoli
and the United States; the offer was rejected when it transpired
that "peace" would require humiliating U.S. concessions. Algiers
also made an offer to mediate, but the effort was similarly
abandoned.

Mostly, though, the Barbary powers harassed the Americans
by increasing the diplomatic pressure. In Tunis, for example, Bey
Hammuda Pasha unexpectedly renewed his demands for an
armed frigate from the Americans. There did not appear to be
anything prompting the bey's sudden burning desire, particularly
as William Eaton had just recently given him his long-awaited
jewels—gold- and diamond-encrusted guns and pistols that
Captain Murray delivered, at a cost to the American taxpayer of
$27,576.96. Eaton simply responded with his usual refusals and
treaty article citations, but it was clear to him that the issue was
not going away so easily. "Yesterday," he reported to the secretary
of state on August 28, 1802, "I was called to the palace. The minister formally demanded of me a frigate of 36 guns. It need not be
thought strange to see me in America this winter. I can neither
yield to nor get rid of the demand." Eaton also encountered open
and flagrant harassment from some Tunisian officials. Similarly,
the bey's minister routinely badgered the consul for being
unfriendly to Barbary interests. The Tunisians also taunted Eaton
for the U.S. naval squadron's performance: "The Minister puffs a
whistle in my face and says, 'We find it is all a puff! We see how
you carry on the war with Tripoli!'" By the end of the year Eaton
wrote the secretary of state, "I cannot serve another summer in
this station."

Richard O'Brien ran into similar difficulties with Dey Bobba
Mustafa of Algiers. The dey began vociferously complaining
about O'Brien's conduct and about the United States' failure to
deliver payment of the military and naval stores. O'Brien tried
to buy off the dey as he usually would, but Mustafa persisted; he
had money, what he wanted were naval stores. By January 1803,

the dey declared that he could find no more reason to remain at peace with the United States, or for Consul O'Brien to stay in Algiers.

On January 25, 1803, Commodore Richard Valentine Morris began to receive these disturbing reports from the U.S. consuls in Algiers and Tunis. O'Brien sent word that the dey refused to receive cash instead of naval stores and that the regency absolutely refused to receive James Cathcart as the new consul general at Algiers (O'Brien had already resigned and James Madison had appointed Cathcart to replace him.) William Eaton, meanwhile, wrote Commodore Morris urging him to assist in Tunis, as the bey was becoming inflexible and American interests were being threatened: "Affairs of incalculable moment to the United States here require the assistance of your counsel, perhaps your force!" Although Morris had spent a considerable amount of time avoiding it, he prepared himself to venture out to Tripoli to confront the pasha head-on. The commodore hoped that a show of force in the region would enable Cathcart to negotiate a new peace treaty.

After a long period of inactivity—there had been, among the crew at least, a fair amount of unofficial activity involving drunkenness, tourism, women, and dueling—off the coast of southern Europe, Commodore Morris set out to Tripoli from Malta on January 29, 1803. By this time, his squadron had grown, as two American frigates had recently entered the fray: the USS *John Adams* (a frigate of twenty-eight guns), commanded by Captain John Rodgers (not to be confused with the USS *Adams*, also of twenty-eight guns, commanded by Hugh G. Campbell), and the USS *New York* (a frigate of thirty-six guns), commanded by Captain James Barron.

Little progress was made on this voyage, however, as the ships were beset by heavy winter gales. On February 10, the three frigates returned to Malta and then nine days later tried for Gibraltar, but stormy whether forced them to the Bay of Tunis. They arrived on February 22, 1803. Their arrival had little affect on the Tunisians, as it had long since been decided that the American commodore had no stomach for war.

Consul William Eaton boarded the *Chesapeake* and informed Commodore Morris of the unfortunate developments. What Eaton neglected to tell Morris, however, was that his personal financial situation was in as perilous a situation as American diplomacy, and, more importantly, that the two had become very much intertwined.

Although it was a policy Eaton decried, the U.S. government paid their consuls less than was adequate with the expectation that the stipend would be offset by commercial enterprise with the locals. Eaton had prospered before the war with Tripoli, but he saw his fortunes greatly diminished because he put his duty before his pocketbook. Even worse, however, he had incurred large debts at usurious rates because he had felt obligated to utilize his own resources to further official business.

While Eaton had not directly indebted his government in any of this, his creditors' lively and not altogether unreasonable expectations were that the U.S. government had unofficially backed his actions. Although Eaton hotly denied that his government would ever pay any of his debts, he occasionally voiced the hope that it would, and he certainly knew what expectations were associated with his station. In any event, he found himself 34,000 Spanish dollars in debt to Hadgi Unis Ben Unis, the chief commercial agent of the Tunisian government, yet he neglected to mention this fact to Commodore Morris despite the obvious way it would compromise any diplomatic proceedings.

Making matters even worse, the Tunisian government was angrily insisting the United States make amends for its recent capture of a valuable Tunisian brigantine, the *Paulina*. Lieutenant Andrew Sterrett's schooner, the USS *Enterprize*, had captured the *Paulina* in January when Commodore Morris learned that she had been planning a blockade run to aid Tripoli. Bey Hammuda Pasha was furious with Eaton, as he considered the U.S. blockade illegal, and he demanded that the ship be returned and that the United States remit damages for the cargo. The bey then threatened to declare war against the United States if his demands were not satisfied.

Consul Eaton apprised Morris of this dangerous and delicate situation and tried to impress upon him the nature and style of Barbary diplomacy and the importance of knowing the nuances of the way the Tunisian game was played. He emphasized his words of caution by highlighting that this would in fact be the commodore's first diplomatic visit to the regency of Tunis since he had entered the Mediterranean. Unfortunately, Eaton's very poor impression of Morris was reciprocated in kind by Morris's attitude toward him. The commodore thus ignored Eaton's advice, went ashore with James Cathcart and John Rodgers in tow, and proceeded directly to the bey and to the business at hand.

Morris demanded an audience with the bey. The interview went very badly, and Commodore Morris did not acquit himself well, particularly once Hammuda pressed the matter of Eaton's debts. Morris's attitude was reflected in his conduct, and he eventually stormed out of the bey's chambers, in gross breach of protocol, making clear that his business was at an end and that Eaton's debts would not be honored. Morris, Cathcart, Rodgers, and their attendants haughtily made their way back to the marina. Their path was blocked, however, and they found themselves confronted by hundreds of armed Tunisians.

In plain sight of three armed frigates and one schooner of the American naval squadron, Commodore Richard Morris, Captain John Rodgers, and Consul General Designate James Cathcart were arrested, hauled back to the palace, and confined. After several days and some awkward negotiations, Eaton did manage to coax the bey into freeing them. The trade-off, however, was that Commodore Morris was forced to pay $23,000 to cover Eaton's debts and had to agree to give up any U.S. rights to the *Paulina*.

While Rodgers remained to settle the arrangements, Morris put out to sea again on March 13, 1803. The commodore blamed Eaton for his incarceration, accusing him of "duplicity" for having lured him into harm's way in order to pay off some debts. It later transpired that the *sahib al-tabi'* had conspired against Eaton to destroy his standing with the bey and pave the way for "an American Consul more pliable to his views." Meanwhile, William

Eaton had clearly exhausted the hospitality of the Tunisian government. Bey Hammuda Pasha deemed him an undesirable, decried him as a madman, and permanently expelled him from the regency. "The Consul," the bey told Commodore Morris, "is a man of good heart, but a wrong head. He is too obstinate and too violent for me. I must have a consul with a disposition more congenial to Barbary interests!"

Commodore Morris reached Algiers on March 19, 1803. After his experience in Tunis, however, he decided to write the dey a letter rather than risk entering Algiers to personally meet with Dey Bobba Mustafa. Lieutenant Sterrett sailed the *Enterprize* into the harbor, picked up Richard O'Brien, and brought him to meet with Morris aboard the flagship.

O'Brien explained that U.S. affairs had deteriorated badly in the regency and urged the commodore to assist. The dey had again refused to accept the $30,000 in lieu of the military and naval store, although he would not allow O'Brien to return the money to the U.S. frigate. He also refused to receive James Cathcart as Richard O'Brien's replacement in the U.S. consul general office.

The squadron sailed off for Gibraltar the very next day. O'Brien and his wife did not sail with them, as Mrs. O'Brien was expecting another child in December, and because they intended to help their future replacements get acquainted with life in Barbary. The commodore reached Gibraltar on March 23, 1803.

As the squadron took provisions at Gibraltar, Commodore Morris contemplated the abysmal job he had performed in the Mediterranean. Indeed, these depressing thoughts had apparently hung over his conscience even before his humiliating diplomatic turn in Tunis. Over the past four months, he had not even bothered to send any report of his activities to the secretary of state. The reports he had sent before that tended to be cryptic and opaque. As Secretary of the Navy Robert Smith had written to Captain John Rodgers, "He [Commodore Morris] has not done anything which he ought to have done. . . . We besides can obtain from him no information what he is proposing to do."

At Gibraltar, William Eaton left the squadron aboard the merchantman *Perseverance* heading for Boston. He was happy to leave Barbary and was eager to file his report with the secretary of state, and perhaps even President Jefferson. James Cathcart also left the squadron at this time. Having been refused at Algiers, and finding none of the Barbary States predisposed to American diplomacy, he had decided to return to his private business ventures. Besides, Commodore Morris had been authorized to negotiate with any of the Barbary powers and made it clear to Cathcart that he would be sent for when and if needed; Cathcart took the hint and made his way back to Leghorn aboard the USS *Adams*.

He would not be out of the picture long, however, as Secretary of State Madison wrote to him on April 9, 1803, informing him that Jefferson was unhappy with the apparent direction of Barbary affairs and wanted him to take action. Even worse, Cathcart learned, Jefferson was prepared to make humiliating concessions to obtain peace with Tripoli and maintain it with Tunis. Madison wrote that Cathcart should no longer consider himself to "be tied down to a refusal of presents" to Tripoli and was duly authorized to pay Qaramanli $20,000 cash up front "and at the rate afterwards of eight or ten thousand dollars a year"—although it was hoped that such concession could be left out of any final public language of a treaty. As for Tunis, Cathcart was empowered to concede to Bey Hammuda Pasha periodic payments "payable in cash and not to exceed the rate of 10,000 per annum, to be paid biennially [if possible]." Cathcart was then instructed to provide a consular present worth no more than "about 4,000 dollars."

None of this came to fruition, however, as Cathcart was already officially unwelcome in Tripoli, and, through correspondence with Danish consul Nicholas Nissen, he easily determined that his proposal would fall far below Qaramanli's expectations. As for Tunis, the effort was similarly rejected. In August 1803, Morris sent Cathcart to Tunis—he had just been officially appointed as consul to Tunis instead of Algiers, and Tobias Lear had been chosen as his replacement in Tripoli—where he made his proposals known during several audiences with the bey.

Cathcart was unwilling to concede in giving the bey a frigate, however, and so the bey rejected the offer and then refused to receive Cathcart as U.S. consul. Bey Hammuda Pasha said that Cathcart was a troublemaker and was responsible for starting the U.S. war with Tripoli, and so was not welcome to try to effect the same nonsense in Tunis. Thus, James Cathcart's diplomatic efforts under Commodore Richard Morris came to nothing.

A year had passed since Commodore Richard Valentine Morris and his squadron had arrived in the Mediterranean. At this time, as was inevitable in such overseas long-term deployments, the squadron was in need of some rearrangement. Both the USS *Constellation* and the USS *Chesapeake*, the first two frigates of the squadron to enter the Mediterranean, were scheduled to return to the United States. So Morris moved his command, designating the USS *New York* as his new flagship. Captain Samuel Barron was given command of the *Chesapeake* and set a course for the United States with Lieutenant Sterrett on board, as well as others whose tours of duty had ended. The very capable Lieutenant Isaac Hull was given command of the USS *Enterprize*.

Finally, in April 1803 Commodore Richard Morris resolved to have another go at Tripoli. The *New York* left Gibraltar, with Isaac Hull's *Enterprize* in company, headed for Malta. Morris intended to rendezvous with the USS *John Adams*, currently engaged in convoy operations in that area, as well as the USS *Adams*, and then sail the squadron against Tripoli. Unfortunately, his initiative was aborted when a stupid accident intervened.

While making toward Malta, on April 25, the *New York* was rocked by an explosion very near the powder magazine. The gunner had carelessly left a lit candle in the storeroom, and after a couple of sparks fell into a bucket of damaged powder that had been collected for fumigation purposes, a fire quickly spread to the powder horns and then to the bulkhead of the marine store, setting off about thirty-seven dozen blank cartridges. As bulkheads blew, fires raged through the ship's interior and the vessel was engulfed in smoke. Fortunately, the main powder magazine did not ignite, and the ship was not destroyed. The fire was eventually put out with wet blankets and buckets of water.

Nineteen officers and men were injured, of whom fourteen later died. Demoralized, depressed, and much the worse for wear, the *New York* continued to Malta. Commodore Morris knew that his flagship required substantial repairs and was no longer fit for service. Despairing of her mission, the *New York* reached Malta on May 1. She and the USS *Enterprize*, which underwent recoppering, remained there for three weeks.

The USS *John Adams*, meanwhile, was sent out to Tripoli on May 3. Upon reaching Tripoli, John Rodgers set the *John Adams* to cruising the area in search of Tripolitan pirates to bring to heel. On May 12 he spotted a quarry, went in pursuit, and quickly captured her: it was the *Meshuda*, now under the Moroccan flag.

After the *Meshuda* had been released from her confinement in the harbor of Gibraltar to the emperor of Morocco, she had sailed to Tunis. There, she had procured military and naval stores intended to help Tripoli against the Americans. Captain Rodgers returned to Malta with his prize in tow on May 18, 1803.

Meanwhile, Commodore Morris received a disturbing dispatch dated March 24 from Dr. George Davis, the chargé d'affaires at Tunis, who had been appointed soon after William Eaton had been expelled. Davis wrote to warn Morris that "a strong armament [was] fitting out at Tunis, and that a junction was intended between the fleet of that power and the Algerines," the intention of which seemed to be a concentrated effort against American shipping. Although Morris fretted over this news and the apparent bad luck that seemed determined to thwart his efforts at saving his career, he decided to continue his mission against Tripoli. On May 20, he, Rodgers, and Hull sailed their ships for Tripoli, arriving two days later at nine in the morning. The USS *Adams* would join the squadron in Tripoli's waters six days later.

Evidently the American ships were imposing enough that Tripoli's harbor batteries opened up on them at first sighting—but before the Americans were in range. Although a good deal of firing and heated activity commenced, the Tripolitans inflicted no damage, as the Americans were safely beyond their reach. Close to shore, Tripolitan gunboats were convoying eleven xebecs, or small lateen-rigged feluccas, the swift-sailing, compact coasting vessels commonly used in Barbary piracy. Morris ordered the Americans to give chase, and the xebecs were cut off from the port at Tripoli, but the gunboats escaped into the harbor, under the batteries.

As the squadron approached, a xebec was spotted to the west and the *Enterprize* was dispatched in pursuit. Isaac Hull sailed close enough to the coast to draw away some harrowing though ultimately ineffective fire from a newly built two-gun battery that had escaped Hull's attention. Hull returned fire, but his broadside was equally ineffective. The Tripolitan boat beached herself rather than face the *Enterprize*, and her crew scrambled to safety while a horde of Tripolitans on shore ran to their defense; the xebec's red flag remained hoisted.

The *Enterprize* fired her long guns in an attempt to destroy the beached vessel and bring down the flag, but to no good effect. Although the desire to send a landing party to burn the vessel was significant, Commodore Morris deemed it an unworthy target for so serious a risk of lives. Although a reasonable decision, it damaged the morale of many in the squadron who had longed for many, many months to engage the enemy.

The next day brought some listless exchanges of cannon fire between the squadron and some Tripolitan gunboats, but nothing of consequence resulted. The day after that was even more tedious and uneventful.

Finally, on May 27, at around 5 P.M. a squadron of nine gunboats and small corsairs were spotted five miles west of the city of Tripoli, very near that newly built two-gun battery. The American squadron advanced immediately, but the wind died too soon and the American warships coasted slowly in.

Once they were within range, they began to fire against the shore battery, but dusk settled over the scene and the enemy was no longer discernible but for the burst of return fire. As one midshipman reported, "It was a most elegant sight, the frequent flash & heavy report of gun boats: the still more frequent broad sides of our squadron formed the most sublime scene you can imagine."

Unable to aim, the Americans soon ceased fire, although just before doing so the USS *Adams* fired a near-disastrous broadside toward the shore, "the greater part of which," as a midshipman later said, "passed through the Mast and rigging of the *John Adams*, but did not damage excepting cutting away the foretop gallant bowlines."

While this bizarre "action" made for an interesting diversion from the tedium of blockade duty, it was also horrendously perilous for the American ships, as they were in the enemy's western horizon and thus easy, illuminated targets without any means of informed defense. Had the Tripolitans simply rowed their ships out to get a better range, they could have easily smashed the American squadron to pieces. Fortunately, the Tripolitans simply continued to fire from shore, advancing not a single boat.

The next day was uneventful, but the day after that, Sunday, May 29, 1803, brought some communication from Pasha Qaramanli and from Danish consul Nicholas Nissen. It was nothing of consequence, mostly just bluster. The effort did, however, convey that the pasha was prepared to talk with Morris. The commodore wrote Qaramanli a letter. On the following day, the squadron encountered a French vessel with a proper passport to Tripoli and learned from the French captain that Tripoli had three pirate corsairs out at sea expected any day now. Commodore Morris spread his squadron out along the length of the harbor to push the blockade to full effect.

That next morning, the USS *Adams* hove out signal that she had spotted a ship to the west of the city, and then she gave chase. The USS *Enterprize* was the only ship fast enough to catch up in time to assist. The *Adams* engaged with an exchange of cannon fire at intervals, and before long the *Enterprize* began exchanging fire as well. The engagement dragged on in a desultory fashion all night, after which the *Adams* anchored near the shore.

The next day, June 1, the *Enterprize* signaled the USS *New York* that ten small craft were unloading wheat in a bay about thirty-five miles northwest of the city and that the *Adams* was keeping watch and "now and then giving them a shot for amusement." At 5 P.M. the *New York* moved in near the *Adams* and anchored in company about a mile off the shore.

The scene was a busy one onshore, as there were roughly one thousand Tripolitans milling about in various forms of activity, including cavalrymen and regular soldiers; there was also an old stone fortification very near the grounded cargo boats that seemed active enough.

The commodore ordered a reconnaissance. At 8 P.M., Lieutenant David Porter and Midshipman Henry Wadsworth—the uncle of future poet Henry Wadsworth Longfellow—led a five-man party armed with cutlasses, muskets, and a pair of pistols each aboard one of the *New York*'s jolly boats, and another five-man team from the *Enterprize* rowed in behind them.

The two American boats approached within pistol shot of the cruisers and cargo boats and near enough to hear the Tripolitans talking to each other distinctly. The team was spotted, and after a brief exchange of fire, they landed safely about a quarter of a mile offshore on a small island. They returned to their ships at midnight, and David Porter reported to Commodore Morris that a landing in force was advisable. The commodore agreed and gave the order.

At dawn the next day, nine boats carrying fifty men and a large quantity of combustibles landed onshore. Midshipman Henry Wadsworth rendered a complete account of the action:

> At 8 o'clock we advanced under the fire from the shipping: there were none of the Enemy drawn up to oppose us on the shore, but they had formed a barricade of the boat sails & yards at the corner of the stone house, from whence they annoyed us, likewise small parties from behind the rocks & little hillocks. The fire Boats went in among the small craft and set them on fire under cover of our musketry. There were many

horsemen prancing about at a distance: some of the bold would take a circuit & come near, one in particular on a Black steed, flourishing his carbine in defiance began his circuit full speed: when he came near several took aim at him: he plunged forward fell & bit the dust.

The shot from the ships brought down several horsemen & foot: Lieut. Porter received a shot through his left thigh, another ball at the same time wounded his other thigh, he set down in the Boat & all pulled on one side to give them fair play on board the ships. Our Ammunition expended & the craft on fire we began to pull off for the ships. The Moment we were out of Musket Shot the Tripolines came down to put out the fire, which, notwithstanding a brisk cannonading from the ships they effected before they were half consumed, for the wheat stowed in bulk prevented the fire from burning briskly. Several masts were left standing. At 10 o'clock we were on board ship . . . [W]e did not accomplish our object fully: for the cargoes must in a great measure remain uninjured. At 11 the squadron weighed anchor and made sail.

This action, the first United States amphibious assault on the shores of Tripoli, was deemed "good sport" by the participants, but it was of little effect. The targets survived, five Americans were wounded, and an unconfirmed number of the enemy fell dead or were injured. Further, this action, like the engagements preceding it, did little to humble and chastise Pasha Qaramanli or otherwise compel him into submission. Still, the pasha was willing to talk, if only because he thought his odds of obtaining American concessions were fairly good.

On June 7, the peace negotiations commenced, but they were fairly brief and compact: Qaramanli pared his demands down to $200,000 cash, plus annual payments of $20,000, and of course full war reparations; Commodore Morris ignored the terms, countering with an offer of $5,000 in cash now and an additional $10,000 in ten years provided the peace was maintained. Needless to say, the negotiations faltered rather directly and were called off entirely the following day.

Commodore Morris left Tripoli aboard the *New York* on June 10 and sailed for Malta to join his wife, who was due to give birth to another child soon. The USS *John Adams*, the USS *Adams*, and the USS *Enterprize* remained in Tripoli to continue the blockade.

Twelve days later, on June 22, Lieutenant Isaac Hull reported sighting a Tripolitan cruiser of twenty-two guns anchored twenty-five miles east of the city, very near the shore. The *John Adams* advanced toward the enemy ship, but as Captain John Rodgers closed in, Tripolitan gunboats launched from the shore in a defensive line, while hordes of Tripolitan infantrymen and cavalrymen moved about excitedly on the shore making general signs of preparation to fight. Rodgers pulled the *John Adams* right alongside the Tripolitan twenty-two-gun cruiser. As he later reported the action:

At 7 Minutes before 9 AM, being in 7 fathoms Water and supposing we were within Point Blank shot of the Enemy Commenced firing which they returned, and a Constant fire was maintained for forty five Minutes, when the Enemy's fire was silenced, at which instant the Crew abandoned the Ship in the most Confused and precipitate manner, for such as her Boats could not carry, jumped overboard and swam to the shore, At this moment being in a 1/4 less 5 fathoms Water, and the Rocks appearing under our Bottom and in every direction round us, I thought it prudent to Ware and lay the Ships head off shore, and in the meantime ordered Lieutenant Hull to stand as close in as Consistent with safety and amuse the Enemy on the Beach, until our Boats could be hoisted out to take possession, At 1/4 before 10 AM, Discovering one of the Enemy's Boats returning to the Ship (whilst in the act of hoisting out our Boats) tacked and renewed our fire, and in a few Minutes after had the Satisfaction to see the Enemy's colors hauled down, at the same time, firing both their Broadsides, which was accompanied by the Ships Blowing up with a Heavy explosion, which Burst the Hull to pieces and forced the Main and Mizzen Masts perpendicularly into the air 150 or 160 feet, with all the Yards Shrouds Stays & [everything] belonging to them.—This Ship was Polacre Rigged Mounting 22 Guns, the largest Cruiser belonging to Tripoli, and to appearance a very fine vessel. From the number of Persons I saw land her Crew must have consisted of more than 200 Men, and from the advantageous position she held, added to the Shoalness of Water outside of her, she ought to have annoyed us very much and have done very considerable damage, yet to the disgrace of Tripoli, we have received no injury.—all the Men which returned to the Ship in the Boat were blown up in her, and I have reason to believe her Captain was among the Number; Several Men which were wounded on the Beach, were seen to be carried off by others, and a vast number must have been Killed previous to their abandoning the Ship. . . . The destruction of the before mentioned vessel, although awful, was one of the Grandest Spectacles I ever beheld.—After a Tremendous Explosion there appeared a Huge Column of smoke, with a Pyramid of Fire darting Vertically through its Center interspersed with Masts, Yards, Sails Rigging, different parts of the Hull & [everything] and the vessel in an instant dashed to Atoms.

This was the single most significant action taken by the U.S. Mediterranean squadron up to this time. Unfortunately, and perhaps remarkably, this great victory further convinced Commodore Richard Morris that the blockade of Tripoli was no longer necessary. Four days after Captain Rodgers had finally turned the tide of battle and taken strong, decisive action, he received orders to raise the blockade, leave Tripoli, and head for Malta. The Tripolitans were thus allowed time to regroup, revive, relax, and return to raiding and attacking American maritime interests.

Morris defended his decision to lift the blockade and abandon Tripoli on the basis that the imminent threat had been neutralized. Tripoli had lost the flagship of her pirate fleet and had just sacrificed the largest and most powerful cruiser in her navy. Furthermore, Morris had managed to disperse most of Tripoli's gunboats, and those that remained were small and unreachable because of the shoal waters. Besides, Commodore Morris deemed the bigger threat now to come from the other Barbary States.

Unfortunately for Richard Valentine Morris's career, President Thomas Jefferson disagreed rather profoundly. On August 31, 1803, Commodore Morris received a letter, dated June 21, from the secretary of the navy. "You will upon the receipt of this," the letter read, "consider yourself suspended in the command of the squadron on the Mediterranean station and of the frigate the *New York*."

Morris was directed to return immediately to the United States aboard the *Adams* and to turn over his command to Captain John Rodgers. Once home, he was asked to explain himself. As his answers were deemed insufficient, President Jefferson subjected his conduct of the mission against Tripoli to a court of inquiry.

The court decided that Commodore Morris "did not conduct himself with the diligence or the activity necessary to execute the important duties of his station" and cited seven specific instances in which he failed because of his "inactive and dilatory conduct" from June 1803 till the lifting of the Tripolitan blockade. He was deemed "not competent to the command of a squadron." For uncertain reasons, Jefferson did not wait to convene a court-martial for Morris, despite the obligation to do so. Instead, the president wrote the secretary of state, who on May 16, 1804, wrote the following to Richard Morris:

> With my letter to you of the 2nd instant I transmitted to you a copy of the opinion of the Court of Inquiry appointed to enquire into your conduct as commanding officer of the late squadron of armed vessels of the United States in the Mediterranean. This opinion having satisfied the President that it is not in the public interest that you should be longer continued in command in the navy of the United States, I have it in charge from him to inform you that he has revoked your commission.

Thus ended the naval career of Richard Valentine Morris.

The United States government had, meanwhile, finally taken the advice of her diplomatic and naval agents in Barbary and decided to build smaller cruising ships to fight in the Mediterranean.

On February 28, 1803, Congress passed "An Act to provide an additional armament for the protection of the seamen and commerce of the United States" and set aside $96,000 to construct or procure four ships equal in size to the USS *Enterprize*, that is, a schooner of up to sixteen guns. The act further enabled and empowered the president to build or purchase gunboats, not to exceed fifteen ships or cost more than $50,000 complete.

Through this act, three ships were built and one was purchased. There were not sufficient resources to provide the gunboats for the next Mediterranean squadron, but it was supposed that they might be procured in Europe. Meanwhile, these shallower-draft ships were prepared, the squadron was pieced together, and the commanding officers were selected.

Captain John Rodgers was instructed to take command of the *New York* and of the squadron until the new commodore, Captain Edward Preble, arrived with the new squadron. Already en route, this squadron included the new flagship the USS *Constitution* (a forty-four-gun frigate); the USS *Philadelphia* (a frigate of thirty-eight guns), commanded by Captain William Bainbridge; the USS *Siren* (a sixteen-gun brigantine), commanded by Lieutenant Charles Stewart; the USS *Argus* (a brig of sixteen guns), commanded by Lieutenant Stephen Decatur; the USS *Vixen* (a twelve-gun brigantine), commanded by Lieutenant John Smith; and the schooner USS *Nautilus* (twelve guns), commanded by Lieutenant Richard Somers. Commodore Preble would also add the USS *Enterprize* to the new squadron, currently commanded by Lieutenant Isaac Hull.

A portrait of Bey Hammuda Pasha, one of the few extant contemporary images of a Barbary pirate in existence

"General" William Eaton, 1808

Tobias Lear

The stranding and capture of the USS *Philadelphia* in Tripoli harbor, October 31, 1803

The ketch *Intrepid*, from a sketch in a letter from Midshipman William Henry Allen to General William Allen, November 14, 1804

The U.S. schooner Enterprize capturing the Tripolitan corsair *Tripoli*, August 1, 1801

Captain William Bainbridge

The destruction of
the USS *Philadephia*
in Tripoli harbor,
February 16, 1804

The explosion of the ketch *Intrepid* in Tripoli harbor, September 4, 1804

Captain Edward Preble

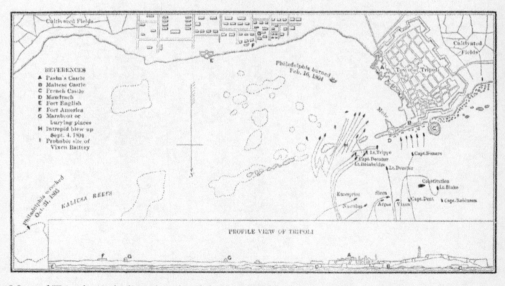

Map of Tripoli, including details of the battle of August 3, 1804, based on a plan drawn by F. C. deKrafft

Attack on Tripoli, August 3, 1804

1. FRIGATE "CONSTITUTION," COMMODORE PREBLE
2. BRIG "SYREN," CAPTAIN STEWART
3. BRIG "ARGUS," CAPTAIN HULL
4. SCHOONER "VIXEN," CAPTAIN SMITH
5. SCHOONER "ENTERPRISE," CAPTAIN DECATUR
6. SCHOONER "NAUTILUS," CAPTAIN SOMERS
7. TWO BOMBS

8. A TRIPOLITAN BRIG
9. SCHOONER
10. ROW-GALLEY
11. A FRENCH PRIVATEER
a. THE BASHAW'S CASTLE
b. FORT SUCHAMEINE
c. CONSULAR FLAGS

e. FORT TURK
f. FORT JEWISH
g. FORT REDONDO, OR THE ADMIRAL'S FORT
h. MOSQUES
o. SIX GUN-BOATS
v. GUN-BOATS

Identification sketch of the attack on Tripoli, August 3, 1804

139

Lieutenant Stephen Decatur
and Midshipman Thomas
MacDonough boarding a
Tripolitan gunboat August 3,
1804

Lieutenant Stephen Decatur

President Thomas Jefferson

James Leander Cathcart

Robert Smith, secretary of the Navy, July 27, 1801, to March 7, 1809

President James Madison

Tripoli Monument,
U.S. Naval Academy,
Annapolis, Maryland

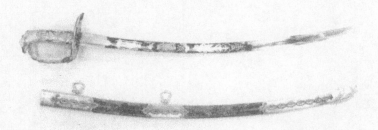

Decatur's dress sword and sheath, presented by Congress for
the burning of the frigate *Philadelphia*, U.S. Naval Academy,
Annapolis, Maryland

Cannons captured from a
Tripolitan gunboat by
Stephen Decatur, August
3, 1804, Leutze Park,
Washington Navy Yard

Map of the Mediterranean Sea by William Berry, 1685

8

The *Philadelphia* Disaster

ONCE IT BECAME clear that the American effort to chastise the pirates was beginning to falter, many in the Jefferson administration began to lose some of their enthusiasm for the campaign. Two Mediterranean squadrons, under two separate commodores, had failed to produce any positive results, and had, if anything, lowered America's standing in the region and throughout Europe. On top of this, fears were running high that both Morocco and Tunis might become actively belligerent as well. By August 1802, Jefferson's cabinet began to grow weary of the slow, long-distance management of hostilities in Barbary. The debate formulated around two options: increasing the resources committed to chastising the pirates, or scaling down operations and preparing to sue for peace on more traditional Barbary terms.

Predictably, Albert Gallatin, Jefferson's secretary of the treasury, thought the war a waste of national resources and urged Jefferson to end it quickly. "I sincerely wish," he wrote on August 16, 1802, "you could reconcile it to yourself to empower our negotiators to give, if necessary for peace, an annuity to Tripoli." Meanwhile Robert Smith, secretary of the navy, urged the president to pursue the war more vigorously against the Barbary pirates: "nothing but a formidable squadron will prevent all the Barbary Powers waging war against us." Jefferson, as per usual, attempted a compromise.

Barbary policy would essentially remain unchanged. The United States would continue to negotiate treaties of amity and commerce with the North African regencies and would continue to give "presents" as necessary to secure the peace. Indeed, Jefferson authorized up to $20,000 for Morocco and Tunis, and even agreed to continue the option of giving unprompted gifts to reward "faithful and friendly conduct." In the matter of Pasha Yusuf Qaramanli of Tripoli, however, Jefferson refused to budge. "It is not thought consistent with the interest or the spirit of our nation (sufficiently manifested)," Jefferson wrote, "after a war so far successful against Tripoli, to finish by paying them a tribute. Besides the dishonor and premature abandonment of the ground our predecessors left us in possession of, it would oblige us immediately to pay a tribute to Tunis and Morocco."

By early 1803, however, Robert Smith was virtually alone in advocating the use of force to chastise Tripoli: "nothing but a formidable force will effect an honorable peace with Tripoli and repress the dispositions of the other Barbary Powers to hostility." Instead of pushing for a compromise position, Jefferson now rejected Smith's view. The goal of Jefferson's Barbary policy was not to obliterate the Barbary regencies and overhaul the long-established system of diplomacy and commerce in Barbary, but merely to control it as the stronger European powers did, and to discourage abuses. Jefferson thought little more would be necessary once the blockade of Tripoli was more effectively established. As he wrote Secretary Smith on March 29, 1803, "I have never believed in any effect from a show of force to those powers. They know they cannot meet us with force any more than they could France, Spain or England. Their system is a war of little expense to them, which must put the great nations to a greater expense than the presents which would buy it off." Jefferson understood the affair in straightforward terms of realpolitik. Force was merely part of the negotiation process—"nothing but the warring on them at times," he wrote, "will keep the demand of presents within bounds."

For Jefferson, the Mediterranean squadron was primarily supposed to bring Pasha Qaramanli's demands back within workable parameters and diminish his bargaining position rather than end the practice of piracy altogether. "The important thing for us now," the president concluded, "is to dispatch our small vessels." The goal was a secure and trustworthy peace, not an end to piracy.

Meanwhile, William Eaton began to lobby Jefferson and his cabinet to try a new approach in Barbary. Eaton had returned to his family in Massachusetts in early May 1803 after four years of service in North Africa. Although pleased to be home, he was eager to help his nation regain some of the honor she had lost to the Barbary pirates. Also, as he was left personally penniless by his service in Barbary, he needed to adjust his accounts with his government. He went to Washington in June to push on both fronts.

Eaton had a scheme he was eager to salvage. Back in Tunis, sometime in June 1801, he had first made contact with Ahmad Qaramanli, the deposed pasha of Tripoli and the older brother of Yusuf. The initial idea behind the scheme had come from James Cathcart in June 1801, but Eaton quickly embraced the plan and made it entirely his own. He thought that Ahmad could be brought under America's wing. In return for America's help in fomenting a rebellion in Tripoli and regaining his throne, Ahmad would establish peace with the United States and operate as an American puppet in the region. Eaton had spent a considerable amount of time, energy, and money on this and had repeatedly advocated it to his government and to the American naval ships in the region.

Unfortunately, he had been unable to rally support for the idea. Washington had not taken it seriously, supposing at the time that its Mediterranean squadron was all that was needed, while the captains of the squadron seemed ill disposed to take suggestions from an opinionated consul who had continually complained of the manner in which they carried out their duties in the region. The ideal time for the plan to be pushed into action had come and gone. Yusuf had gotten wind of the scheme and tried to have his brother killed, so Ahmad had fled. Now that America's Barbary affairs had begun to resemble a pig's breakfast, however, Eaton thought he could persuade the president and his cabinet to support his scheme.

Captain Edward Preble received his orders from the secretary of the navy on May 21, 1803. "Reposing in your skill, judgment and bravery the highest degree of confidence," the secretary's dispatch read, "the President has determined to commit the command of his [Mediterranean] squadron to your direction." Preble's flagship for this squadron was to be the forty-four-gun frigate USS *Constitution*.

Edward Preble, born in 1761 in Falmouth (near Portland), Maine, entered upon his naval career in 1778 as a seaman aboard a privateer. He served in the Massachusetts state navy and then joined the merchant marine after the war. Preble sought action, however, and tried in vain to procure a naval commission when Congress founded the U.S. Navy. Eventually he was given an appointment in 1798, during the Quasi-War with France, and soon he was promoted to captain owing to his talents and abilities at sea. Preble distinguished himself in this service, and he commanded the first U.S. warship to fly the American flag in the Indian Ocean.

The new six-ship squadron, which was to be joined by the USS *Enterprize*, already in the Mediterranean, would be the largest American squadron yet to be sent into that sea. Commodore Preble was resolved to command actively and effectively. Not only did he wish to make a good account of himself, he also knew that the president was eager for reports of action and successes following the Richard Morris fiasco in naval operations and the James Cathcart disappointment in diplomacy.

Commodore Edward Preble's mission was first and foremost to introduce some effective activity into Barbary affairs so as to bring Yusuf Qaramanli to terms, as well as to stem the tide of bad news and bring some peace and order back to the U.S.-Barbary relationship. On July 14, 1803, Preble received his operational orders. He was "at liberty to pursue the dictates of [his] own judgment," provided he kept Washington at least loosely informed, kept "a vigilant eye over the movements of all the other Barbary Powers," maintained a blockade of Tripoli, and focused his efforts to "annoy the enemy" with "all the means in [his] power."

Despite some initial delays from repairs, provisions, construction, and the finding and training of the crews, Preble's squadron was falling into shape. The twelve-gun USS *Nautilus* sailed on June 30 under the command of Lieutenant Richard Somers; the thirty-six-gun USS *Philadelphia* sailed out on July 18 under the command of William Bainbridge; Lieutenant John Smith's twelve-gun schooner, the USS *Vixen*, set out on August 3; the sixteen-gun USS *Siren*, commanded by Lieutenant Charles Stewart, sailed on August 27; and the sixteen-gun USS *Argus*, commanded by Lieutenant Stephen Decatur, sailed on September 8. The *Constitution*, which had required significant repairs, finally set out on August 14, 1803.

The *Constitution* had a smooth and fast voyage, arriving in Gibraltar on September 12. The voyage allowed Preble and Tobias Lear, the new consul to Tripoli, to commiserate a little on how best to bring Qaramanli to heel, and along what course Barbary affairs ought to proceed. Colonel Lear had been General George Washington's military as well as personal secretary; he had also served (1801–1802) as the U.S. consul at Cap-Français at the time of the French attempt to reconquer Haiti and had maintained American rights during the bloody uprising in Santo Domingo. Although in many respects an odd man, Lear was a brave, loyal, and crafty patriot, and he and Preble seemed to get along well enough during the voyage.

Early in the course of this voyage, Commodore Preble earned the enmity of many of his men for running a very tight ship and for having a very quick, ferocious temper. The divide between him and the men under his command was rendered more pronounced by the dramatic age difference—twelve years separated Preble and the second oldest officer in his squadron. Fortunately for Preble, a run-in with a foreign vessel helped win over most of his crew.

At sunset on September 10, 1803, two days before the USS *Constitution* was to hit Gibraltar, a sail was spotted ahead to the southeast. By 8:30 P.M., however, the *Constitution* suddenly found herself nearly on top of this unidentified ship—she looked very much as if she could be a warship. Preble called the crew to quarters and then hailed the mystery ship.

"What ship is that?" asked Preble.

"What ship is that?" came the reply.

"This is the United States frigate *Constitution*. What ship is that?" Preble demanded.

"What ship is that?" came the reply.

"This is the United States frigate *Constitution*. What ship is that?!"

"What ship is that?"

"I am now going to hail you for the last time. If a proper answer is not returned, I will fire a shot into you."

"If you fire a shot, I will return a broadside."

"What ship is that?!"

"This is His Britannic Majesty's ship *Donegal*, eighty-four guns, Sir Richard Strachan, an English commodore. Send your boat on board."

Commodore Edward Preble was far too proud for such taunting nonsense, and his temper erupted and ran quite away from him. He scrambled to the netting, secured a foothold, and personally shouted back, "This is the United States ship *Constitution*, forty-four guns, Edward Preble, an American commodore, who will be damned before he sends his boat on board of any vessel!"

Climbing down from the nettings and turning back upon his crew, Preble shouted very loudly to the men on the quarterdeck, "Blow your matches, boys!"

All communication ceased, and a silence filled the air. Although only a few minutes passed, it seemed like an eternity to the men aboard the *Constitution*. Finally, a boat was heard approaching slowly toward the ship. An English officer came aboard and explained that his ship was indeed a British frigate, but not the *Donegal*. She was the *Maidstone*, commanded by Captain George Elliot.

The *Maidstone* had sighted the *Constitution* earlier that afternoon but was concerned she was a hostile ship; Captain Elliot had come closer to inspect, but had not realized in the darkness just how close the two ships had gotten until it was too late. After that, Elliot was simply trying to buy his crew some time to get to quarters and man their defenses.

Although the crisis was diverted and both vessels were able to stand down and relax, Commodore Preble's actions in standing up to the British had a dramatic affect upon his crew and substantially boosted morale.

Two days later, on September 12, 1803, the *Constitution* entered the Straits of Gibraltar and headed directly to Tangier. Commodore Preble hove to in the harbor at 10 A.M., raised the U.S. flag as well as his colors, and fired a shot to signal U.S. consul James Simpson to send out a boat to greet him. Nothing happened at first, although before too long the Swedish consul hoisted its flag over the consulate. Preble fired another signal, yet this second shot seemed to elicit no response at all. What had become of U.S. consul James Simpson? Clearly something was amiss.

The *Constitution* sailed across the strait and made Gibraltar by midday. Once moored in the port at Gibraltar, Captain Bainbridge and U.S. consul John Gavino brought Preble up to speed. Emperor Mawlay Souleïman of Morocco seemed to be involved in assisting Tripoli against the United States. By August 1803, Gavino had received reports that Morocco had two pirate cruisers actively seeking American merchant captures. The Americans had captured one of these ships, the *Mirboka*, and learned that the orders to attack American shipping had come from the governor of Tangier. Meanwhile, Consul James Simpson was under house arrest by the governor of Tangier, Alcayde abd al-Rahman Hashah, who demanded that Simpson would be released only when the *Mirboka* was returned. Because of the actions of Governor Hashah, it wasn't exactly clear whether or not Morocco was actually at war with the United States.

With such a delicate, difficult, and uncertain situation before him, Commodore Edward Preble became convinced that an active, aggressive, campaign was in order. "I suspect the demands of the Barbary Powers will increase," he wrote, "and will be of such a nature as to make it imprudent for our government to comply with. . . . I believe a firm and decided conduct in the first instance towards those of them who make war against us would have a good effect." Preble ardently believed that "the Moors are a deep designing artful treacherous set of villains and nothing will keep them so quiet as a respectable naval force near them."

On the afternoon of September 13, a very unhappy Richard Morris arrived aboard the *New York*. Although Morris had already received notice of his suspension and recall, Captain John Rodgers had not had the chance to relieve him of his command and take charge of the squadron before Preble arrived to assume supreme command. This created an unfortunate complication between Rodgers and Preble. A natural rivalry and mutual hostility already existed between them, since although Preble was more than a decade older, Rodgers was actually the senior officer, as he had received his captaincy just before Preble. Now, after enduring Morris's lethargic approach to Barbary affairs, Rodgers felt robbed by having to surrender his frustratingly short-lived command of the Mediterranean squadron. That this command was going to Edward Preble, a junior officer he greatly disliked, simply added insult to injury.

As Preble's squadron was still missing two ships, the *Siren* and the *Argus*, and he knew he would need to show substantial force before Morocco if the situation was to be contained and neutralized, he sent Rodgers a conciliatory note. Rodgers agreed for the good of the nation to cooperate in a show of force against Morocco, but he otherwise refused to accept Preble's authority.

Commodore Preble now had enough of a force at his disposal for him to take the fight to Mawlay Souleïman. The *Philadelphia* and the *Constitution* were ordered to take up the blockade of Tripoli, while the rest of the squadron sailed to Tangier, entered the harbor, and took their position. Preble sent word to Emperor Souleïman that the United States was prepared for action if Morocco had indeed declared war. Emperor Souleïman sent word back that his recent forays into piracy were merely retribution for the earlier U.S. capture of the *Meshuda*.

Several days of negotiation passed before Souleïman came to terms. The original 1786 treaty was once again ratified, this time on October 11, 1803. The peaceful resolution of the conflict was attributed mostly to the awesome show of American force in the harbor, coupled with the stern and distinctly unaccommodating countenance of Commodore Preble. Word quickly spread, and American prestige soared very high.

The effort furthered the perception that the United States was now more than willing to settle such matters with serious force. Commodore Edward Preble described his progress in a letter to his wife, Mary:

> I have been so engaged in official duties since my arrival on this station that for many nights in succession I have slept without taking off a garment, excepting my coat, as I have often been called upon ten times in a night. I returned here from Morocco a few days since, where I have been to negotiate a peace with the Emperor, whom I found at war with the United States on my arrival here. During my stay of fourteen days at Tangier, his principal port, all the men in our ships slept at quarters, prepared for battle. It has so far been a hard service, but I have the satisfaction of having succeeded in my negotiations, and an honorable peace is established. This, I presume, will be highly gratifying to our government. . . . I have undertaken an arduous task, but hope to get honorably through and return to you, never again to separate.

By the time Commodore Preble returned to Gibraltar on October 15, 1803, the USS *Siren* had arrived. Due to an unfortunate run-in with the British over the defection of three of that ship's crew, however, Preble had to find a new base of operations for the squadron that was not under direct British command. Thus, the squadron was moved to Syracuse on the island of Sicily, a tad farther out from Tripoli, but a manageable port nonetheless.

As the realities of the task before him became clearer, Preble began to worry. He sent the *Siren* off to Leghorn to procure some of the consular presents that Tobias Lear would need when he entered Algiers.

Lieutenant Stephen Decatur, now in control of the *Enterprize*, having switched commands with Isaac Hull, was dispatched to convoy a storeship to Syracuse. The *Constitution* and the *Nautilus*, commanded by Richard Somers, would head first to Algiers to land Lear so that he might take up his consular post, as well as show the flag, meet and greet a few officials, and so forth, before continuing on to Syracuse. The *Argus* was to spend the winter cruising the Straits of Gibraltar, just in case Morocco reneged.

Preble understood that he would need all his ships and commanders if the Tripoli blockade were to succeed, and even then the forces at his disposal might prove insufficient. He pored over maps of the region, studying and planning for that theater of engagement. Meanwhile, he sent to the secretary of the navy for more resources and more ships. Unfortunately, the weather was against him.

By the middle of October, Commodore Preble realized that the onset of winter would prevent his conducting any naval engagement more substantial than an occasional blockade. He hoped, however, that the time would be sufficient for the reinforcements he had sent for to arrive. Fearing for loss of time and momentum, he decided to establish the blockade and do his best to hold the line until the spring. Meanwhile, he had plenty of business to attend to. "I have an arduous task to perform," he wrote to Mary in early November, "but hope to acquit myself honorably. I am determined to oblige the Pasha of that regency [Tripoli] to make peace with us on terms which are admissible or to destroy his city." To help ensure success, he explained, "I am in treaty with the King of Naples for a supply of gunboats to assist my squadron, which I have no doubt will be readily granted as he is the inveterate enemy of the Tripolines. I wish to close the war with the Barbarians by conduct which shall establish our naval character among them and make them have a respect for peace." Despite his steely determination, Edward Preble expected to work hard for victory: "My duty has been hard and fatiguing since I came on this station and must expect it will be very much so at the siege of Tripoli."

Having set his mind round his task, Preble declared on November 12 that the city and regency of Tripoli was in a state of blockade and that anyone venturing into these waters risked capture by the American squadron. Two days later, the *Constitution*, the *Argus*, and the *Nautilus* set off for the Barbary Coast. They headed first to Algiers and landed Colonel Tobias

Lear, his family, and his suite. After a couple of pleasant days in the city, Commodore Preble sailed eastward toward Tripoli.

On November 24, the *Constitution* came upon the British thirty-eight-gun frigate HMS *Amazon*. Preble spoke with the ship's commander and received some stunningly bad news regarding the USS *Philadelphia*. He immediately set a course for Malta in hopes of verifying the report. On November 27, the *Constitution* reached Valletta harbor. From there, he received letters from Captain William Bainbridge detailing the situation. More details would become available over the next few weeks.

When the USS *Philadelphia* and the USS *Vixen* reached Tripoli on October 7, 1803, Captain Bainbridge had immediately established the ordered blockade. For the next two weeks the American warships cruised the area. The schooner *Vixen*, being a smaller-draft vessel, would try to flush the enemy away from the shoal waters, while the *Philadelphia* would try to control the situation offshore. The two weeks passed at an interminably slow and frustrating pace. On October 22, Captain Bainbridge sent the *Vixen* off to cruise between Cape Bon and the island of Marettimo to follow up on a report of two Tripolitan cruisers in the area.

Finally, on October 31, at 9 A.M., the *Philadelphia* was cruising five leagues east of the city when she sighted a foreign ship to the westward, standing before the wind. She gave chase, and the foreign ship hoisted Tripolitan colors and made a run for Tripoli, hugging the shoreline. By 11 A.M., the *Philadelphia* was making eight knots and gaining quickly on the blockade runner. Because he was in uncharted and possibly shoal water, Bainbridge moved carefully. He was determined, however, to take the prize and continued in hot pursuit. As the Tripolitan cruiser began to break farther away, Bainbridge opened fire with his eighteen-pounders.

Throughout the chase Bainbridge had set three different leadsmen to make soundings to be sure that he did not run his ship aground. At about 11:30 A.M., however, the *Philadelphia* suddenly found herself in shoal water, a mere seven fathoms deep. Bainbridge called off the chase immediately and proceeded to beat out to sea.

The *Philadelphia* did not get very far.

The ship suddenly shuddered as it struck ground. The *Philadelphia* had shot up on a hidden reef, bringing her to an abrupt stop. The U.S. frigate was stranded, five or six feet out of the water, just three or four miles northeast of the enemy harbor of Tripoli and only a mile and a half from the shore.

The enemy vessel the *Philadelphia* had been chasing, Bainbridge observed, avoided the shoal and sailed safely off to the harbor of Tripoli. Coming from that harbor, however, were nine Tripolitan gunboats heading directly for the now immobilized and impotent warship.

Captain Bainbridge tried everything he could to free his ship. First he tried to crowd on sail to shift her forward off the reef; then, in an effort to shift her astern, he tried to lay the sails back, cut three anchors away from the bow, hove overboard all the cannons except for those well aft, and proceeded to smash the water casks and pump their drinking water out of the flooded hold. Then he tried cutting away the foremast; this in turn tore down the main topgallant mast. Nothing seemed to be working.

The Tripolitan gunboats had gathered within range now and had begun to open fire. The *Philadelphia* returned fire as best she could, but it was merely enough to hold the cautious Tripolitans to their position. The U.S. frigate had no effective means of protecting herself, while the enemy gunboats had no problems maintaining a steady fire.

As the afternoon wore on, the situation seemed desperate. Bainbridge and his officers decided to surrender to the enemy.

The Americans flooded the magazine, disabled the remaining guns, destroyed all the signal books, threw shot into the pumps, and drilled holes in the bottom. The *Philadelphia* struck her colors.

Oddly, however, Captain Bainbridge neglected to destroy his personal papers—from which the pasha would soon discover the size and makeup of the American squadron, its perceived weaknesses and strengths, and even its projected movements. Although Commodore Preble would never learn of it, William Bainbridge, by neglecting to destroy these papers, effectively supplied Qaramanli with hard and invaluable intelligence.

The Tripolitans had little difficulty saving the ship. The scuttling of the frigate had been done poorly, and within a few days the sea level had risen due to a storm. In little time the *Philadelphia* was off the reef and brought into port, under the harbor battery—they even salvaged the cannons that had been thrown overboard. The ship would need a new foremast, but it was otherwise in excellent condition and would surely become the finest pirate ship in all of Barbary.

The Tripolitans wasted little time in repairing the damage and refitting the *Philadelphia* for Barbary service. The ship's entire complement of 307 men, Captain William Bainbridge included, were taken captive.

Pasha Yusuf Qaramanli of the city and regency of Tripoli was positively euphoric.

Edward Preble's plans for Tripoli were immediately laid waste by the *Philadelphia*'s capture. The vessel now posed an immediate threat to American interests, as well as to Preble's squadron. American prestige had been riding high after the demonstration of naval strength in Tangier, but it was now unbelievably low—so low in fact, that Preble worried that Tunis and Morocco might declare hostilities.

Commodore Preble's vision of a single brilliant, shining moment that would humble the pasha and end Barbary piracy against the United States seemed now a distant, imponderable fiction. Pasha Yusuf Qaramanli had 307 hostages with which to stave off any decisive action, regulate American terms, and perhaps ensure the faithful execution of virtually all of his demands.

Edward Preble had a handful of small vessels, one forty-four-gun frigate, and no solid plans.

From Malta, Preble immediately sailed to Sicily to establish the American resupply base in Syracuse and refit the *Constitution* for the winter months. Mostly, though, he needed time to regroup and reconsider the situation. He prepared several dispatches notifying Washington of the *Philadelphia*'s capture and renewed his request for more resources and more ships. He wanted a frigate to cover the Straits of Gibraltar, thereby freeing the smaller and more useful schooner *Argus*, and he requested a frigate to replace the *Philadelphia*. If he was given such a force, Preble convinced himself, he could force Qaramanli to terms without the United States having to ransom the 307 men of the captured warship. The USS *Nautilus* sailed for Gibraltar with these dispatches on December 15, 1803.

With no hope of regaining his position of power without reinforcements, Commodore Preble returned to the only two options left to him. He could attempt to recapture the *Philadelphia*, or he could destroy her. Given his resources and the likely chances of success, Preble opted for the more practical course of action. As he explained to Secretary of the Navy Smith, "I do not believe the *Philadelphia* will ever be of service to Tripoli. I shall hazard much to destroy her. It will undoubtedly cost lives, but it must be done."

On December 17, the *Constitution* and *Enterprize* set a course for the coast of Tripoli. Preble was determined to keep the blockade up for as long as the weather permitted, but he would break for winter, as these waters would soon be far too forbidding. He assigned the *Enterprize* the task of reconnoitering the *Philadelphia*'s location and determining her position.

Preble's luck was set to change.

On the morning of December 23, in Tripolitan waters, the *Constitution* sighted a foreign vessel on the southwestern horizon. Preble immediately went in pursuit, signaling to the *Enterprize*, which was much closer to the ship, to do so as well. Then the wind veered to the southwest, putting the foreign vessel dead to windward, steering toward the American frigate. Preble was flying English colors as a *ruse de guerre*.

The foreign ship, a lateen-rigged ketch of the sort common to Turkish and North African ports, identified herself as the *Mastico*, and although she sailed under the Ottoman pennant and was commanded by a Turk, she also carried an assortment of Tripolitan officers, soldiers, and slaves, and had arms and personal effects from officers aboard the *Philadelphia*. Commodore Preble was certain he would be able to claim her as a lawful prize. The English colors were struck, the American flag was raised, and the commodore declared the *Mastico* as a prize. A crew took the ship to Syracuse, where she would be detained until her papers could be translated and the lawfulness of her seizure adjudicated.

Once the *Mastico*'s month of quarantine ended and her crew was taken away as prisoners, she was renamed the *Intrepid* and was fitted out with a heavy quantity of arms and combustibles for a special mission in Tripoli. Preble also sent the USS *Siren*, disguised as a merchantman. The mission was straightforward: destroy the *Philadelphia*.

The plan was simple. The *Intrepid* would sail into the harbor of Tripoli with Americans hidden below deck. She would come alongside the *Philadelphia* and the crew would board and burn her. As the *Intrepid* was a Tripolitan lateen-rigged ketch, the odds were pretty good that she might slip into the harbor without attracting too much attention. The plan was exceedingly dangerous, and Preble thought it likely he would lose many good men in the effort. Either way, he expected to hear word of the mission's outcome before too long.

The *Intrepid* sailed out of Syracuse under the command of Lieutenant Stephen Decatur at 5 P.M. on February 2, 1804. She traveled in the company of the *Siren*, commanded by Lieutenant Charles Stewart. The *Siren*'s job was to cover the *Intrepid*'s retreat and so was to take a position at the mouth of the harbor of Tripoli.

Several days passed without any news of the *Intrepid* or the *Siren*, or of any action in Tripoli. Commodore Preble grew impatient and anxious for the safety of his men and the success of their mission.

A hard gale had ripped through the area from February 6 through February 9, and Preble's increasing unease became discernible to his squadron. Every passing day worsened his mood and inflamed his anxiety. On February 12, he ordered a lookout to be maintained at the *Constitution*'s masthead. Far too much time had elapsed, and he despaired that both the *Intrepid* and the *Siren* had been lost to Tripoli.

On February 7, the two raiders arrived off Tripoli, but their first attempt to carry out the mission was thwarted by the inclement weather—the same gale that was vexing Edward Preble's nerves. The storm finally passed on the tenth, but the two ships had been carried far to the east, away from Tripoli. Five days later, on February 15, they finally made their way back toward the waters off Tripoli, and at 5:30 P.M. they sighted Point Tagiura, just east of the city. Standing a good distance off the coast to avoid detection, they finally tacked in toward Tripoli at around 9:30 P.M. for a second attempt. They were unable to get any positive bearings, however, so nothing could be done till morning; they could not, after all, advance against a harbor they could not find. Lieutenants Stewart and Decatur agreed to try again the next day.

Although the morale of the *Intrepid* had been high at the outset of the mission, little kept the cramped and uncomfortable volunteers going but the leadership of Lieutenant Decatur. The tall, dark-haired, broad-shouldered, earnest twenty-five-year-old Stephen Decatur had a warrior's mentality and the charisma of a natural leader. He was also a glory seeker and was eager to strike a blow against the enemy. With Decatur in the lead, it was widely felt, they would prevail no matter the conditions.

On February 16 the morning was bright, the sky was clear, and there was a healthy breeze in the air. The *Intrepid* stood in once again toward Tripoli at around 11 A.M. flying British colors, with a makeshift drag out astern and plenty of canvas atop to slow the ship's advance and make her appear as if she was laden with heavy cargo, pushing to make the harbor before dark. No more than six or eight men were allowed on deck at any one time, and these were dressed as Maltese mariners. The disguise appeared to have the desired effect.

As night fell, the *Intrepid*'s drags were taken in so that she was within two miles of the harbor's eastern entrance. She was supposed to wait for boats from the *Siren*, which would then accompany her under cover of darkness, but there had been no sign of that vessel for the last three miles. The breeze was growing faint, however, and Decatur did not want to risk exposure by having to break out the sweeps to reach the *Philadelphia*. He decided they would proceed without the *Siren*'s accompaniment. "The fewer men," he added, quoting *Henry V*, "the greater share of honor."

Later that evening, around 7 P.M., the *Intrepid* entered the harbor. From this point forward, she was directly under the shore batteries; complete silence was maintained. Due to light winds, she covered the distance to the captured ship in just over two hours. Moving within hailing distance of the *Philadelphia*, she was hailed and challenged by the watch on the frigate. It was claimed that the ship—a ketch laden with cattle for the British garrison at Malta—had lost her anchors during the recent gale. The ruse worked, and the *Intrepid* was given permission to make fast to the *Philadelphia* until daybreak. A line was extended and received, and the *Intrepid* began to haul in. Soon she would be alongside the *Philadelphia*.

As she glided into position, one of the Tripolitan guards who had been standing at the *Philadelphia*'s bulwarks caught sight of something aboard her that gave them away. "Americanos! Americanos!" he shouted. The captain of the watch frantically ordered the tow line cut. It was, however, already too late.

The official order "Board!" was given as Lieutenant Decatur leapt over the side.

The Americans rushed the ship. There were only seven or eight guards at watch, and all but two of these were quickly overwhelmed with sabers and tomahawks rather than pistols. Two of the Tripolitans went over the side; the rest were killed in the noisy action. The *Philadelphia* was secured in about five minutes.

Now, however, it was just a matter of time before the Tripolitan gunboats and shore batteries—already showing signs of life—mounted a defense.

Quickly, combustibles were distributed to predetermined sections of the berth deck, storerooms, and the cockpit. Decatur shouted the order "Fire!" signaling the men to ignite their combustibles and head quickly back to the *Intrepid*. The fire spread rapidly and uncontrollably. Decatur waited until every man had safely left the blazing *Philadelphia* before leaping into the *Intrepid*'s rigging as it swung away. The mission had taken about twenty minutes.

Finally, the Tripolitan defenses kicked into action, opening fire with ferocity the moment the burning *Philadelphia* lit up the harbor. The *Intrepid* scrambled to make her escape amid the barrage of cannonade and musketry. Between her sail and the sweeps, she made a brisk pace away from the scene and cleared the harbor out of reach of the guns. Near the entrance of the harbor, she met up with the earlier-expected launch and barge with reinforcements from *Siren*. The two ships were reunited around midnight.

On Sunday, February 19, at 10 A.M. the *Intrepid* and the *Siren* arrived off the entrance of the harbor at Syracuse. The *Constitution* made signal 227: "Business or enterprise, have you completed, that you was sent on?" The answering flags were hoisted on the *Siren*, signaling 232: "Business, I have completed, that I was sent on."

The ships entered the harbor to the jubilation of the entire squadron and a roar of three cheers.

Lieutenants Decatur and Stewart went aboard the *Constitution* to make their report. Decatur was that day recommended for captain, and soon afterward the promotion went through. At twenty-five, he became the youngest man appointed captain in the U.S. Navy. Congress awarded him a sword and gave the crew of the *Intrepid* two months' pay. On May 22, 1804, Secretary of the Navy Smith wrote Decatur a letter informing him of his new commission and expressing President Jefferson's "thanks for your gallant conduct on this occasion." He requested that Decatur in the name of the president "thank each individual of your gallant band for their honorable and valorous support, rendered the more honorable from its having been volunteered."

In Tripoli, Decatur's exploits were less well received. The burning hulk of the *Philadelphia* had broken free of her mooring cables, and she drifted ashore very near Pasha Qaramanli's castle before finally exploding. The eruption shook the entire water-front. As one of the American prisoners described the scene, "Tumult, consternation, confusion and delay reigned in every section of the town and castle."

The former crew of the *Philadelphia* was awoken early the next morning in their prison. The wardens "rushed in amongst us," one of the Americans noted, "and began to beat every one they could see, spitting in our faces and hissing like the serpents of hell." The warship's former officers were not exempt from Qaramanli's wrath. The pasha gave orders that the officers be confined under lock and key to their quarters, with additional guards posted outside the door. A few days later, the officers were transferred from quarters in the castle to a dungeon next to the palace. Still enraged, Pasha Yusuf Qaramanli let it be widely known that he might retaliate by setting fire to each and every American prisoner, and he even had special combustible shirts made of "hemp cloth, and well saturated with melted brimstone" ready for each man. Fortunately, wiser counsel prevailed, and Pasha Qaramanli's wrath soon cooled.

9

American Gunboat Diplomacy

COMMODORE EDWARD PREBLE was in much better spirits following the destruction of the USS *Philadelphia*. To his mind, American honor had been restored, and Pasha Yusuf Qaramanli had been, at the very least, humbled if not actually chastised. Although Preble had accomplished little more than to remove part of the enemy's advantage—and one that had been gained as a direct result of American incompetence—the momentum was undeniably his. Stephen Decatur's mission had been styled "the most bold and daring act of the age" by Admiral Horatio Nelson, and the prestige of the United States was soaring very high.

Eager to relax a bit for the duration of winter, Preble dispatched ships to maintain the blockade of Tripoli and to courier dispatches. He wrote again to the secretary of the navy requesting resources and reinforcements, but otherwise he settled in and contemplated his next offensive. "My heart is fixed," he wrote, "on obliging him [Pasha Qaramanli] to sue for peace, and I hope yet to make him consent to sign a treaty as favorable as ours with Morocco without a cent for tribute."

The USS *Constitution* sailed to Malta on March 2, 1804, where Commodore Preble intended to remain just a few days before returning to Syracuse to prepare for his operations against Tripoli. While he was there, however, credible rumors surfaced suggesting that Tunis was preparing to declare war on the United States. Preble knew that Bey Hammuda Pasha was still irritated about Commodore Richard Morris's capture of a Tunisian ship, so he thought it irresponsible to ignore the possibility of a declaration of war.

The thought of conflict with Tunis particularly worried Preble, as he thought his squadron could not perform well against an additional belligerent nation in Barbary. Tunis had, as far as Preble could ascertain, one thirty-six-gun frigate operational and ready for cruising, one frigate under construction that would be between thirty-six and forty-two guns, thirty-two xebecs with somewhere between six and thirty-six mounted guns each, thirty galleys armed with one or two guns each, and at least ten gunboats.

By comparison, the United States' Mediterranean squadron now consisted of one frigate, two brigs, and three schooners. Also, Preble's force already had to divide its time among patrolling Tripoli, cruising the Straits of Gibraltar to keep an eye on Morocco, and periodically dispatching vessels to maintain the lines of communication or convoying American merchant ships. Should Tunis declare war, the Mediterranean theater of battle would become far too large for his resources to cope with.

Once again, Commodore Preble began to lobby his government for reinforcements. He wrote privately to the secretary of war that he needed two more frigates and two more brigs if he was to beat the Tripolitans into submission without recourse to paying ransoms or promising tribute. Later, he wrote again surveying American interests in the region, pointing out the increase in commercial activity and profit and asserting that all could be lost because of foolish economies with naval expenditures. "I feel extremely desirous," he wrote in one of his appeals, "of serving my country. Give me the means and I will do it."

Meanwhile, the *Constitution* returned to Syracuse on March 17. The next day, Preble received notice from Robert R. Livingston, U.S. minister to France, that he had, on his own initiative, successfully persuaded the French to intercede with Tripoli on behalf of the United States. Preble was dubious of the arrangement, as he believed that the French largely embraced the interests of Tripoli over those of the United States. The commodore made it clear to Livingston that he did not particularly appreciate the interference, but he reluctantly agreed to meet with the French consul in Tripoli.

The *Constitution* made for Tripoli on Wednesday, March 21, 1804. A week later, just off Tripoli's coast, on Wednesday, March 28, Preble and Bonaventure Beaussier, the French consul in Tripoli, dined aboard the warship. Beaussier was eager to assist, but he made it plain that the United States could not hope to negotiate a peace without purchasing it at some expense, and that nothing could be done about ransoming the prisoners without also entering into peace negotiations. The audience quickly fell apart. Preble refused on principle to purchase peace; he intended to win the war through force of arms. As he wrote in his diary later that day, "We must, therefore, depend wholly on our own exertions for effecting a peace, which can only be done by an increase of our force and a number of gun and mortar boats to batter down his [Qaramanli's] castle and town."

Preble next set sail for Tunis, eager to evaluate the situation, flex a little muscle, and sooth the bey's temper a bit. Expecting a possible surprise attack, the *Constitution* and the *Siren* both approached the port ready for a fight. George Davis, the U.S. chargé d'affaires, apprised Preble of the situation on the ground and informed him that the bey was expecting the commodore to land and attend to an audience with him. Unwilling to comply with what seemed a possible trick—after all, Commodore Morris had been arrested and detained on his visit to Tunis—Preble took refuge in his chronic ailments, claiming that his ulcers had begun acting up again and he was becoming very ill—which, as it happens, was quite true.

Preble explained this in a letter and then added that he was a new commodore, not Morris, and so was not familiar with the *Paulina* affair and was not authorized to make any reparations for Tunisian vessels that had been seized while running the blockade of Tripoli. He told the bey that Tobias Lear was authorized to negotiate and expressed his hope that Lear would arrive at Tunis very soon.

Davis returned the next day to the city and met with Bey Hammuda Pasha to deliver Preble's message. The bey was not amused; he threatened war should Preble leave the harbor without bringing the matter to a satisfactory conclusion.

Commodore Preble decided the whole affair was merely a pretext for some excuse to declare war. He was determined to leave and call Bey Hammuda Pasha's bluff. The *Siren* was ordered to await word from Davis, while the *Constitution* sailed to Malta. Fortunately, Davis managed to persuade Bey Hammuda Pasha to wait for Tobias Lear to arrive. A six-week grace period was granted to the United States before the bey would once again demand restitution.

From April 6 through 11, Commodore Preble remained sick with fever in his cabin aboard the *Constitution*. On April 12, former U.S. consul general Richard O'Brien visited him in Malta. At Preble's request, O'Brien had left Algiers with his family a few weeks earlier. Commodore Preble had initially wanted O'Brien to assist in negotiating with Qaramanli; now, however, the commodore proposed that O'Brien, in consultation with Tobias Lear, sail to Tunis to assist Chargé d'Affaires George Davis in negotiating with the bey (Lear was unable to leave his posting at Algiers at that time). O'Brien agreed to help.

Richard O'Brien landed at Tunis on April 24. During the first week of negotiations, the bey obstinately haggled over various gifts and proposed substitutions. Finally a deal was struck, but it required every bit of hard cash left to the American squadron. The United States would pay Bey Hammuda Pasha $5,000 in reparations and agreed to give $8,000 as an annuity in addition to the previously agreed-upon stipulations of the original treaty. The deal was finalized on April 29, 1804, and O'Brien was picked up by the *Constitution* on May 2. He reported the successful but degrading business to Preble. The commodore's faith in force over tribute was reaffirmed very strongly.

Back at Tripoli, Preble was determined to smash some sense into Qaramanli. The plan was to compel the pasha to terms by hitting the Tripolitan coastal towns and cities hard from just offshore, capturing them as needed, and driving the refugees into the city of Tripoli, which would be subject to a truly effective blockade using shallow-draft gun- and mortar boats. Preble also intended to maintain a steady bombardment of the city itself.

To put this plan into action, he would need shallow-draft gunboats that could hug the shore at close enough range to fire upon the enemy with great effect. These boats would also have the advantage of being able to take after the Tripolitan gunboats and xebecs without fear of running aground on the reefs. Besides the gunboats, Preble also needed mortar or bomb ketches with the capability to deliver shot over the city walls.

Although both boats were fairly common in the Mediterranean, they did not prove so easy to procure, as none of the southern European nations wished to antagonize the North African states by helping the United States. Fortunately for Preble, the Kingdom of the Two Sicilies was an eager exception. Years of chronic hostilities and piracy by the North African states against the kingdom practically guaranteed that the king of Naples would be enthusiastic about assisting Preble. Preble did, however, need to actually go to Naples and submit his request.

Therefore, the *Constitution* made her way to Sicily and then sailed on, dropping anchor at Naples on May 9, 1804. Preble met with General Sir John Acton, the British prime minister of the Kingdom of the Two Sicilies, in an effort to advance his request to the king. He asked to borrow eight gunboats, two mortar boats, two floating batteries, eight long brass cannon of either twenty-four or thirty-two pounds, and supplies of powder, shot, shells, muskets, and sabers. On May 13 he was informed that the king had agreed to lend him everything in the request, although the number of long guns and gunboats had changed slightly, from eight to six.

Commodore Preble spent the next few days busily loading cannon, powder, cartridges, and other supplies. As soon as the long guns were to hand, he decided to mount them on the *Constitution*'s upper deck rather than on charter merchantmen to turn them into floating batteries. To augment his squadron and man the additional boats and guns, he also got permission from the king to sign on ninety-six Neapolitan seamen. Everything was fully loaded and ready on May 19, and Preble took the *Constitution* off to Messina, Sicily, to pick up the gunboats and mortar boats.

Upon arrival in Messina, Preble inspected the gunboats on loan to him—everything was set for them to go right out to sea. The lateen-rigged gunboats were, however, built for harbor defense, not swift sailing or maneuvering. Each was sixty feet long, twenty-five tons, and flat-bottomed, making sailing or rowing very cumbersome and sluggish; each boat was equipped with a long twenty-four-pounder in the bow that could pivot slightly, but its fire was essentially limited to wherever the bow pointed. The two mortar boats were similar, but they were equipped with a twenty-six-pound cannon mounted forward, as well as a fourteen-inch brass mortar with about a mile-and-a-half range using Neapolitan powder. The bomb ketches required about three weeks of work before they would be ready to sail. As the schooner USS *Nautilus* was also at Messina at this time undergoing recoppering and some refitting, Preble took most of that vessel's crew with him to man his gunboat flotilla, including Lieutenant Richard Somers, who was made commander of the new task force of gunboats.

On Wednesday, May 30, 1804, at 10 A.M., the *Constitution* and the gunboat flotilla set sail for Syracuse, which they made two days later. Although Preble had set out fairly optimistic that he would succeed, by June 1 he began to have serious doubts. As he noted to his wife:

> I shall then attack the Pasha's city and castles and hope with this additional force to our little squadron to be able to effect an honorable peace, although I by no means place too much dependence on success. The city of Tripoli is strongly fortified and defended by a large force of gunboats. I am astonished that our government have not sent out a reinforcement of ships. It is now nearly eight months since the loss of the *Philadelphia* and nothing has arrived to replace her. The season for action has already arrived, and, as the fine weather continues but about

three months so that gunboats can navigate these seas with safety, I shall be obliged to attack Tripoli under many disadvantages for want of more ships or I shall lose the season by letting it pass off without attempting anything. This I am determined not to do.

Unbeknownst to Commodore Edward Preble, however, President Thomas Jefferson had made two pivotal decisions related to the question of reinforcements—both of which were to have a direct effect on Preble's designs.

On March 19, 1804, President Jefferson had finally received Commodore Preble's first dispatch detailing his Tripolitan activities. It was only now and from this report that Jefferson first learned of the grounding and capture of the frigate *Philadelphia* and the imprisonment of all 307 members of her crew. Jefferson despaired that his first two commodores had utterly failed to do anything significant against the pasha of Tripoli, while his third, Preble, had so far given the enemy a U.S. frigate and 307 hostages. The news did little to convince his cabinet that the war effort was going well or had so far justified the expense poured into it.

This news dropped during a time of national budget worries. Jefferson's Louisiana Territory land deal had been popular, but the interest on the loan undertaken for the deal persuaded Jefferson and Albert Gallatin, the secretary of the treasury, that economies needed to be made in the national budget. Bad news in the Mediterranean did not bode well for further naval outlays. Yet the *Philadelphia* disaster was a double-edged sword that on the one hand offered strong support for cutting back on naval expenditures, and on the other simultaneously presented a strong reason to devote more resources to regain the national honor.

Jefferson was strongly committed to balancing the budget through trimming expenditures, but he was also strongly committed to taming Tripoli, both in principle and in public. Indeed, the war had so far proved fairly popular—the public seemed to love the occasional successes—and there had as yet been no substantial losses. In the end, Jefferson's original impulse to fight the pirates trumped his administrative urge to cut expenditures.

Although Jefferson did not know how the public would respond to the news of the *Philadelphia's* capture, he thought it likely to stir sentiment toward an even more robust policy in Barbary. He brought the matter before Congress, informing legislators of the disaster and suggesting that the news "renders it expedient to increase our force, and enlarge our expenses in the Mediterranean, beyond what the last appropriation for naval service contemplated."

American public opinion seemed uniformly outraged by the loss of the warship and the imprisonment of her crew. Only six days later, on March 26, 1804, the Eighth Congress passed "An Act further to protect the commerce and seamen of the United States against the Barbary Powers." The act established a new tax on all import goods to defray the cost of building more U.S. naval ships and authorized the president to order "warlike operations against the regency of Tripoli, or any other Barbary Powers." This new "Mediterranean Fund" was designed to cease three months after a peace treaty with Tripoli had been ratified, assuming the United States was not at war with any other Barbary power. The act also appropriated $1 million to pay for immediate expenses.

President Jefferson moved energetically to get reinforcements to the Mediterranean squadron operational and mobilized. This new detachment was to be a squadron of four frigates—the USS *Congress* (thirty-six guns), under the command of Captain John Rodgers; the USS *Essex* (thirty-two guns), under Captain James Barron; the USS *Constellation* (thirty-six guns), under Captain Hugh G. Campbell; and the flagship, the USS *President* (forty-four guns), under Captain George Cox—all under the general command of *Commodore* Captain Samuel Barron.

As Barron was senior to Preble, Jefferson had no choice but to confer on him overall command of the Mediterranean squadron, making him the new commodore. Secretary of the Navy Smith wrote Edward Preble on May 22 informing him both of the forthcoming reinforcements and of his being superseded in command by Commodore Samuel Barron. The secretary labored hard to soften the blow to Preble, explaining at length that the president had "of necessity . . . been obliged to send out two gentlemen senior to yourself in commission. Be assured, sir, that no want of confidence in you has been mingled with the considerations which have imposed upon us the necessity of this measure."

The secretary's letter, which would not actually reach Edward Preble until August 7, 1804, did rather little to salve the wounds it inflicted on his ego.

By June 2, 1804, the frigate *Constitution* and the flotilla of gunboats were safely anchored in the harbor at Syracuse. The commodore met up with the *Enterprize* and the *Intrepid*, which had recently been converted into a floating hospital. Preble ordered the *Enterprize* to continue on to Tripoli and meet up with the *Siren*, the *Argus*, the *Vixen*, and the *Scourge* (a blockade runner taken as a prize and retrofitted for the squadron) to maintain the blockade. Lieutenant Somers was ordered to remain in Syracuse and oversee the readiness of the gunboats.

The *Constitution*, meanwhile, set sail on June 4 to make another sweep of Malta, Tunis, and Tripoli in hopes of gaining more intelligence that might be useful in the upcoming campaign. Preble also made one last attempt at regular diplomacy with Qaramanli, but the effort failed. As Preble knew full well, Qaramanli had yet to be given any reason to change his position. Preble was back in Syracuse by June 25.

The preparations for battle were completed fairly quickly. On July 12, Commodore Preble was ready to attack Tripoli with his six gunboats (numbered 1 through 6), two bomb ketches, and with the *Enterprize* and the *Nautilus* in company (both had rejoined the flagship toward the end of June). Tripoli was still under blockade from the *Siren*, the *Argus*, the *Vixen*, and the *Scourge*. The next day, Friday, July 13, the squadron set sail from Syracuse to Malta.

The reinvigorated naval force reached Malta on July 16, and after five days of bad weather gathered just off Tripoli on July 25. With one frigate, three brigantines, three schooners, two bomb ketches, six gunboats, and combined personnel of 1,060 men, the U.S. squadron was grossly outnumbered but determined to prevail.

Tripoli was no easy target, and Pasha Qaramanli had been preparing for this assault for some time. The town was protected by a thick, fortified wall and was defended by shore batteries and forts—one of which had been recently built by the forced labor of the American prisoners taken from the *Philadelphia*.

Tripoli had 115 large guns mounted in her defense, ready to strike at a moment's notice, and her navy fielded nineteen gunboats, two galleys, two schooners, and a brigantine and had well over 25,000 men under arms for defense against any American onslaught. The Tripolitan navy was out in force, in line of battle, just behind the Kaliusa and Ra's al Zur reefs that served as the harbor's northern perimeter—this natural barrier had netted Tripoli the *Philadelphia*, and militated against any large-draft vessels entering from this side.

When the weather finally permitted, on August 3, 1804, the American squadron advanced to within about two miles of the Tripolitan Molehead Battery. At noon, Commodore Edward Preble scanned the enemy through his glass.

He saw that the Tripolitan gunboats had split into two divisions and had advanced beyond their protective reef; he also observed flags flying on the castle, the batteries, the warships in the harbor, and the gunboats. He noted that the fortifications were filled with troops and that large numbers of spectators were crowding the roofs and terraces, no doubt eager to see Tripoli's defenses dispatch the infidel American squadron.

As long as the gunboats were outside the harbor rocks, however, this also meant that they had advanced beyond the range of the shore batteries and so were without effective supporting fire. Commodore Preble saw his advantage and signaled for his captains to come within hailing distance of the *Constitution*. Once they were close, he gave the signal to "prepare for battle."

Preble ordered his gunboats to split into two equal divisions: Gunboats No. 1, No. 2, and No. 3, commanded by Richard Somers, James Decatur (brother of Stephen), and Joshua Blake, respectively; and Gunboats No. 4, No. 5, and No. 6, commanded by Stephen Decatur, Joseph Bainbridge (brother of William, still held captive in Tripoli), and John Trippe.

Preble's plan was very simple: the two gunboat divisions were to stand in and engage the Tripolitan flotilla. Once the battle commenced, action would be dictated by opportunity and circumstance. The *Constitution* was to direct the action and remain offshore, to prevent falling afoul of shoal waters and unmerciful reefs.

At 12:30 P.M. the *Constitution* moved farther inshore to gain a better position, but this maneuver seemed to confuse the squadron, and the ships drifted out of formation. Preble backed the *Constitution*'s main topsail to afford some time for his squadron to reform, but the *Nautilus*, with Gunboat No. 1 still in tow, was too far behind and off to the left to catch up; Preble signaled her at 1:15 P.M. to make more sail. Finally, fearing that the afternoon would be lost and the weather would dissipate, he advanced, signaling the squadron to follow his motions.

By 2 P.M. the squadron was in better formation. The *Constitution* stood in, the *Nautilus* had fallen behind, and the *Siren*, the *Vixen*, the *Enterprize*, and the *Argus* were spread out eastward. Preble signaled for the gunboats to advance and attack.

They did so, but for some reason none of the gunboat commanders had the presence of mind to station anyone to look out for the commodore's signals. For the next two and a half hours of battle, they were out of contact with Preble and either acted at their own discretion or followed the lead of their fellow commanders.

At 2:30 P.M. the *Constitution*, along with the *Enterprize*, the *Nautilus*, the *Argus*, the *Siren*, and the *Vixen*, stood in toward the harbor batteries. The bomb ketches, meanwhile, were also advancing toward Tripoli, just west of the gunboat divisions.

Bomb ketch No. 1 fired first at 2:45 P.M., followed immediately by No. 2. One of these shots exploded very near the Molehead

Battery; the other went over the walls into the town. After the first shot, the Tripolitan batteries came alive and began firing rapidly and wildly at the U.S. squadron, but the Tripolitan gunners had yet to get the range, and the U.S. ships were entirely untouched by this fevered activity. Preble was eager to get his batteries into play to return fire and by 3 P.M. maneuvered to do so.

When the order was given for the gunboats to advance, No. 1, commanded by Richard Somers, was too far off to be of any use or direction to gunboats No. 2 or No. 3, and it seems these two boats simply attached themselves to Captain Stephen Decatur's division, behind Gunboat No. 4. Decatur stood in toward the enemy, while all the other gunboats, except for No. 1, fell in behind him. This division swiftly made its way toward two Tripolitan boats just outside of the harbor rocks, got within point-blank range, and poured eight or nine balls into the enemy vessels. One shot evidently hit home, as both enemy ships immediately retreated behind the rocks, out of reach of Decatur's ships.

Captain Decatur then turned his attention to the sixteen Tripolitan ships anchored leeward. Just before 3 P.M., his boats closed to within twenty yards of the enemy, firing canister, grapeshot, and musket volley upon musket volley. The fire was punishing, and the Tripolitans cut their moorings to retreat into the harbor beyond Decatur's reach. Decatur continued westward, eager to engage the enemy. Fortunately, he was in line to run up into the eleven remaining Tripolitan ships—these did not retreat.

The American gunboats bored in on the Tripolitan vessels, all the while firing round shot. Foolishly, some of the Tripolitans fired their pistols before they were within range, and many were then too busy to reload in time.

Once he was close enough, Decatur delivered a canister of 432 musket balls, known as a "boarding dose," which ripped into the Tripolitans.

Determined to take a prize, Decatur surprised the nearest Tripolitan ship by boarding her—the traditional Barbary modus operandi. The Tripolitans were thoroughly terrified, as they had been told many times by Yusuf Qaramanli that the Americans were cowards, "a sort of Jews, who have no notion of fighting."

Decatur and nineteen of his men from No. 4, screaming and yelling, armed with boarding pikes, dirks, cutlasses, pistols, tomahawks, and axes, grappled and boarded the first Tripolitan ship. She had thirty-six defenders. The battle lasted about ten blood-soaked minutes, and Decatur showed no mercy; sixteen Tripolitans killed, fifteen wounded, and five captured. "I always thought," Decatur later wrote, "that we could lick them in their own way."

Gunboat No. 1 never managed to close in with the division and join their fight. Instead, Captain Richard Somers moved within range of the Molehead Battery and maintained fire upon that position. As he later reported it, "By this time there was five of the enemy's gunboats of the lee line under way, advancing and firing. When within point-blank shot I commenced firing on the enemy with round and grape. They still advanced until within pistol-shot when they wore round and stood in for the batteries. I pursued them until within musket-shot of the batteries, which kept up a continual fire of round and grape. Three of their boats had got in behind the rocks." Captain Somers found himself under heavy fire, unable to maneuver the boat out of range. Luckily, one of the bomb ketches fired into the battery, creating enough diversion for No. 1 to escape. "I then wore and stood off," he reported; "the boat has received no damage, and but two of the men slightly wounded."

Just behind No. 4's attack, James Decatur in No. 2 made for the second Tripolitan vessel in the line, poured some twenty-four-pound round shot into her, and then unleashed close-range musketry and blunderbuss fire. After a few jarring minutes, the Tripolitan boat struck her colors in submission. It appeared as if all but three of the Tripolitan's crew had been killed. It was, however, only a *ruse de guerre*.

No. 2 came alongside, and James Decatur, the brother of No. 4's Stephen Decatur, leapt from his gunboat to the enemy

vessel to claim his prize. At this exact moment, Tripolitan muskets were raised and fired. One shot hit Decatur in the head, and
he fell in the water between the two boats; he later died some
moments after being brought aboard the flagship.

Confused by the enemy action, No. 2's second in command,
Midshipman Thomas Brown, allowed the crew to focus on fish-
ing the body of their commanding officer out of the water rather
than on pursuing the enemy. The Tripolitan vessel broke away
and made for the harbor. Just as Midshipman Brown made ready
to pursue, however, No. 2 took fire from another Tripolitan ship.
Although this attack was beaten off, the Tripolitan vessel that had
mortally wounded James Decatur escaped. No. 2 disengaged and
tacked away from the battle.

Gunboat No. 6, under the command of John Trippe, attacked
a third Tripolitan ship. As No. 6's stern made contact with the
Tripolitan vessel, Trippe, Midshipman John D. Henley, and nine
other men leapt on board the enemy ship. Before any more of the
complement could follow, No. 6 fell off suddenly and was unable
to maneuver back toward the enemy.

Trippe and his men suddenly found themselves alone, cut off
from their shipmates, up against overwhelming odds: eleven
against thirty-six. Trippe and Henley led their men head-on into
the melee of fierce Tripolitans. Trippe engaged the Tripolitan
captain, a massive, hulking figure, over six feet tall. Lunging
toward the enemy captain, he shattered his cutlass against his
opponent's scimitar. He jumped and grabbed the Tripolitan, but
was easily thrown to the deck; they struggled, and Trippe managed to wrench the scimitar away from the Tripolitan, slicing his
hand in the process.

Other Tripolitans came to their captain's assistance, and
Trippe was soon taking multiple blows; he began bleeding pro-
fusely from eleven separate wounds. He still had the Tripolitan
captain's scimitar, however, and managed to engage him head-on
and inflict three different wounds. The two men continued to
fight, undaunted and unfazed. Trippe offered to spare the captain's life should he choose to surrender, but the mighty

Tripolitan refused, eventually outfighting Trippe, who finally collapsed on the deck from loss of blood and exhaustion.

Just then another American lunged with a boarding pike and caught the Tripolitan captain in the groin, lifting him off the deck; he came crashing down, quite dead. The Americans soon gained the advantage and the Tripolitan crew surrendered.

Trippe, revived and back on his feet, granted quarter and prevented a general massacre of the Tripolitan sailors. The prize was secured; fourteen Tripolitans had been killed, and twenty-two were taken prisoner, seven of whom had been wounded.

After Stephen Decatur captured, secured, and manned his first Tripolitan prize, he learned that his brother James had been mortally wounded through treachery. Decatur became enraged, or perhaps deranged (depending on how one reads the various accounts of what happened). He spotted another enemy vessel just leeward, outside the rocks, and decided immediately that it was the ship of his brother's slayer—a belief he persisted in all the rest of his days. Although there was very little chance that Decatur actually seized the right ship, he was convinced vengeance was his—and legend records it as so.

Decatur immediately took No. 4 off in hot pursuit.

He had only a skeletal crew at his disposal, having sent men off to occupy his first prize, yet he chased this fresh quarry undaunted. Coming alongside her, he boarded her in an instant. Followed by Midshipman Thomas Macdonough and eight other men, Decatur advanced with his cutlass against the Tripolitan's twenty-four-man crew.

Captain Decatur and his men mercilessly slashed and hacked their way through the defenders. Amid the ensuing carnage, the Tripolitan's captain, a stout Turk, was spotted. Decatur ran forward. The Turk lunged at him with a long boarding pike. Decatur deflected this with his cutlass, but the blade hit the iron and snapped at the hilt.

Unarmed, Decatur was slashed at and wounded slightly in the arm and chest. The enemy captain tried again with the pike, but Decatur managed to wrest it from the mighty Turk's grip. He jumped the Turk, grabbing him by the throat, and the two men fell wrestling to the deck.

As the two men grappled, with Decatur on top, another Tripolitan rushed to his captain's aid with raised scimitar in hand. Fortunately, an American sailor, Daniel Fraser (some reports have it as Reuben James), deflected the blow away from Decatur's head. Fraser, according to legend, was already wounded in both arms, but he was determined to sacrifice his life for his captain, and so positioned himself over Decatur, effectively offering his head instead of his captain's; the blow glanced off Fraser's head— he caught the blade at the top of its downward arc—inflicting a dangerous but miraculously nonlethal wound. The Tripolitan was dispatched by the pistol shot of another American sailor.

Decatur and the Turk continued to thrash about on the deck, and the superior might of the Turk enabled him to roll over on top. Using his not insignificant mass, the Turkish captain pinned Decatur to the deck and produced a yataghan from his sashband. He raised the dagger up in an arc and thrust it straight down toward Decatur's chest. Just in time, Decatur freed his left arm and desperately grabbed the Turk's wrist, halting the blade's plunge.

During this brief arm wrestle, Decatur managed to find a pistol in his jacket pocket with his injured right hand, and reached over his assailant, pressing the muzzle of the pistol into his back. He fired into the man. The massive Turk's grip relaxed on the yataghan, his power melted away, and he slumped forward onto Decatur and died.

When the boat was finally secured, twenty-one Tripolitans had been killed or injured, and three were taken prisoner. Between Decatur's two prizes, only four Americans were wounded, while thirty-three Tripolitans had been killed and nineteen had been wounded. As Decatur later reported his activities of the day, "I boarded and carried two of them and was successful in bringing them off." In a letter to a friend, he boasted, "Some of the Turks died like men, but much the greater number like women."

The *Constitution*, meanwhile, saw action as well. At 3 P.M., as most of the gunboats followed No. 4's lead, Preble brought his flagship within six hundred yards of the Molehead Battery. He spotted reinforcements making toward the U.S. gunboat flotilla, and signaled the *Enterprize*, the *Nautilus*, the *Argus*, the *Siren*, and the *Vixen* to "Cover the boats!" Throughout the engagement, Preble directed covering fire for his gunboats.

The ships stood in close to the gunboat engagement and delivered fire upon the Tripolitan vessels starting out from the harbor. The *Constitution*'s heavier firepower was brought to bear as well, as Preble fired his starboard bow guns and his bow chasers at the western end of the Tripolitan line.

The *Constitution* then wore to the west, bringing her port battery into service. The aft, or rear, division focused on the Tripolitan reinforcements, the center division focused on the pasha's castle, and the forward division opened up on the Molehead Battery and the Tripolitan vessels farther west down the line. Preble then concentrated grapeshot on the Molehead Battery and the Tripolitan boats, effectively tearing up the Tripolitan counterattack. No further attempt was mounted to cut off the American gunboats or reinforce the Tripolitan vessels.

Preble's flagship took heavy fire, but the Tripolitan gunners were off their mark. It was estimated that over two hundred shot fell within sixty feet of the flagship, but only nine balls actually hit. Most of the damage was to the rigging, as the Tripolitan batteries consistently overshot the hull. Preble attributed the *Constitution*'s lack of damage to his tactic of running in close to the battery positions, ensuring the guns were off target, and to his use of grapeshot, dissuading the enemy gunners from risking the exposure needed to service and re-aim the cannons. He also noted the aid of the poor marksmanship among the Tripolitan gunners.

By 4:30 P.M. the day's action had dissipated. The remaining enemy vessels had either retreated into the harbor or taken shelter under the Tripolitan fortifications. Preble signaled the squadron to "Join company as soon as possible," and the prizes were slowly towed away. The American gunboats and bomb ketches disengaged and began pulling toward the *Constitution*.

Although most of the American commanders did well against overwhelming odds, Commodore Preble was discouraged and disappointed. Three small Tripolitan vessels had been captured, but little else had been accomplished. Even though the American "victory" was embarrassing to Tripoli, the effort did little in the way of convincing Pasha Yusuf Qaramanli that the American force was overwhelming. The American squadron withdrew, anchoring about fourteen miles northeast of Tripoli.

The next morning, a French vessel of four guns called *Le Rusé* approached with a message from Bonaventure Beaussier, the French consul. "On the occasion of your approach with an offensive force," Beaussier's message read, "I have submitted various considerations to the Pasha." However, Qaramanli's exact words were recorded in Beaussier's private notebook. The Pasha had replied, "I would rather bury myself under the ruins of my country than basely yield to the wishes of the enemy."

Beaussier also noted that "the whole city is in arms . . . the troops, the gunners and the bombardiers exhibit outwardly the greatest courage; women and children have been sent into the country." For some reason, Preble mistakenly thought Qaramanli was ready to talk, so he persuaded the *Le Rusé* to return to Tripoli bearing a message for Beaussier: if Qaramanli was at all disposed to negotiate, tell him that the offer of $40,000 for ransom, plus a $10,000 consular present, was good until U.S. reinforcements arrived—they were expected any day. After that no money of any sort would be offered. Preble also convinced the captain of the *Le Rusé* to carry back fourteen of the most seriously wounded Tripolitan prisoners. The next day, the *Le Rusé* returned to Tripoli with Preble's message.

Consul Beaussier thought Preble's desire to negotiate at this time a serious tactical blunder, and one that would reflect poorly on his desire to be seen as a determined enemy. Qaramanli flatly refused the offer and interpreted the return of the prisoners as an indication of Preble's refusal to treat them humanely.

August 5 was spent in preparation for another assault. The *Vixen* ran in toward Tripoli to reconnoiter the harbor, the batteries, and the fortifications. Preble had the three Tripolitan prizes converted into gunboats to join the squadron, and all the ships were resupplied from the *Constitution* for another attack. These preparations were not completed until late on August 6. The attack would commence early the next day.

West of the city of Tripoli lies a shallow bay that was not visible behind the batteries of the city's harbor. Preble's junior officers, principally Charles Stewart, urged the commodore to send the gunboats and bomb ketches into this bay to attack the city and bombard her unimpeded by the harbor batteries, all of which were turned away from this location.

The plan seemed simple enough, and the shallow bay had the added benefit of being entirely unapproachable from the city's harbor. The Tripolitans would have to leave their harbor and sail beyond her protective reefs in order to run down and attack the American gunboats. Preble would thus be able to cut these off from the city with his brigs and schooners and capture them.

Qaramanli would have to either endure the attack without response or risk losing his gunboats. "I think a blow in the face," Richard O'Brien said in dissent of this plan, "is better than a kick in the stern [rear]." In the end, however, Commodore Preble decided to embrace the stratagem.

The squadron began to move on the morning of August 7. The *Constitution* was forced to sit this engagement out, as a strong current mixed with a light wind to prevent smooth navigation; she was the only ship too large for sweeps (rowing with large oars). At 10 A.M. Preble signaled the squadron to "advance in a line abreast." By 10:30 A.M. the ships were rowing in formation toward the shallow bay, immediately west of Tripoli.

The nine American gunboats closed in. Unfortunately, there was a strong westerly current that made a hash of their formation as they were swept leeward. They tried to row in and form a new line abreast, but the effort merely resulted in confusion. By noon, the campaign had made little progress. By 1:30 P.M., the *Constitution* was able to get a bit closer to observe more clearly.

At 2:30 P.M. the gunboats entered the eastern end of the bay and immediately came under heavy fire from the shore. Although Preble had not discovered it in advance, the Tripolitans had fortified the bay.

An hour later, in the thick of battle, Gunboat No. 9, one of the three recent additions to the American flotilla, unexpectedly exploded. The force was immense; the blast silenced both the American gunboats and the Tripolitan batteries. Men and body parts were projected above the cloud of smoke before plunging down into the sea.

Evidently the magazine of No. 9 had blown up, as her stern and midsection had vanished; only her bow remained, although this slowly settled into the water while several men reloaded in preparation to fire one last time. The gun slid underwater before discharging, and the men gave three cheers as they sank into the bay.

Of No. 9's complement, ten men had been killed, including her commanding officer, Lieutenant James R. Caldwell; two were wounded, four men seriously so, and twelve escaped unscathed. Although the explosion was initially attributed to enemy shot, the culprit was later determined to be an errant piece of flaming wadding that had accidentally entered the magazine from one of the other American ships.

The pause in battle lasted only a few minutes before the Americans harnessed the full weight of their collective desire to avenge their fallen comrades. But, by 5:30 P.M., as the wind began to shift unfavorably, Preble signaled for the squadron to disengage and pull back. Once again, the attack had accomplished little to nothing. The American gunboats did manage to get within range of the city and lob in a few shots, but most of the shells hit the Jewish quarter. Although a number of fires were started as a result, the city was mostly made of stone, mortar, and mud, and so these blazes were of little consequence. There was also some building damage sustained from direct hits, but nothing substantial.

Commodore Edward Preble knew that he had done nothing so far to compel Pasha Qaramanli to terms. Unfortunately, he also knew he was running out of time.

Two hours before the engagement ended, a strange sail had been sighted and the *Argus* dispatched in pursuit. After the battle, the *Argus* signaled the *Constitution* with the news that "Strange ships in sight are friends." It was the frigate USS *John Adams*, commanded by Master Commandant Isaac Chauncey and carrying fresh dispatches from Washington.

It was here that Commodore Preble learned he was to lose command of the squadron to Samuel Barron. He was deeply wounded, as his private journal records: "How much my feelings are lacerated by this supercedure at the moment of Victory cannot be described and can be felt only by an officer placed in my mortifying situation." Officially, he made noises, particularly in his official dispatches, that he intended to wait for Commodore Barron before taking any further action beyond maintaining the blockade. In reality, however, his activities became frantic and focused.

Eager for a victory of some sort, Preble began a desperate negotiation with Qaramanli. He raised his offer of $50,000 to $120,000, while bluffing that a force would soon arrive that could enable him "to destroy all the seaport towns in Tripoli." The negotiations faltered, but Preble thought he could maintain pressure on Qaramanli by continuing to attack.

He spent the next twelve days trying to mount a third attack on Tripoli; a night bombardment finally commenced at 1 A.M. on August 24. The performance of the American squadron was pathetic. Every single shell fell short. Pasha Qaramanli thought the war was truly going swimmingly now, and Tripolitan morale was running very high.

Preble tried again on the night of August 28, 1804. At 1:30 A.M. the gunboats, in the now usual two-division formation, under Decatur and Somers, respectively, went in toward the harbor, accompanied by the *Siren*, the *Argus*, the *Vixen*, the *Nautilus*, and the *Enterprize*, and took up positions close to the rocks, anchoring at 3 A.M.

The brigs and schooners were just outside in support positions; the ships' boats remained with the gunboat flotilla to assist in boarding enemy vessels. Lacking any sure signal at night,

Preble simply fired a rocket to signal an advance to attack. The squadron began to unleash a heavy, steady fire until daylight—about two and a half hours of continuous firing.

At dawn Preble moved the *Constitution* in toward the harbor and signaled the gunboats to cease firing and retire out of range. By 6:15 A.M. the *Constitution* was within four hundred yards of the harbor rocks, and Preble opened fire on the Tripolitan vessels that had engaged the American squadron, sinking one ship and forcing two others to run onshore, all the rest retreated to safety deep in the harbor.

Preble silenced several of the Tripolitan batteries and maintained a steady fire upon the pasha's castle, the Molehead Battery, and the seaward fortifications. Although the Tripolitan defenses returned fire whenever possible, the *Constitution* was too close to sustain any serious damage. By 7 A.M. the American squadron was safely out of range, and the *Constitution* had retreated four miles north of the hostile batteries, anchoring in safety.

The Americans had lost one of the *John Adams*'s boats that had been in company with the gunboat flotilla; three men had died, and a fourth was wounded. All the ships in the squadron sustained only minor damage, mostly to the rigging and sails. Preble was convinced, however, that Tripoli had suffered mightily under the attack.

The next day he sent the brig *Argus* to communicate with French consul Beaussier to discern the pasha's mood and see if he were any nearer considering serious peace negotiations. Once again, Preble had miscalculated. His attacks had done very little real damage to Tripoli, and his efforts at negotiations made matters worse.

Consul Bonaventure Beaussier explained that every time Preble followed an attack with another offer to negotiate, Qaramanli took it for weakness, or figured that Preble was perplexed or perhaps was under orders to obtain a peace. Either way, Yusuf already believed he had the stronger position and was not willing to lose his psychological edge. Besides, since the commencement of Preble's attacks, the people of Tripoli had rallied behind Qaramanli and were adamant that they would stay the course and humble the infidel would-be conquerors. Preble's options were limited. As Beaussier wrote to Talleyrand, the French minister of foreign affairs:

> Now Preble can hope for success only when his four additional frigates arrive—but this prince is not afraid of their guns either. Unless Preble succeeds in striking great blows, Tripoli will yet cause the United States to repent her vain attacks, and the regency will gain the glory of having resisted the reinforced squadron. This is what the Pasha desires most of all, that the powers of Europe and Africa may form a favorable opinion of his resources and his courage. From the outset, it would have been more appropriate and more adroit [for Preble] to have attacked vigorously and continuously, without entering into any negotiations. The Barbary regencies are skilled at putting up a good front with tiny means, but most especially when they see that one treats them with circumspection.

Although Preble despaired of scoring any significant victory before Commodore Barron's arrival, he decided to try again one last time in early September. For his fifth assault on Tripoli, he would send a fireship, or an "infernal," into the harbor while his gunboats bombarded the city.

As early as August 29, Preble had begun converting the *Intrepid* for her final mission. She was loaded up with five tons of powder, one hundred thirteen-inch shells, and fifty nine-inch shells, and a whole room was filled with combustibles through which the powder keg could be easily ignited.

Preble hoped the *Intrepid* could slip through the harbor, close in near the fortress, ignite the combustibles, and get the crew safely away before the ship exploded. Given the frustration of the Americans in their campaign against Tripoli, it is perhaps not so surprising that there was an abundance of volunteers for this extremely hazardous mission. Commodore Preble selected Lieutenant Richard Somers, Midshipman Henry Wadsworth, and acting lieutenant Joseph Israel to lead the mission, along with ten enlisted men.

At 11 P.M. on September 1, the *Intrepid* advanced toward the harbor, but unfavorable winds forced her back. Her presence had gone undetected, however, so the element of surprise was not yet lost.

The evening of September 4, at 8 P.M., the ship set out again toward the harbor of Tripoli, accompanied by the *Argus*, the *Vixen*, and the *Nautilus*. At 9 P.M. the *Argus* and the *Vixen* hove to, while the *Nautilus* continued until she was within seven hundred yards of the western passage into the harbor. The *Intrepid* was very near her target now, just three-quarters of a mile away. When she reached the western entrance, however, two alarm guns were fired from the Tripolitan batteries. It appeared as if she had entered the harbor, but it was unclear. Roughly ten minutes passed in total silence.

At 9:47 P.M. there was an abrupt blinding flash of light and a massive explosion. "How awfully grand!" one midshipman later reported. "Everything wrapped in dead silence made the explosion loud and terrible. The fuses of the shells, burning in the air, shone like so many planets. A vast stream of fire, which appeared ascending to heaven, portrayed the walls to our view." The harbor was rocked by the concussion, but little else transpired as a result of this "infernal." Clearly, the mission had been fouled up, as the combustibles did not blaze before the powder blew, and the *Intrepid* had not gotten near enough to the target to even so much as scorch the walls of the harbor fortress. The Tripolitans recovered the grossly disfigured and mangled corpses of the *Intrepid's* thirteen-man crew two days later. It was some time before their bodies were buried, however, as Qaramanli found that their presence substantially boosted Tripolitan morale.

Commodore Edward Preble had plainly and utterly failed. As Danish consul Nicholas C. Nissen wrote on September 30, 1804, "I must candidly tell you that all the attacks of the squadron, except that of 3rd August have had very little effect, and the damage done of absolutely no consequence." Aggravated and depressed, Preble decided by dawn of the next morning, September 5, to end offensive operations. The gunboat flotilla was to be disarmed, and the *John Adams*, the *Siren*, the *Enterprise*, and the *Nautilus* headed for Sicily late the following afternoon, with the eight gunboats and two bomb ketches in tow. By 6:30 P.M., they made sail. The *Constitution*, the *Argus*, and the *Vixen* remained to maintain the blockade of Tripoli.

At noon on Sunday, September 9, the frigates *President* and *Constellation* were sighted and soon after identified. Commodore Samuel Barron had finally arrived to assume command of the United States' Mediterranean squadron. With him was an overeager William Eaton, newly titled a U.S. "Naval Agent for the Barbary Regencies."

10

General Eaton's Advance

COMMODORE SAMUEL BARRON, unlike the previous three United States commodores, had already served in the Mediterranean. He had commanded the *Philadelphia* in that first Mediterranean squadron. Although he had spent most of his time patrolling off Gibraltar and blockading the Tripolitan flagship *Meshuda*, he had a very clear understanding of the Barbary situation. Further, he had presided over the court of inquiry that had investigated Commodore Richard V. Morris's mishandling of the second Mediterranean squadron. Barron was thus intimately familiar with President Jefferson's instructions and expectations in Barbary even before he actually received his orders.

Commodore Barron's objectives were clear. He was to maintain the blockade of Tripoli whenever weather permitted and use every means in his power to "annoy the enemy so as to force him to a peace honorable to the United States." Although Tripoli was the primary target, his commission and his authority, as with his predecessors, extended to all the Barbary States. Unlike his predecessors, however, Barron was to command the single largest naval force his country had ever unleashed on active duty: six frigates, the USS *President* (forty-four guns), USS *Congress* (thirty-six guns), USS *Constitution* (forty-four guns), USS *Essex* (thirty-two guns), USS *Constellation* (thirty-six guns), and USS *John Adams* (twenty-eight guns); two brigantines, the USS *Siren* and USS *Argus* (both of sixteen guns); and three schooners, the USS *Vixen*, USS *Nautilus*, and USS *Enterprize* (each of twelve guns). He was also authorized to obtain and use as many gunboats as he thought necessary to augment this armada. Thus, when Captain Samuel Barron took command of the U.S. naval forces in the Mediterranean in September 1804, President Thomas Jefferson had high hopes of rapid progress against Tripoli.

Yet Barron's command began at a rather sluggish pace. By the time he finally reached Edward Preble, on September 9, 1804, he was nearly a month behind schedule. Barron and the four new frigates for the squadron (the *President*, the *Congress*, the *Essex*, and the *Constellation*) had put out to sea from Hampton Roads, Virginia, on July 5. Although they had crossed the Atlantic in just over two weeks, coming in sight of the Azores by midday July 21, inclement winds prevented them from reaching Gibraltar until August 12.

When Commodore Barron arrived, he received reports from the U.S. consul in Tangier that the emperor of Morocco's navy had been behaving suspiciously. Barron left the *Congress*, commanded by Captain John Rodgers, and the *Essex*, commanded by his younger brother Captain James Barron, off Gibraltar to keep watch over Moroccan activities and resumed his course on August 16. The winds remained difficult, however, and a week's passage put him no farther than Cape Gata. He put in at Malta on September 5 before sailing on to Tripoli. By the time he finally made Tripoli on September 9, the weather was not likely to permit much action for very long, so the commodore decided to suspend further offensive actions altogether. He was content to wait rather than rush forward with his plans.

From September 9 through 13, Captain Preble remained off Tripoli, maintaining the blockade and conferring with Barron. Although Secretary of the Navy Robert Smith hoped and expected Preble to remain in the Mediterranean and serve under Barron, Preble had decided to head home. While he was willing to serve under the thirty-nine-year-old Samuel Barron, who was four years his junior, he was most unwilling to play a subservient role to John Rodgers, who was senior in commission but over ten years his junior, and their mutual dislike remained pungent. "He never shall command me," Preble once declared of Rodgers, "while I have command over myself." Edward Preble intended to return home at the earliest opportunity.

During the last five days of his service off Tripoli, Preble made his final contribution to his nation's war with that regency. Part of his discussions with Commodore Barron involved a risky and unusual plan energetically and tenaciously proposed by William Eaton, who was also a passenger aboard the *President* and had spent much of the transatlantic crossing trying to convince Barron to embrace his scheme. Eaton had come recommended to Barron by Secretary of the Navy Robert Smith, and had general authorization to proceed, subject to Barron's assent and discretion. Commodore Barron was generally tepid about the strategy, and through most of the Atlantic crossing sought refuge from Eaton's continuous sales pitch in the qualified statements of endorsement from the secretaries of state and navy, both of whom, echoing President Jefferson, thought it a long shot but one worth taking.

Eaton was discouraged to find Barron less than enthusiastic. The commodore kept vacillating between backing Eaton's scheme and dropping it, and he refused to promise any men, weapons, or ammunition. Not only was Eaton under Barron's direct orders, but the practicability of his scheme rested completely in the commodore's level of commitment. As he complained to Secretary Smith, "I cannot forebear, however, expressing on this occasion the extreme mortification I suffer on account of my actual situation, destitute of commission, rank, or command, and, I may say, consideration or credit, and even without instructions for the regulation of my conduct while ostensibly charged with the management of an enterprise on which, perhaps, depends the successful issue of this war."

In its most mature formulation, Eaton's plan was straightforward: the U.S. squadron would assist Ahmad Qaramanli, the exiled elder brother of Pasha Yusuf, to lead a revolution in Tripoli, stage a coup, regain the throne, and thereby install and obtain a ruler responsive to the United States and obligated to support America's interests in the region. Eaton had earlier, and at his own expense, secured Ahmad's interest and cooperation, but Commodore Morris had disdained the plan.

Although pleased to finally get his plans under way, Eaton was greatly disgusted with President Jefferson, "a man," he wrote to a friend, "the most fortunate in contingency—the most base in calculation." To Eaton, his plan with Ahmad Qaramanli was simple and Jefferson either supported it or he did not. The wavering and the hedging struck him as cowardice and cynical computation. At first Jefferson had seemed enthusiastic and made noises of support, but two months later, "on the first symptom of a reverse in his [Ahmad's] affairs, discouragement superceded resolution with our executive, and economy supplanted good faith and honesty . . . supplies . . . are withheld. The President becomes reserved." Eaton was further upset that he was being sent out without any substantive proof of Jefferson's backing—no written orders, no letter of alliance for Ahmad, no stipulation that Commodore Barron would actually support the scheme or make supplies available. Eaton had, he lamented, "nothing but a general and vague discretion of my agency in the affair . . . in case the project should seem feasible." Fortunately, he had an ally in Edward Preble.

Preble was familiar with the scheme, and he had even met with Ahmad Qaramanli's representative in November 1803. Preble had shown some mild enthusiasm for the endeavor and had continued to consider it an option as late as April of 1804. He had only come to abandon the idea in favor of direct offensive action after he had been given to believe by French consul Beaussier at Tripoli that Ahmad was broke, unpopular, and an alcoholic.

Now, however, Preble's enthusiasm for the project was reawakened, and he threw his support behind the scheme. Finally, the cautious and indecisive Commodore Barron accepted this opinion, and he, Preble, and Eaton coordinated their plans.

On September 13, 1804, Commodore Samuel Barron issued secret orders—orally, not in writing—to Isaac Hull, commander of the *Argus*, granting Hull broad discretionary powers to assist and facilitate Eaton's plans to support Ahmad Qaramanli. These orders were issued in Eaton's presence, and he and Hull later put them in writing for the official record. Since Ahmad had fled Barbary and taken refuge in Egypt to escape his brother's assassins, Hull was instructed to take Eaton to Egypt to make contact. Hull was authorized to assure the deposed pasha that Commodore Barron would "Take the most effectual measures with the forces under my command for cooperating with him against the usurper, his brother, and for reestablishing him in the regency of Tripoli."

That same day, the USS *Constitution* parted company with the USS *President* and set a course for Malta for some refurbishing. Although no longer in command, Captain Preble had all sorts of loose ends to tend to—social visits, account closures, people to thank, and so forth. He also agreed to try and once again secure gunboats and bomb ketches from Naples for Commodore Barron's offensive use against Tripoli. The *Constitution* was reassigned to Captain Decatur, and Preble was moved to the USS *John Adams*, but as a passenger, not a commander. Captain Preble would not leave the Mediterranean for another three and a half months.

When he finally did so, reaching New York on February 25, 1805, he discovered that his countrymen hailed him as a hero. He wrote to his wife, Mary, "I cannot but be a little flattered with the reception I have met with here, the people are disposed to think I have rendered some service to my country." Although he had left the Mediterranean thoroughly depressed with his performance and unhappy over the circumstances of his having lost command of his squadron, the nation welcomed him openly and warmly. He received accolades from the president, from Congress, from various dignitaries and foreign governments, and even from Pope Pius VII, who declared, "the American commander, with a small force and in a short space of time, has done more for the cause of Christianity than the most powerful nations of Christendom have done for ages." Congress later awarded

Preble a gold medal for his services in the Mediterranean. The greatest tribute, however, came in the form of a very warm letter of regret signed by fifty-three of his officers, those who would later proudly proclaim themselves "Preble's Boys."

Shortly after assuming command from Edward Preble, Commodore Samuel Barron was stricken with a serious liver disease, which was incapacitating and seemed at times nearly fatal.

Despite having such obvious difficulties with leading the squadron, Barron refused to hand over his command to John Rodgers, his immediate second. Although he came to delegate routine and rudimentary responsibilities to Rodgers in November, he insisted on directing the important matters himself. Once he was too sick to remain at sea, however, he moved ashore to Syracuse. There he remained through the winter of 1804 and into the spring of 1805, teetering back and forth from recovery to near death.

One of his officers, despairing of any recovery, noted that Barron's ailment would essentially "disqualify him from transacting any business, his mind being so much impaired as scarcely to recall anything that transpired from one day to another." As there was no leadership to turn to on the quarterdeck of the flagship and little more emanating from the sickbed, the war against Tripoli faltered. The Mediterranean squadron remained directionless, and the war received virtually no planning during the summer of 1805.

While Commodore Barron writhed in bed, struggling to stay alive, determined to remain in command of his squadron and recover in time to lead his ships against Tripoli during the summer, his advisers fought for access, influence, and power. Captain John Rodgers, Barron's second in command, Captain James Barron, his younger brother and closest confidant, and Colonel Tobias Lear, the negotiator and diplomat, all fought with each other for access to the commodore. Each of these potent personalities tried desperately to sway policy to favor their designs.

Under Commodore Morris, John Rodgers had lived a life of frustration. Where he sought action, Morris sought quiet. The thought of playing a subordinate role to another inactive commodore was torturous. Rodgers desired not only action but also glory and leadership over others. More importantly, he had no intention of allowing Lear to get the upper hand.

James Barron was loyal and protective, but he was also given to bouts of crippling depression over his brother's condition. The younger Barron also tended to promote both pessimism and defeatism, and inclined like his elder brother, toward hedging and inactivity.

Tobias Lear, meanwhile, intended to force Barbary affairs back toward diplomacy. He had been ignored and pushed to the periphery under Commodore Preble, but he was now determined to assert himself and control Barbary policy as much as possible.

Thus, Rodgers and Lear were both hoping to dominate Commodore Barron's thinking, while James Barron tried to dominate his brother's attention. The results, however, did little to advance American interests in any concerted fashion.

The only definite action under way would be Eaton's, although even this resolution to back Eaton, taken in mid-September, was rendered uncertain and pushed into some operational confusion as Samuel Barron began to waver again. Almost from the moment Preble left his conference table and Eaton stopped pushing to get Barron on his side, the commodore began to shy away from his decision to support Eaton's scheme. The matter was not helped by the fact that Tobias Lear opposed the plan and very actively tried to kill and derail it at every turn.

Lear considered Eaton's plot an ill-conceived "experiment" and thought that America could obtain respect in Barbary only by winning peace with Tripoli without outside help. He considered Eaton an insane romantic and a fundamentally unsound player in American affairs in the region. Further, he doubted Ahmad's abilities and thought Yusuf unlikely to ever surrender or give up his hostages without some honorable, diplomatic solution—one that would probably entail some token cash ransom. Commodore Barron spent October and half of November reconsidering his decision to support Ahmad Qaramanli.

With nearly two months of inactivity passed, William Eaton despaired. Convinced that Barron would fritter away more time, he sought and obtained Edward Preble's assistance. Preble was still in Syracuse at this time and was happy to help spur Barron to action; after so many months of frustration, both men agonized over the commodore's placidity. It pained Preble to think that he was denied the privilege of command just as his country finally committed sufficient resources to the Mediterranean squadron, while Eaton saw the opportunity for victory slipping further away with every day lost to ponderous indecision.

After Preble weighed in again on the matter, Barron vacillated back toward supporting Eaton's scheme. Finally on November 14, 1805, Barron ordered the *Argus* to take Eaton off to Alexandria, Egypt, to search for Ahmad Qaramanli.

Unfortunately, neither Preble nor Eaton realized that Commodore Barron's understanding of the endeavor had shifted and that their plans were no longer in accord. Barron had dispatched Eaton expecting that Ahmad Qaramanli would be brought back to Syracuse for further conference over the matter. In Barron's mind, he had not yet committed to any definite action, only to further and more active consideration. Besides, as he explained in a letter to a very agitated Consul General Lear, "should we succeed in getting him [Ahmad] here, I shall take no ultimate measures, without informing you of them."

Yet Eaton and Preble thought more decisive action had been authorized: Eaton would contact Ahmad, raise an army, march with this force against Yusuf, capture the city and harbor fortification at Derna, and then march on toward Benghazi and then Tripoli. Eaton expected the U.S. Navy to transport them from Benghazi to Cape Misurata, across the Gulf of Sidra, and then attack Tripoli from the rear, maybe augmented with a detachment of marines, while the squadron bombarded from the sea.

When Eaton sailed to Egypt aboard the *Argus*, this confusion of purpose had not been identified and so was not addressed. Eaton assumed authorization had been granted for a rigorous and robust operation. Once he landed at Alexandria on November 26, 1804, he steamrolled ahead with a small detachment of U.S. Marines led by Lieutenant Presley Neville O'Bannon.

Finding Ahmad Qaramanli was to prove more difficult than Eaton had imagined. From the British consul in Alexandria, he learned that Ahmad had gone to Cairo and had joined a band of Mamluks, the minority element that was fighting against the Ottoman authorities. Undeterred by the obvious dangers, Eaton dispatched messages to Ahmad informing him of his presence and intentions, and then planned to lead a very small expedition up the Rosetta branch of the Nile to find Ahmad. Throughout, he and his party would need to keep mindful of Arab brigands, trigger-happy Turkish troops, and paranoid Mamluk rebels. On November 28, 1804, he reported to the secretary of the navy that he planned to initiate his trek that evening "with Lieut. O'Bannon, Midshipmen Danielson, Richard Farquhar, ESQ., four servants and a Turkish guide, all in a good state of defense to Grand Cairo in prosecution of the object of our voyage hither. The interior of this country being in a general state of revolt renders traveling somewhat dangerous. If no accident occur to prevent, I shall in due season report in details; otherwise I beg leave to refer you to Captain Hull."

Due to contrary winds and various dangers from the locals, Eaton and his group did not begin their journey until after the start of Ramadan (the ninth month of the Muslim lunar calendar). As Eaton knew from his experiences as a Christian consul in Tunis, traveling through this contested terrain during the holy month would be particularly perilous.

Finally, on December 4, they embarked early in the morning for Cairo. Eaton charted two *marches*, a sort of schooner developed for the Nile. Their tour "sailed tranquilly along the beautiful banks of the Nile," stopping occasionally at local villages, where they saw abject poverty, extreme misery, and famine-induced rioting; at one stop they encountered cheering crowds who mistook them for British soldiers, and at another they took some aimless hostile fire and fled upriver.

On the morning of December 8, they entered Cairo as "American Officers of the army and navy, whom curiosity had brought from Malta to Egypt," were given a grand reception through advance word from Captain Vincents (secretary to the British minister, whom they met in Rosetta), and were also granted an audience with the viceroy for the next evening. While venturing around Cairo, Eaton met one of Ahmad's trusted aides, from whom he discovered that Ahmad had taken up with a band of Mamluks, three thousand strong, camped out in El Minya, 120 miles up the Nile. Even worse, eight thousand Turkish soldiers were currently besieging this Mamluk encampment. Eaton dispatched another letter to Ahmad via a courier.

"Coffee, pipes and sherbet were served in oriental style," Eaton noted, and the "customary salutations" were "passed and repeated" with "questions on indifferent subjects asked and answered." Finally, Viceroy Ahmad Pasha Khorshid signaled for his court to retire to give them privacy, and then he observed to Eaton that "it seemed to him our visit to this country, at so critical a moment, must have something more for its object than the mere gratification of curiosity." Eaton responded with "a candid explanation" of his business.

Viceroy Khorshid was intrigued by their mission and flattered by Eaton's candor and diplomacy. "He approved our resolution," as Eaton put it, and he furnished them with a letter of safe conduct through the Turkish-secured areas.

Some difficulties later arose, however, when the French consul maliciously "insinuated" that they were "British spies in American masks" and that their desire to find Qaramanli was "aimed at nothing but an intercourse with the Mamelukes." Eaton admitted that Ahmad had taken up with the Mamluks, but he explained that Ahmad was driven by desperation and fear and asked the viceroy to be lenient. In this way, Eaton managed to talk the viceroy into granting Ahmad Qaramanli a letter of amnesty for associating with the Mamluks and a letter of safe conduct "to pass the Turkish army and leave Egypt unmolested." All that was left was to make positive contact with Ahmad and find some way of extracting him from the Mamluks without "exciting suspicions of treason which might prove fatal to him."

Fortunately, Eaton made the acquaintance of a colorful yet hardened mercenary called Eugene Leitensdorfer, who, for a $50 cash advance, was willing to rescue Ahmad from his predicament and sign up for their expedition in Tripoli. Leitensdorfer had had many identities and at least as many names; his real name was Gervasio Prodasio Santuari. He was a thirty-two-year-old Tyrolese soldier of fortune who had served in and deserted the Austrian, French, and Turkish armies and had been variously employed as a peddler, a café proprietor, a Capuchin friar, a conjurer, a theater producer, a Bedouin, a dragoman, a faith healer, and a dervish, among other odd jobs. Leitensdorfer was a most unusual and persuasive character; Eaton agreed and paid him $50.

Eugene Leitensdorfer and a companion rode via dromedary almost nonstop to El Minya. Once there he easily ingratiated himself among the Mamluks, made contact with Ahmad Qaramanli, and persuaded him to slip out quietly with him into the desert to catch up with Eaton. Ahmad agreed, and within a few days they were on their way down the Nile. For rendering this service, Eaton made Leitensdorfer his adjutant.

Eaton received his first communication from Ahmad on January 8, announcing that he was en route to join the expedition. Eaton waited in Cairo and had several letter exchanges with Lieutenant Hull, who was growing anxious and impatient. He then received word that Ahmad changed his plans; he would now rendezvous with Eaton at Alexandria with about thirty followers in tow. Eaton and his party left for Alexandria on January 19, and on February 5 they finally met up with Ahmad just outside of Alexandria.

Ahmad was nervous and afraid. He had earlier written to Commodore Barron to check up on Eaton, to verify that the expedition was authorized and that Eaton actually represented the United States. Barron had responded positively, from which dispatch Ahmad came to believe the United States would support his campaign completely and be the source of unlimited funds. Eaton encouraged this belief, up to a point, telling Ahmad not to worry about money, "for the occasion demands heavy expenditure. It is a matter of making war, and war calls for money and men." Eaton remained, however, very conscious of their finances and grew increasingly worried about whether his government would supply the cash or cover his debts. "I calculate the whole expenditure of cash in this expedition," he wrote to the secretary of the navy on February 13, "including expenses in Egypt, will amount to twenty thousand dollars. Further disbursements and supplies will be necessary to carry this plan into final effect. But to indemnify the United States, I have entered into a convention with Ahmad Bashaw [Ahmad Pasha] to pledge the tribute to Sweden, Denmark, and the Batavian Republic, which convention I shall reduce to writing and forward by Captain Hull, if time permits; otherwise by the earliest occasion."

Tenaciously focused on his ultimate goal, Eaton began to recruit an odd and decidedly motley assortment of mercenaries, both Christian and Muslim. Ahmad, for his part, had decided against traveling to Derna aboard the USS *Argus.* He hoped to gather desert Arabs along the way, he thought it unsafe to enter Alexandria with an armed retinue, and he worried that his loyalists might disperse should he be seen to leave without them. Eaton concurred. "I am to join him [Ahmad] with a detachment from the city next Sunday," he reported to the secretary of the navy on February 13, and proceed with him to Bomba [just east of Derna] at the end of five hundred men, and there take post. Meantime Captain Hull repairs to the rendezvous [Syracuse] for suitable reinforcements and supplies to secure an establishment at Derna and Bengazi. Those provinces in our possession will cut off from the enemy and turn into our channel a source of provisions and will open a free intercourse with the interior of the country. I have requested of the Commodore for this purpose an hundred stands of arms, with cartridges, and two field pieces, with trains and ammunition, and also a detachment of one hundred marines, if necessary, to lead a *coup de main*.

Lieutenant Isaac Hull expected Eaton to return with Ahmad and his forces to the *Argus*, whereupon he would courier them to Derna or some other suitable local in the regency of Tripoli. Instead, Hull found that Eaton would march with Ahmad directly from Alexandria overland to Derna. Uncertain of how to proceed and eager to report back to Barron, Hull left Eaton a small detachment of one lieutenant (O'Bannon), seven enlisted marines, and a midshipman (Pascal Paoli Peck) onshore and sailed the *Argus* from Alexandria on February 19, supplied with letters to Commodore Barron from Eaton and Ahmad requesting supplies and reinforcements.

Thirty miles southwest of Alexandria, at Burg el Arab, Eaton and Ahmad Qaramanli gathered and amassed a diverse (roughly) four-hundred-man army of Muslims and Christians, including some forty veteran Greek infantrymen, a sixty-man troop of Arab cavalry and a large rabble of Arab "foot soldiers," a twenty-five-man team of artillerymen, Ahmad's suite of ninety men, and assorted renegades, mercenaries, and soldiers of fortune from Europe and the Levant. Eaton also employed the services of the men who had been left behind by Captain Hull of the *Argus*.

On March 6, 1805, *General* William Eaton, as he began to style himself, and Ahmad Qaramanli initiated the expedition, leading their ragtag army across more than five hundred miles of uninviting desert landscape.

Eaton's campaign was a most unhappy affair. Religious friction and anxiety were very strong, and on various occasions the

Muslims threatened the Christians with mutiny, massacre, and abandonment. The terrain proved extremely inhospitable, as did many of the native tribes, and food and fresh water proved hard to come by with any regularity. Further, Eaton was in a hurry, for he learned that word of their expedition had reached Pasha Yusuf and that a large detachment of mounted warriors had been dispatched to Derna to reinforce the city. During the expedition Ahmad Qaramanli exhibited cowardice and fits of depression. Most of Ahmad's "loyalists" suffered from lack of determination, greed, and cowardice. Arab thieving was a continuous problem, as was their loyalty—Eaton had to routinely stave off disaster with money or promises of money. "Cash," he lamented continuously in his journal, "is the only deity of the Arabs."

After more than three hundred miles of hard marching, the entire expedition nearly ended—once again—in catastrophe.

The thirsty, haggard, and nervous army had finally found a natural supply of water, and Ahmad seemed determined to halt the march for at least a day, perhaps longer. It was not yet 10 A.M., however, and Eaton was concerned that they were running out of time, both to meet up with Lieutenant Hull and the *Argus* at Bomba and to make it to Derna before Yusuf Qaramanli's reinforcements arrived.

Eaton quickly surmised Ahmad's real intentions for the delay: the courier they had dispatched to Bomba had not yet returned. This was a source of continual tension, as Ahmad and the Arabs continued to worry that Eaton had misled them to their death in the desert. Ahmad proposed that another be sent and that they wait here by a good water supply until the courier returned with definite assurance that the *Argus* was waiting for them at Bomba with their supplies.

Water they had, but, Eaton argued, their food was running out. They had only six days' half-ration left, all rice; the bread and meat and condiments were all gone. Every day they lost or made slow progress was one day more for Yusuf's support troops to beat them to Derna. They could not afford to waste any more time.

Ahmad refused to budge.

"He said," Eaton noted in his journal, "the Arab chiefs were resolved to proceed no further till the camp shall have recruited themselves by a little repose." Eaton responded that if the Arabs "preferred famine to fatigue, they might have the choice." He ordered their ration stopped and the food supply locked up. If he could not persuade them to march, he would starve them into it. Lieutenant O'Bannon and the marines were ordered to stand on guard in front of the supply tent.

The stalemate lasted a few hours.

At midafternoon, Ahmad had his silk pavilion taken down and his baggage packed; he mounted his horse and led the Arabs into marching formation. Eaton was pleased until Ahmad made it plain he intended to return to Egypt.

Eaton forced himself to remain silent, stand back, and watch what happened next. Experience had taught him not to show his hand with the Arabs any sooner than he had to. Careful observation confirmed his worst fear—that another Arab mutiny was afoot.

He quickly made his way to the marines and was relieved to learn that Lieutenant O'Bannon had recognized the danger as well, immediately reinforcing his marines with soldiers from the contingent of Greek cannoneers.

The mounted Arab mob took this as their cue and approached the supply tent, shouting war cries.

Eaton's soldiers did not waver.

The charging Arabs were nearly on them now, but O'Bannon and the marines stood their ground. The Arabs assembled in an offensive line. An hour passed in deadlock. Eaton, O'Bannon, the marines, and the cannoneers remained composed and unruffled. The Arabs remained rather less so, and Ahmad was positively beside himself with anguished indecision. Finally, he managed to persuade the Arabs to dismount and disperse. He called for his tent to be pitched again.

Eaton ordered Lieutenant O'Bannon to have the marines perform the manual of arms. O'Bannon gave the commands, and his marines smartly executed the manual, smacking their rifles as they raised, shouldered, and pointed them.

"In an instant," Eaton noted in his journal, "the Arabs took an alarm, remounted and exclaimed, 'The Christians are preparing to fire on us!'"

The Arabs mounted up and some two hundred of them wheeled their horses and charged. The horde rushed Eaton's men, yelling and waving their rifles and scimitars.

Eaton, O'Bannon, and the defensive line of marines and soldiers stood their ground. As suddenly as they had charged, the Arabs, their bluff called again, broke away and circled back into a dusty tangle of horses and men. The frustrated mob grew angrier—and more confused. Some of the Arabs aimed their rifles at the marines.

Eaton's line stood firm.

Eaton immediately surmised that the first sign of fright would encourage the more hotheaded Arabs and likely end the entire expedition with a full-scale Christian massacre. He dismounted his horse and handed his rifle, pistols, and scimitar to an astonished O'Bannon. Visibly unarmed, he walked straight into the mob milling around Ahmad. A column of unsteady muskets rose and aimed at his chest. Most of the Arabs were frightened, but some were hot and seemed ready to kill. A loud clamor arose from the Arab ranks, and Eaton found his voice drowned out as he tried to address the mob.

He calmly and imperiously raised his hand as a signal for attention. With that, some of Ahmad's officers rode out with sabers drawn and positioned themselves between Eaton and O'Bannon's line of defense.

William Eaton was now entirely cut off from his troops.

He quickly surmised that Ahmad's officers were in fact interposing themselves between him and the mutineers. Seizing the moment, he walked up to Ahmad, who clearly remained unsure which way to move, asked him to dismount, took him by the arm, and led him away from the tumult. One Arab protested; Ahmad smacked him with the flat of his scimitar. Eaton calmly took control of the situation and asserted his will on Ahmad.

As he later recorded in his journal, "I asked him if he knew his own interests and friends. He relented, called me his friend & protector—said he was too soon heated and followed me to my tent—giving orders at the same time to his Arabs to disperse." Ahmad then embraced O'Bannon with an enthusiasm of respect, calling him "the brave American."

Shaken by the close call, Ahmad apologized and proposed that Eaton rescind his order and issue some rice. Eaton promised to reissue rations on the condition that the Arabs agree to march next morning. Ahmad agreed. Eaton ordered a ration distributed; and, he wrote, "the camp again resumed its tranquility."

"We find it almost impossible," Eaton wrote dejectedly in his journal, "to inspire these wild bigots with confidence in us or to persuade them that, being Christians, we can be otherwise than enemies to Mussulmen. We have a difficult undertaking!"

Fortunately, the march proceeded with comparative gusto. Although the dangers and problems of dissension, insubordination, mutiny, and thievery continued off and on, Eaton managed to persuade, cajole, and lead his army to Bomba.

The only binding element and driving force of the expedition was William Eaton. Through him, it seemed virtually anything was possible. As Lieutenant O'Bannon once remarked, "Wherever General Eaton leads, we will follow. If he wants us to march to hell, we'll gladly go there. General Eaton overcomes every obstacle. He is the great military genius of our era!"

By mid-April, Eaton's forces met up with the *Argus* and the *Hornet*—a sloop of ten guns that had been purchased at Malta to reinforce the Mediterranean squadron—at the Gulf of Bomba. The American show of support and the fresh provisions were a welcome relief and helped stave off another potential mutiny. Thus invigorated, the army resumed the march for Derna, and the *Argus* and the *Hornet* set off to rejoin the squadron with plans to rendezvous with Eaton's army.

11

To the Shores of Tripoli

THOUGH COMMODORE SAMUEL BARRON had once again decided to support William Eaton's scheme, U.S. consul general Tobias Lear's influence and interference were still firmly felt. Barron wrote Eaton a lengthy dispatch that mapped out a strategy and complimented him on successfully pushing the expedition forward but then proceeded to hedge and protect himself for the record.

Under Lear's influence, Barron set down, for posterity, his concern that Eaton had pushed the United States government into commitments beyond his authority: "I feel it my duty to state explicitly that I must withhold my sanction to any convention or agreement committing the United States or tending to impress on Hamet Bashaw [Ahmad Pasha] a conviction that we have bound ourselves to place him on the throne." As far as Barron was concerned, he had authorized no absolute commitment of any kind. He planned to support Ahmad in battle, "but," he added, "should the Bashaw be found deficient . . . or that it appears that we have been deceived with regard to the disposition of the inhabitants, he must be held as an unfit subject for further support."

Although Eaton recognized Lear's handiwork in Barron's equivocation, he found the letter more heartening than disturbing; after all, Commodore Barron clearly intended to support him a while longer. Indeed, initially Barron had seriously considered sending the *Congress* with heavy artillery to support the army against Derna. He only refrained from doing so because he had no reliable charts of those waters and so, with the memory of the *Philadelphia*'s fate in mind, feared for the frigate's safety. The

Nautilus was dispatched instead, augmented by the *Argus* and the *Hornet*.

Eaton's forces took up a position outside the city of Derna on April 25. Within a few hours, Eaton noted, several of the local sheiks "came out to meet the Bashaw [Pasha] with assurance of fealty and attachment." More usefully, they also gave him valuable intelligence of the enemy's strength and position. The USS *Nautilus* arrived on April 26, 1805, and Eaton began to plan.

The city of Derna, in the province of Cyrenaica in the regency of Tripoli, stood across the Wadi Derna, which carried water from the hills into the Mediterranean across a narrow stretch of land just southeast of Cape Bu Azza. The east bank of the Wadi Derna was the Bu Mansur quadrant, reaching out to the harbor, protected from the north and northwest by a sea battery, armed with eight nine-pounder guns, on the Ras el Matariz promontory.

On the left bank of the riverbed, in the center of the town, stood the castle of the bey, which was armed with a ten-inch mortar. On the left bank of the Wadi Derna lay the other three quarters of the city: El Gebila, nearer Cape Bu Azza; El Bilad, under the hills; and El Mogar, named after the caves that were used by the locals for housing.

Being more Cyrenaican in ethnicity, the residents of the left-bank settlements tended to be more favorable to Ahmad Qaramanli's cause than were those of the Bu Mansur, who tended to be more Tripolitan and so more loyal to the current regency. El Bilad was, however, completely inaccessible to Eaton's army from the direction of their approach. The residents of El Gebila and El Mogar were disinclined to be helpful while the bey of Derna remained in control of the city.

Eaton would have no choice but to concentrate most of his forces on the Bu Mansur quarter. Making matters worse, the bey of Derna had been preparing for Ahmad's advance for some time.

He had strengthened the Bu Mansur fortifications and defenses, seized all the arms of the majority pro-Ahmad contingency, and entrenched himself with about eight hundred troops.

Yet Eaton remained optimistic that he would prevail, even despite the fact that Commodore Barron proved improvident in his commitment of manpower. While his forces prepared for battle, William Eaton, as was still the custom of officers and gentlemen at this time, sent the following ultimatum to the bey of Derna:

> Sir, I want no territory. With me is advancing the legitimate Sovereign of your country. Give us a passage through your city, and for the supplies of which we have need, you shall have fair compensation. Let no differences of religion induce us to shed the blood of harmless men who think little and know nothing. If you are a man of liberal mind, you will not balance on the propositions I offer. Ahmad Bashaw [Ahmad Pasha] pledges himself to me that you shall be established in your government. I shall see you tomorrow in a way of your choice. Eaton.

The bey of Derna was fiercely loyal to Pasha Yusuf Qaramanli, his cousin and brother-in-law. Without reflection he scrawled his reply:

"My head, or yours. Mustapha."

On April 27, 1805, the *Argus* and the *Hornet* finally arrived to join the *Nautilus*. Eaton met with the commanders of the three ships and went over their battle plans once more to assure coordination for a joint attack on the city from sea and land. A field gun was offloaded from the *Argus*, and then Lieutenant Hull drew her off into the bay of Derna in position to fire her twenty-four-pounder guns against the fortified buildings around the Bu Mansur fort. Meanwhile, the *Nautilus* and the *Hornet* drew in to provide close support and to sweep the bey's batteries on the Ras el Matariz promontory.

The attack began at roughly 2 P.M. on April 28. The naval bombardment commenced in earnest, and on land the "fire became general," Eaton noted, "in all quarters where Tripolitans and Americans were opposed to each other."

Just a hundred yards off the harbor fortification, the *Hornet* unloaded a broadside against the eight nine-pounder guns of the Bu Mansur water battery. At the same time, half a mile off the city, the *Nautilus* lobbed her shells over the walls and into the center of town, and the *Argus*, just a little farther out into the bay, concentrated her fire into the city as well.

William Eaton divided his men into two units. He, Lieutenant O'Bannon, and his contingent of marines led the Greek artillerymen, the Christian mercenaries, and about fifty Arab foot soldiers in an assault against the barricades and against some enemy forces in a ravine at the southeast section of the city, while Ahmad Qaramanli led several hundred mounted Arabs around the city to attack from the south.

Ahmad used his force to secure an old castle on the heights (just above El Mogar) that overlooked the town and deployed his cavalry in the hills to the southwest, putting them in a position to cut off the garrison's retreat and to hold up any potential reinforcements from the west.

To Eaton's surprise and relief, Ahmad acted with bravery, energy, and intelligence. Indeed, Ahmad Qaramanli appeared, for the first time since the expedition had begun, to command his men with great force and purpose, as if he were a natural leader.

The *Hornet*'s fire was regular and concentrated, and after an hour's heavy pounding, the enemy gunners abandoned their station. The water battery of Bu Mansur was silenced and evacuated. Unfortunately, most of its men joined the defenders at the southeastern barricades, increasing the firepower brought to bear on Eaton and O'Bannon's position. The attackers' lone artillery piece was early rendered useless, as one of the Greek artillerymen, taking heavy fire, forgot to remove the rammer before firing, sending both rod and ball into the city. With the loss of the cannon, the situation became critical, as Eaton's unit was pinned down and taking heavy fire.

The men grew uneasy, and it seemed to Eaton that his forces would not stand. "The fire of the enemy's Musketry became too warm and continually augmenting," he reported later to Commodore Barron. "Our troops were thrown into confusion and, undisciplined as they were, it was impossible to reduce them to order." Without hesitation, Eaton took the only option he saw and ordered a full bayonet charge: "We rushed forward against a host of Savages, more than ten to our one."

The sheer bravado of the scene proved too disconcerting for the defenders: "They fled from their Coverts, irregularly, firing in retreat from every palm tree and partition wall in their way."

From one of these parting shots, Eaton "received a ball through my left wrist, which deprived me of the use of the hand and of course of my rifle." Characteristically, he simply wrapped his arm in a makeshift bandage and sling, grabbed a pistol with his right hand, and continued to charge ahead. With the American marines in the lead, Eaton's forces stormed the ramparts and advanced straight to the harbor. The defenders retreated to their right flank across the Wadi Derna. The Americans quickly secured the southeastern section of the city.

Lieutenant O'Bannon, his marines, and Midshipman George Mann of the *Argus* led a section of these forces—initiating what would soon be thought of as the finest tradition of the United States Marine Corps—straight to the fort, where they "passed through a shower of musketry from the walls of houses, [and] took possession of the battery." Then Lieutenant O'Bannon "planted the American flag upon its ramparts, and turned its guns upon the enemy."

The enemy troops were driven out of their positions, directly toward Ahmad and his forces, who had swept around to the western section of the city. Ahmad's cavalry thrashed the retreating garrison, and the bey's palace was taken. The defenders of Derna were routed.

The city of Derna was entirely in Eaton's possession by 4 P.M.

Even though William Eaton's scheme with Ahmad had piqued Yusuf Pasha, it was not clear that the stated goal of restoring

Ahmad to the throne would work. In fact, even after Derna was captured there was little in the way of popular uprising or revolutionary fever against Pasha Yusuf among the locals.

Most of the Bu Mansur quadrant, and a smattering of people throughout the city, remained loyal to the reigning pasha. Although the rest were nominally pro-Ahmad, it is very likely that they expected Yusuf's advancing troops to smash Eaton and Ahmad's forces to pieces; the exact number of the "reinforcements" Yusuf had reportedly sent tended to increase substantially with every telling. Expecting the worst, Eaton strengthened the city's defenses, and "raised parapets & mounted guns towards the county to be prepared against all events."

Hassan Agha, the commander of the Janissary soldiers who had been ordered to raise reinforcements, was making slow progress. Therefore, Yusuf Qaramanli's reinforcements, which had been requested on March 4, did not arrive until May 8, eleven days after Derna had been taken. On May 13, after having recruited as many loyalists as he could, Hassan Agha finally attacked. Although Yusuf's army was soon enough repelled, they returned the next day, and the next, and the next. Derna was under siege; not only was the town subject to attack and constant raids, but the city's food and supplies were entirely cut off. Due to lack of resources, the primary defense of Eaton and Ahmad's forces came from the *Argus*'s guns. Their prospects of long-term success appeared bleak, at least initially.

In fact, things were going reasonably well. Although the defense of Derna was tiring and cost far more lives than its capture, the effort seemed to be paying off. Hassan's army suffered substantial desertions, some to the country and some to Derna, and at least one commander sent word to Eaton that he and his 150 men would join Ahmad if he could guarantee protection from Pasha Yusuf's revenge. Hassan had tremendous difficulties inducing his Arabs to fight. Eaton's spies daily brought reports of desertions and near mutinies in the enemy's ranks.

As long as Eaton and Ahmad could hold on, they had a fighting chance of success. They were, however, quickly running out of resources and food. It seemed that only a serious commitment of money, supplies, and manpower from Commodore Barron could save the endeavor. As Eaton noted in his correspondence to Barron, "With the aids contemplated by government to have been furnished Hamet Bashaw [Ahmad Pasha] when in the position he now holds, I have no doubt but he may proceed to the walls of Tripoli."

Eaton also began to worry that the commodore's support, weak at the outset, was not substantial enough to furnish additional supplies. "[T]here is one discouraging circumstance" to the option of providing more resources to Ahmad, Eaton confessed to Barron; that was the thought that "these aids are to be withdrawn at any period when the enemy shall propose terms of peace which may be accepted by the agent of government on the spot." If Ahmad "is to be used solely as an instrument," Eaton continued, to the "attainment of an object exclusively to the advantage of the United States, without any consideration to his future existence and well being, I cannot persuade myself that any bonds of patriotism dictate to me the duty of having a chief agency, nor indeed any, in so extraordinary a sacrifice. Certainly the enemy will propose any terms of peace with us the moment he entertains serious apprehensions from his brother. This may happen at any stage of the war most likely to rid him of so dangerous a rival, and not only Hamet Bashaw, but every one acting with him must inevitably fall victims to our economy!"

Commodore Samuel Barron, meanwhile, continued to vacillate in his support of Eaton's activities. Under the withering assault of Tobias Lear, Barron increasingly believed the Ahmad expedition a bad idea, and one unlikely to succeed. Besides, Lear began to suspect that the matter could be resolved diplomatically, without the bedridden Barron having to engage in any lengthy and dangerous campaign.

As late as December 1804, Consul General Tobias Lear had been receiving feelers from Qaramanli about renewing peace talks. It seemed that the pasha was growing worried, not just about the expedition of William Eaton and his brother in the

Cyrenaica province, but also at the expected summer assault from Barron's squadron. Although Qaramanli knew that Commodore Barron was ill, he also knew that Captain John Rodgers, the most likely replacement commodore, was itching for a fight and, like Preble, preferred to negotiate from the mouth of a cannon.

Still, when Qaramanli's formal terms of peace were proposed on April 21, 1805, Lear and Barron rejected them outright. The thought of spending $200,000 for peace and ransom seemed absolutely outrageous to both of them, plus Qaramanli wanted restitution for the war. Still, Lear believed the terms were but an opening through which his masterful diplomacy could extract an "honorable peace." Exactly what this meant was, to Lear, straightforward: the United States would pay nothing for peace; would allow an exchange of prisoners with Tripoli; would only consent to pay ransom for American prisoners once the U.S. store of Tripolitan prisoners had been exhausted; and would make peace only if there was some credible expectation of permanence.

By this time, Commodore Samuel Barron knew that he would not recover from his illness sufficiently to lead the squadron into battle against Tripoli during the summer. Indeed he was preparing to fully resign his commission to Captain Rodgers. The commodore, spurred by his dyspeptic younger brother James, also began to assume the worst for a summer campaign against Tripoli because they had been unable to procure gunboats from Naples and thought they would get none from Venice. (Unbeknownst to Barron, Edward Preble, upon his return to the United States, had overseen and secured ten gunboats—one would eventually be lost in the Atlantic crossing—and two bomb ketches for the Mediterranean squadron.) So, between Barron's depression and his brother's defeatism, Tobias Lear's calls for diplomacy seemed worthwhile.

Commodore Barron consented on May 18, 1805, to allow Lear to make a credible attempt at peace negotiations. Lear was shipped to Tripoli aboard the *Essex*. Four days later, on May 22, Captain Samuel Barron resigned his command. Captain John Rodgers became commodore of the Mediterranean squadron.

Consul General Lear arrived in Tripoli on May 26, and negotiations began in earnest three days later.

During the talks, Pasha Qaramanli tried to use the American prisoners as leverage; he even threatened to execute them if he felt pushed to take extreme measures to save himself. It was fairly clear, however, that he would do no such thing; he was losing support from a populace far more eager to be done with the whole affair than to be bombarded into submission on account of Yusuf Qaramanli's demands for tribute.

"Money is not my object at present," Yusuf related in a message to both Lear and Commodore Rodgers, "but a peace on terms that will not disgrace me hereafter." As the American prisoner Dr. Cowdery noted in his journal on May 28, 1805, "the Bashaw [Pasha] showed the greatest anxiety for peace. He was sensible of the danger he was in from the lowness of his funds and the disaffection of his people." When Yusuf finally learned that his brother Ahmad had successfully taken and held Derna, he was very eager for peace—particularly since the former bey of Derna had exaggerated the numbers of Ahmad's forces so as not to be too shamed by having lost the city.

Understanding what was required to settle the matter, Consul General Lear gave Yusuf Qaramanli a face-saving opportunity for peace. He offered a nominal $60,000 in ransom for all the American prisoners, and he expected peace to be made without cash payments of any kind. Qaramanli readily accepted this proposal, provided that the Americans withdrew entirely from Derna, and provided—this stipulation was kept very secret—that Yusuf be allowed to keep Ahmad's family hostage (he had detained them sometime back to try to keep his elder brother's activity in check). Lear readily accepted these conditions, and although the final treaty retained language that explicitly provided for the release of Ahmad's family, they agreed to a secret clause that allowed the pasha's stipulation to stand.

The Americans were freed, peace was declared, and Ahmad Qaramanli was betrayed without a moment's hesitation. The treaty was settled on June 3, 1805, and later ratified by the United

States on April 17, 1806. Lear's secret clause was not included in the version of the treaty that was submitted to Congress, and President Jefferson later maintained that it was kept secret from him as well.

On June 11, 1805, the frigate *Constellation* anchored in the bay off of Derna. William Eaton hoped this was a sign that the commodore had finally decided to support his mission without reservation. Captain Hugh Campbell sent an officer ashore with fresh dispatches.

Eaton learned of the peace treaty, and was flattened. He was convinced that with just a little bit of support to tip the balance, victory was certain. Once the shock wore off, he became furious and horrified at his country's betrayal. As he wrote to the commodore:

> You would weep, sir, were you on the spot to witness the unbounded confidence placed in the American character here, and to reflect that this confidence must shortly sink into contempt and immortal hatred. You would feel that this confidence, at any price, should be carried through the Barbary Regencies, at least to Tripoli, by the same means it has been inspired here. . . . But if . . . we are compelled to leave the place under its actual circumstances, humanity itself must weep. The whole city of Derna, together with numerous families of Arabs, who attached themselves to Hamet Bashaw [Ahmad Pasha], and who resisted Yusuf's troops in expectation of succor from us, must be abandoned to their fate. Havoc and slaughter will be the inevitable consequence, not a soul of them can escape the savage vengeance of the enemy. . . . Could I have apprehended this result of my exertions, certainly no consideration would have prevailed on me to have taken an agency in a tragedy so manifestly fraught with intrigue, so wounding to human feelings, and, as I must view it, so degrading to our national honor.

The dispatches made it clear that Eaton was under orders to evacuate. Ironically, that day also saw the final assault of Hassan Agha's troops against Eaton and Ahmad's forces at Derna. The

Tripolitan army had not fared well; among the desertions Hassan Agha suffered was his treasurer, who ran to Egypt with all of the troops' wages. Although this final push was a heady affair, Ahmad's forces won the day, and the siege ended. Allowing the men their victory, Eaton waited till the following morning to inform Qaramanli of his government's decision.

Ahmad Qaramanli took the news relatively well and accepted Eaton's offer to evacuate with the Americans. Great care must be taken, he pointed out, to ensure that their men did not learn of this treachery and betrayal, otherwise they would all be slaughtered. Thus Eaton was forced to carry out a secret evacuation of Ahmad, his retinue, and all the Christians.

The deception worked rather well.

Eaton told their forces that the enemy had rallied and was prepared to attack again shortly. He distributed extra rations and ammunition, and even dispatched spies and lookouts to track enemy movements. He then made a show of inspecting the garrison, and at 8 P.M. he placed the marines on patrol in a visible position, just to make certain that everyone would be able to spot an American. While the marines stood on display, the *Constellation*'s boats silently hauled the Christians off to safety.

Eaton then sent for Ahmad, as if to request a formal audience. Qaramanli knew the signal and quickly went to the fort with his full retinue, all of whom quickly made their way off in the boats. Eaton then sent off the marines and American officers. Once he knew everyone was out of harm's way, he entered his boat and rowed out to the American ships. As he departed, the deception was discovered.

Under the protection of the night's darkness, Eaton watched as the soldiers and civilians at Derna began to panic. In the midst of the confusion, shots were fired aimlessly out toward the American ships; shouts, exhortations, and curses were heard as well—some addressed to Ahmad and some to Eaton. The last Eaton saw of Ahmad's troops was a fevered assault of the tents, baggage, and horses left behind; in short order everything was pillaged and stolen away into the countryside.

The next morning a representative from Pasha Yusuf Qaramanli was dispatched from the *Constellation* under a flag of truce to declare a general amnesty to the people of Derna provided they lowered their arms and pledged their allegiance to the regency. On his return to the frigate, he reported to Eaton that "nothing but despair depicted itself in the visages of the few wretched inhabitants who remained." He said that they rejected Qaramanli's amnesty deal, "declaring that they knew his perfidy too well to suffer themselves to be ensnared by it."

As the *Constellation* pulled away from Derna, Eaton sat down in his cabin with his journal and his thoughts:

"In a few minutes more, we shall loose sight of this devoted city, which has experienced as strange a reverse in so short a time as ever was recorded in the disasters of war; thrown from proud success into an abyss of hopeless wretchedness. Six hours ago, the enemy were seeking safety from them by flight—this moment we drop them from ours into the hands of this enemy for no other crime, but too much confidence in us."

12

American Peace

THROUGH SHEER FORCE of will, William Eaton transformed a somewhat unlikely scheme into a bold and effective strike into enemy territory. The fall of the fortified city of Derna represented a major blow to Yusuf Qaramanli's sovereignty. Derna was the second largest city of the regency of Tripoli and the organizational and military center of the Tripolitan province of Cyrenaica. As Tobias Lear wrote Eaton, on June 6, 1805 (the day after the peace treaty was signed), "I found [during negotiations with Yusuf] that the heroic bravery of our few countrymen at Derna . . . had made a deep impression on the Bashaw [Pasha]."

Clearly the tide of the war had turned in America's favor. Yet instead of advancing the cause, pushing the war forward, and defeating Yusuf Qaramanli outright or otherwise bringing his days of piracy to an end, the United States settled for an immediate "peace" induced with a $60,000 "ransom." While the arrangement freed the hostages and obliged Tripoli to end its war against American shipping, it did nothing to penalize Qaramanli or actually restore national honor, and it tied treaty fulfillment to the promises of a murdering pirate. Even worse, the cause of Ahmad Qaramanli was abandoned, sacrificed for expediency.

William Eaton was beside himself with anger at what he considered the timorous and dishonorable conduct of U.S. consul general Tobias Lear and their boss, President Thomas Jefferson. "If . . . fratricide, treason, perfidy to treaty—already experienced, and systematic piracy, be characteristic guarantees of good faith," he wrote to the secretary of the navy, "Mr. Lear has chosen the fittest of the two brothers for his man of confidence."

Jefferson declared "victory," but the "peace" proved rather political.

The United States had been quick to declare victory over Tripoli and by extension the pacification of all of Barbary. Through the many plays, books, poems, and paintings that emerged from the celebration of this victory, it was thought that American honor had been restored and the nation's backward and beastly enemies vanquished. As Francis Scott Key rendered it in the song that he would nine years later rewrite as "The Star-Spangled Banner":

> In conflict resistless each toil they endur'd,
> Till their foes shrunk dismay'd from the war's desolation:
> And pale beam'd the Crescent, its splendor obscur'd
> By the light of the star-bangled flag of our nation,
>   Where each flaming star gleam'd a meteor of war,
>   And the turban'd head bowed to the terrible glare.
> Then mixt with the olive the laurel shall wave,
> And form a bright wreath for the brow of the brave.

Jefferson's war against the Barbary pirates was, at the time and for a while, a massive success for the young Republic. The Jeffersonians compared the conflict to the Revolution, with its heroes ranked beside those that won American independence. While the revolutionaries bested the British and established their liberty, this generation stood up to and defeated the tyrants of Barbary who had plagued Christendom for centuries. America's victory in Tripoli, further, was a testament to American ability, might, ingenuity, and enterprise. Jefferson won peace through strength, and the young nation still managed to escape the entanglements of the Old World. Jefferson's war carried the promise, it seemed, of beginning another noble chapter of American history, one that demonstrated that America would be a force to be reckoned with around the globe. The war in Tripoli can even claim the first U.S. war memorial.

Unlike some of America's later military conflicts, however, Jefferson's war with Tripoli never really escaped its own politics in terms of the national collective memory. The war and its victory did not remain long in the national consciousness. Although its memory is forever enshrined in the Marine Corps hymn— "From the Halls of Montezuma/To the Shores of Tripoli"—its history is little more than trivia, relegated to one or two lines in presidential biographies. The grand Tripoli Monument, transferred in 1860 from the Capitol grounds in Washington to the Naval Academy in Annapolis, today stands forgotten and ignored by the general public.

Early in the war, Jefferson's party, the Democratic-Republicans, embraced every success as a testament to their president's leadership and vision. When Stephen Decatur performed "the most bold and daring act of the age" with his nighttime assault on, and destruction of, the USS *Philadelphia* in the harbor of Tripoli right under the nose of the enemy, he became their poster boy for the defense of liberty. By claiming Decatur as their champion, the Democratic-Republicans were able to embrace the navy, politically stealing it from the Federalists. Under the previous Federalist administration, Jefferson's party had vilified the navy and pushed at every opportunity to retard its development. Yet now they were the Navy Department's firmest friends.

When, however, victory was finally declared over a year *after* Decatur's famous mission, it became clear to the president's opponents that the Democratic-Republicans had milked the achievement dry. Many acts of heroism took place in the intervening year between Decatur's success and the war's end, and the Federalists were able to find their own hero to rally behind—William Eaton.

The desert march to the shores of Tripoli, the capture of Derna, and the planting of the American flag on the enemy's ramparts captured the American imagination. Even better,

Eaton's mission—unlike Decatur's—actually did help end the war rather directly. The Federalists were eager to raise "General" Eaton up as their champion—and beat Thomas Jefferson and Tobias Lear over the head with him in the process.

William Eaton returned to the United States in November 1805, a conquering hero. Edward Preble captured the national mood exactly when he wrote to Eaton, "The arduous and dangerous services you have performed have justly immortalized your name, and astonished not only your country but the world. If pecuniary sources and naval strength had been at your command, what could you not have done?" Eaton went to Richmond, Virginia, and then to Washington, D.C., and was overwhelmed by his reception in both cities.

The media buzz lasted for several weeks, and Eaton enjoyed every moment of it. Various embellished accounts of the "great American victory at Derna" circulated, as did flattering biographical sketches and editorials of exaltation. On November 16, a testimonial dinner was held in his honor at the Eagle Tavern in Richmond, Virginia, attended by various notables, including John Marshall, United States Supreme Court chief justice. In Washington, Eaton was pleased to encounter Federalist members of both the House and Senate showering him with adulation and praise, and local newspapers announced his triumphant return.

Eaton's sudden hero status left President Jefferson and the Democratic-Republicans in an unusual position. The administration was eager to enjoy its "victory" over Tripoli, but if it acknowledged that the president had backed Eaton's scheme, the peace treaty might look like a betrayal of principle and the abandonment of an ally. But to ignore or even attack Eaton might also fuel the Federalists and tarnish the peace with Tripoli. The president resolved, it seems, to try to have it both ways, congratulating him at the beginning and then discrediting him when he proved openly troublesome.

The administration honored Eaton in private and in public: a private dinner with Jefferson, and then, on November 28, a public banquet attended by public officials, members of Congress, and other important personages. On December 3, 1805, Jefferson even praised Eaton to Congress by referencing "the successful enterprise on the city of Derna" that had been "gallantly conducted by our late Consul Eaton." Jefferson even allowed that Eaton's efforts "contributed doubtless to the impression which produced peace."

Within a few days, however, the good cheer started to ebb as the peace treaty began to circulate. To the Federalists and others, the $60,000 payment to Pasha Yusuf Qaramanli and the abandonment of Ahmad tarnished Jefferson's glorious peace. The Federalists saw their opening and pounced. By the time the treaty was officially submitted to the Senate for ratification on December 11, 1805, it was already a political football.

William Eaton became a willing foil in the efforts to embarrass the administration and correct the wrongs perpetrated against the national honor—and he thereby became an avowed enemy of the Jefferson administration. He was eager, as well, to adjust his financial accounts with the U.S. government and to persuade Congress to give financial relief to Ahmad Qaramanli, who had been left destitute by American betrayal. The Democratic-Republicans, of course, repaid this activity in kind, and every aspect of the Tripolitan business quickly became a four-month-long partisan slugfest, replete with derisive name-calling, character assassination, and bitter accusations of misconduct and deceit.

Determined to establish that Tobias Lear had disgraced the nation, the Federalists in the Senate held a formal investigation into Lear's conduct and the administration's backing of Eaton's scheme, while the House of Representatives was making formal inquiries into the precise nature of the alliance between the United States and Ahmad Qaramanli in its consideration of

Ahmad's application for relief funds. Jefferson was forced to provide all the relevant correspondence, reports, and dispatches, and had to subject himself to congressional scrutiny. Various people were brought forward to give evidence that Pasha Yusuf Qaramanli was nearly beaten and broke; that Eaton's forces would have had no great difficulty in taking Tripoli; that the American prisoners were not in any grave or immediate danger should Eaton's forces advance on Tripoli; that Commodore Barron, while ill, was under the undue influence of Tobias Lear; that Lear was violently opposed to Eaton's scheme; and that Lear had made a secret arrangement with Pasha Yusuf regarding the return of Ahmad's family that was in direct violation of article three of the treaty.

Finally on March 17, 1806, the committee published its report. In every respect, the report backed Eaton's own account of what transpired. Commodore Barron was absolved of any wrongdoing owing to his illness, and the committee recommended that some remuneration be established for Ahmad Qaramanli. The report made a special point of attacking Tobias Lear: "the committee are compelled by the obligations of truth and duty, to state further, that Mr. Lear . . . appears to have gained a complete ascendancy over the commodore . . . dictated every measure . . . paralyzed every military operation by sea and land, and finally . . . entered into a convention with the reigning Bashaw [Yusuf] . . . by which . . . he stipulated to pay him sixty thousand dollars, to abandon the ex-Bashaw [Ahmad], and to withdraw all aid and assistance from his army." The committee also accused Lear of selling out Ahmad's family, and made clear its collective view that Eaton and Ahmad's mission would have been a complete success with minimal aid and support and financial expenditure from the United States, and would thereby have "established a peace with the Barbary powers, that would have been secure and permanent, and which would have dignified the name and character of the American people." William Eaton was ecstatic.

The next day Senator Stephen R. Bradley of Vermont—one of Eaton's allies, although he was part of Jefferson's party—

introduced a resolution to express congressional gratitude to Eaton and his marines and suggested that Congress name some small parcel of public land "Derna," the acreage of which was to be doled out to them. There was also consideration of granting Eaton a resolution of "thanks," a ceremonial sword, and even a highly coveted gold medal. There was much acrimonious discussion, but nothing was ever approved. Lengthy and bitter debate continued following the March 21 introduction of a bill for Ahmad Qaramanli's relief.

In the end, the Senate ratified the peace treaty with Tripoli on April 12, 1806, by a vote of 21 to 8. The Federalists did not manage to derail the treaty, but they did embarrass and, at junctures, discredit President Thomas Jefferson and forever tarnish the career of Tobias Lear. (Thomas Jefferson and James Madison saw to it that Lear continued in government employ until his death; he committed suicide in 1816.)

Eventually, Congress voted, in 1806, to salve its conscience and pay Qaramanli $2,400 for his troubles, and then gave him a pension of $200 a month for life, while some of Eaton's own financial claims for reimbursement were finally, and grudgingly, admitted in 1807, and he was paid $12,636.60.

Ahmad Qaramanli and William Eaton remained friendly for some time after their evacuation from Derna, and they maintained a periodic correspondence for a time. Congress finally compelled Jefferson to make Pasha Yusuf release Ahmad's wife, his three sons, and his unmarried daughter in October 1807; the family joined Ahmad in exile. They remained exiled in Syracuse, Sicily, living among the Americans stationed there, until Pasha Yusuf once again offered to appoint his brother to serve as bey of Derna in 1809. Two years later, Ahmad once again fled to Egypt to save himself from his brother's treachery, and he remained there in relative poverty until his death.

William Eaton, meanwhile, had been greatly disillusioned. The Commonwealth of Massachusetts awarded him 10,000 acres in the District of Maine (then part of the Massachusetts Commonwealth) in March 1806, and he was popularly elected to the state legislature in May 1807. Had Eaton ended his involvement with Washington politics there, he likely would have ended his days as a popular local celebrity.

He returned to Washington, however, to try again to close his accounts with Congress. While there he became embroiled in the affairs of Aaron Burr, former vice president to Thomas Jefferson. Back in the winter of 1805–6, Burr had cultivated a friendship with Eaton and now tried to involve him in his schemes to divide the Louisiana Territory from the Union. Eaton rejected Burr and went straight to Jefferson with his accusations, eventually giving a deposition. In January 1807 a grand jury decided there was no case against him. More evidence surfaced, however, and Burr was made to stand trial for treason in May 1807.

Although William Eaton was expected to begin his stint in the Massachusetts state legislature, he spent the entire session in Richmond, Virginia, as a star witness for the prosecution. The defense labored hard to discredit his testimony. He returned bitter and angry to his home at Brimfield, Massachusetts, and immediately alienated the local Federalists in the next session of the state legislature with his vicious and injudicious comments against the presiding judge—Chief Justice John Marshall, a Federalist icon. Eaton was not nominated for a second term.

William Eaton, his public life in shambles, retreated to the safety of an alcoholic stupor. After spending much of his wife's fortune on booze, he was forced to sell most of his holdings in Maine. His drinking increased, and he began to suffer from gout and rheumatism. "Fortune has reversed her tables—I am no more Eaton," he wrote to one of his closest friends on June 15, 1810. "I live, or rather stay in obscurity and uselessness." He continued, "The wound I received on the coast of Tripoli, and others more early, have deprived me of an arm's use and the use of a leg— Want of economy, which I never learned, want of judgment in the speculative concerns of private life, which I never studied, and, what is more, privation of the consideration of a government which I have served, have unmanned me."

The forty-seven-year-old William Eaton died a year later, on June 1, 1811, at his home in Brimfield. His death received little public notice.

Although the American "victory" proved problematic and the "peace" too political, the war ended rather well for the other participant.

Pasha Yusuf Qaramanli was greatly pleased with the outcome of the war. Although it had proved costly in the short term, it was an unqualified Tripolitan success in the long term.

America sought to break Yusuf, to chastise him, and even to overthrow him, yet they retreated at the first opportunity, delivering peace terms he was willing to accept. The United States sent several squadrons to the region to attack Tripoli, yet it was Yusuf who captured an American frigate—the single most valuable naval capture in the whole of Barbary history—and enslaved her entire crew without a single defensive shot being fired. Despite years of blockade, his cruisers managed to routinely get his ships in and out of the harbor. When a peace treaty was finally negotiated, the United States paid Yusuf $60,000 for his troubles— a small sum but rich with symbolism. Further, the new peace treaty made no reference to Algiers backing its fulfillment. Regionally, Yusuf Qaramanli became a symbol of Islamic fortitude. He proved that the regency of Tripoli was independent of the other Barbary powers, and he proved that Tripoli's pirate navy was a force to be reckoned with. In relative terms, Tripoli prospered. Yusuf Qaramanli continued to rule until 1834.

To this day, the history of this American war with Tripoli stands, in the region, as a testament to the leadership and rule of Pasha Yusuf Qaramanli.

13

The Lessons of War

ALMOST FROM THE moment of independence, the United States of America was compelled to grapple with the pirates of the Barbary States. The effort proved both challenging and exhausting, and in many ways it forced the young nation to mature, progress, and advance in directions the revolutionary founders had not entirely imagined or foreseen.

From 1776 to 1784 the Americans attempted to engage the protection of the European nations from the threat of Barbary piracy. These efforts failed. By 1785, America recognized the necessity of following the European path of opening diplomatic relations with North Africa. Before long the continued piracy against American shipping and enslavement of American citizens had taken its toll, and the United States grew determined to fight the pirates just as soon as it had the means to do so, but, as the means were not yet available, it resolved to continue to follow the European example of paying bribes and tribute. This confused desire to both fight and appease resulted in the birth of the United States Navy, but with the understanding that peace would trump naval buildup.

By 1801, however, America realized that without a strong projection of force abroad, its maritime interests would never be secure. The war with Tripoli was an opportunity for the United States to chastise the pirates and demonstrate that it could project its might even in a transoceanic conflict four thousand miles from home. Following the cessation of the Tripolitan war, however, the United States continued to pay tribute to Algiers and Tunis, and Pasha Yusuf Qaramanli continued to rule in Tripoli. Barbary piracy continued unabated.

In the course of America's fight against the Barbary terror, the nation tried appeasement, diplomacy, the threat of force, and war. Although the United States settled for peace in 1805, it seemed clear that war, or at least the judicious and credible threat of force, was far more eloquent a method of persuasion with Barbary than money or goodwill. For many years William Eaton argued that the only way to end Barbary piracy against America was to destroy it and teach the world that the United States would never give in to terror or sacrifice its principles and honor in the name of expediency.

Although Eaton did not live to see it, his argument was to prove wholly valid.

Despite America's claim to have vanquished its foe and restored national honor, the other Barbary regencies continued periodically to cause trouble. When Tunis made problems and threatened hostilities, Commodore John Rodgers sent an overwhelming force—the *Constitution*, the *Constellation*, the *Essex*, the *John Adams*, the *Siren*, the *Nautilus*, the *Enterprize*, the *Hornet*, and some gunboats that had been recently obtained in the Adriatic—to Tunis under a flag of truce. With this naval squadron standing in the harbor of Tunis in a line that, according to one witness, "stretched athwart the harbor from one end to the other," on August 1, 1805, Commodore Rodgers sent the bey a note asking whether he wanted war or peace—it was clear which the commodore preferred.

The bey quickly agreed to negotiate, and the matter was eventually settled with "presents" back in the United States following a lengthy visit and negotiation with the bey's ambassador, a Turk named Sidi Souleïman Mellimelli. Rather than congratulate Rodgers, however, Jefferson was displeased with the show of force to threaten Tunis. As he wrote apologetically to Bey Hammuda Pasha on June 28, 1806, "I learned with great concern that the Commander of our Squadron . . . had done this in a manner not consistent with the respect due to your Excellency's character, nor with the friendship which I bear you . . . of this he will be made duly sensible on his return home."

The Mediterranean squadron remained in place for a little while. Commodore Rodgers stayed near Syracuse during the fall and into the winter until, on November 28, 1805, he received notice from the secretary of the navy, dated August 5, suggesting that he begin sending back the American squadron as soon as some of the ships could be spared from active patrolling. As long as the United States appeared to be at peace with the Barbary powers, President Thomas Jefferson and Secretary of the Treasury Albert Gallatin hoped to reduce expenditures.

Commodore Rodgers balked. He thought the decision improvident, and he fully anticipated belligerence to break out at a moment's notice. He believed the presence of his squadron essential to the security and promotion of American interests in the region, and he intended to delay the breakup of his Mediterranean force as long as possible. Unfortunately, Jeffersonian parsimony won out, and on October 12 Rodgers was sent direct and clear orders to reduce the size of the squadron in the Mediterranean "without any unnecessary delay" by sending home the *Constellation*, the *Congress*, the *Essex*, and the *John Adams*, as well as three of the five smaller ships. The commodore received this dispatch on January 25, 1806, and promptly responded that the secretary was not as well informed of the situation as he was, and so he again refused to comply with the recall.

Although John Rodgers had bought himself some time, he had also pushed his luck; even though he had found technical reasons to assert his authority, the technicalities could not be extended indefinitely, and there was other business back home for which he was needed. Finally, on March 22, 1806, Secretary Smith ordered Rodgers home directly. On May 27, 1806, Rodgers conferred command of the *Constitution* and of the U.S. squadron to Hugh G. Campbell. He returned home aboard the *Essex*.

Soon after John Rodgers left, the squadron was reduced per the wishes of the secretary of the navy. By spring 1806, only the

Constitution, the *Enterprize*, and the *Hornet* remained in the Mediterranean. Although the U.S. government had intended to keep this force on more or less permanent station in the region, they too were soon recalled following the deteriorating relationship between Great Britain and the United States. Indeed, virtually every ship in the navy was kept at home for much of this period, excepting brief and infrequent European cruises.

President Jefferson signed the Embargo Act on December 22, 1807, bringing virtually all American foreign trade to a screeching halt and also having a crippling effect on American domestic economic activity. The increasing aggression with Great Britain did not abate, and so after James Madison became president, handily winning the 1808 election, the act was replaced on March 1809 by the Nonintercourse Act, which opened up trade with the rest of the world, but forbade it with Great Britain or France. Neither act, nor any of the measures that followed them, had much effect. Slowly, the nation geared up for war against England. Consequently, from 1807 through 1815, the United States essentially ignored the Barbary States, and all of its interests in the region remained undefended.

Despite Jefferson's glorious 1805 victory in Tripoli, the Barbary States were not permanently humbled out of the piracy game. Having failed to heed the lessons of the past, the United States neglected to arm for peace. As William Eaton had warned, "How often is the maxim repeated in America, 'to preserve peace, be prepared for war'? But how should this preparation be productive of its object, if the world are ignorant of it? If this precaution be necessary to preserve peace among civilized nations, how much more so among savages who have no restraint but fear? Having never seen the quiver they have no desire for the olive branch." Thus, America was caught unawares when Barbary affairs became difficult following the retreat of the U.S. Mediterranean squadron.

Although Tripoli had been pacified recently enough, and Tunis remained more or less in line, Algiers was itching for a fight and could not resist American merchant vessels now that their protection had disappeared.

Algiers decided—based on the regional understanding of America's performance against Tripoli and the recent evacuation of American forces from the Mediterranean—that American shipping was vulnerable and that the Americans had no stomach for war. Once again, America looked ripe for the picking. So Algiers let loose its cruisers, attacking three ships, and seizing two of them and enslaving their crews (the third ship escaped after the American sailors attacked the Algerine prize crew that was to sail the vessel to Algiers). The appeasement process continued again, and the reversal of America's position in the region was more or less reestablished.

Nevertheless, Algiers remained peaceful enough toward the United States, in large part because the stipulated naval and military stores arrived very promptly for several years. Also, when in July 1809 Algiers once again requested the use of a United States ship to convoy an Algerine ambassador to Istanbul, both Lear and the captain of the American ship complied immediately.

"If the United States persists in resignation and passive obedience," William Eaton had warned, "they will find that *Qui se fait brebis le loup le mange*. He who makes himself a sheep must expect to be devoured by the wolf."

Sure enough, the favorable disposition Algiers exhibited toward the United States changed in July 1812.

The dey had grown annoyed because some of the American naval and military stores had been arriving behind schedule. With further promptings from the prince regent of Great Britain, the dey sent his cruisers out looking for American ships and, after accepting additional bribes from Tobias Lear, expelled him from the regency. On July 25, 1812, Lear left with his wife, his son, and three other American nationals. American affairs were left in the hands of the Swedish consul, John Norderling.

Algiers was unable to find very many American ships in the Mediterranean. War had already broken out between the United States and Great Britain, and the British had already seized some of those ships foolish enough to do business in unprotected waters. But Algiers did manage to snag one prize. On August 25, 1812, the brigantine *Edwin* of Salem was taken en route from Malta to Gibraltar. Captain George C. Smith and his ten-man crew were taken prisoner and enslaved in Algiers. Later a Spanish ship was also taken, and one American, a Mr. Pollard, was found aboard; he was immediately taken to Algiers and thrown in prison with Captain Smith.

In 1813 a new U.S. consul was appointed to Tunis, Mordecai Manuel Noah, and he was instructed to try to arrange for the release of the twelve American prisoners in Algiers. He was only partially successful, however, as his agent obtained the release of two Americans after having spent $4,000 in the process. Ten Americans were left behind in the prisons of Algiers.

As the American war with Great Britain finally came to a close, and the Treaty of Ghent, signed in that Flemish city on Christmas Eve, finally made its way to the United States for ratification in February 1815, President James Madison was finally able to tend to other pressing business abroad. Less than a week after peace was declared, Madison approached Congress regarding the new Barbary problem. On February 23, 1815, he sent a closed session message to a joint session of Congress:

> Congress will have seen, by the communication from the Consul General of the United States, at Algiers, . . . the hostile proceedings of the Dey against that functionary. These have been followed by acts of more overt and direct warfare against the citizens of the United States trading in the Mediterranean, some of whom are still detained in captivity, notwithstanding the attempts which have been made to ransom them, and are treated with the rigor usual on the coast of Barbary. . . .
>
> The considerations which rendered it unnecessary and unimportant to commence hostile operations on the part of the United States, being now terminated by the peace with Great Britain, which opens the

prospect of an active and valuable trade of their citizens within the range of the Algerine cruisers; I recommend to Congress the expediency of an act declaring the existence of a state of war between the United States and the Dey and Regency of Algiers; and of such provisions as may be requisite for a vigorous prosecution of it to a successful issue.

A week later, on March 2, 1815, Congress responded by declaring war on Algiers, granting the president the authority to take whatever measures he deemed necessary. President Madison had been waiting for this opportunity and was pleased to have enough vessels at his disposal to handle this matter properly. Unlike Thomas Jefferson, Madison was eager to pursue the war against the Barbary terror with real gusto.

"Our language to them," William Eaton had once written, "should be the language of the gospel: 'I have this day set before you life and death, choose you which you will.' Without a language like this, and an attitude to support it," he had warned his countrymen, "to think of reciprocity is idle, since here are no commercial interests to induce it."

President Madison formed two squadrons, one under the command of Commodore William Bainbridge and the other under the command of Commodore Stephen Decatur. Bainbridge's squadron was fitted out at Boston, Decatur's at New York. Secretary of State James Monroe instructed Bainbridge, Decatur, and William Shaler, the new consul general for the Barbary States, to try to obtain peace as soon as possible, to free the American prisoners, but to pay no tribute, and to promise no "presents."

Commodore Decatur's squadron put out to sea first on May 20. Decatur's fleet consisted of his flagship, the brand-new frigate *Guerriere* (forty-four guns), accompanied by two frigates, the *Constellation* (thirty-six guns) and the *Macedonian* (thirty-eight guns). She also sailed in company with two sloops-of-war, the *Epervier* (eighteen guns) and the *Ontario* (sixteen guns); three brigantines, the *Firefly*, the *Spark*, and the *Flambeau* (each of fourteen guns); and two schooners, the *Torch* and the *Spitfire* (both of twelve guns). A few days after sailing, however, the squadron hit bad weather and the *Firefly* had to return for repairs.

They cleared the Straits of Gibraltar on June 15, 1815. En route, Decatur was informed that Algerine cruisers had recently returned from an Atlantic cruise and were likely to be just ahead of them. The commodore went in hot pursuit, and on June 17 he spotted the Algerine flagship, the *Meshuda* (forty-six guns), commanded by Ra'is Hammida, off Cape Gata and gave chase. Ra'is Hammida frantically beat a course for Algiers, but Decatur had superior might at his disposal and quickly mobbed the enemy.

The USS *Constellation* opened fire at long range, lightly wounding Ra'is Hammida with the first shot. *Meshuda* replied and then tried heading for the Spanish coast and the refuge of a neutral port. The *Guerriere* was now able to draw close, and the *Ontario* was able to cross her bow. At such close range, Ra'is Hammida had his men open musket fire on the American frigate, wounding some of her crew. Decatur was too busy trying to get alongside the *Meshuda* to reply with musketry.

Finally, the *Guerriere* was alongside the *Meshuda*. Decatur poured a demoralizing and destructive broadside into her, making a mess of her deck. As Ra'is Hammida had been wounded by the *Constellation* and was unable to stand, he was sitting on the ship's deck feeding orders to the crew, trying desperately to run the battle. A forty-two-pound shot from Decatur's broadside met with the Algerine admiral and ripped him in twain. A second broadside sent most of the crew running belowdecks. Only a handful of musketeers kept up the fight.

Decatur held his fire and drew ahead. The *Meshuda* had not struck her colors. The *Epervier* came up on the enemy's starboard and unleashed nine broadsides into her. The Algerine musketeers tried valiantly to return some fire, but musket balls were no match against cannonballs. The *Meshuda* brought down her flag and surrendered.

Commodore Decatur tallied up the day's effort. Four hundred and six Algerine prisoners were taken, many of whom were wounded; the *Meshuda* suffered thirty deaths. The *Guerriere* had four men killed and ten wounded—one man was killed and three wounded by enemy fire, while three had been killed and seven wounded by the explosion of a gun. *Macedonian* took the *Meshuda* under convoy to Cartagena, Spain, as a war prize.

Decatur was continuing on toward Algiers when, on June 19, an Algerine brigantine, the *Estedio* (twenty-two guns), was spotted off of Cape Palos. The squadron gave chase and once again overpowered the enemy. The *Estedio* surrendered after feeling the accuracy of American firepower: twenty-three bodies were strewn about the deck; eighty men were taken prisoner.

Commodore Decatur reached Algiers. He and William Shaler, the new peace negotiator, quickly forced Algiers to terms. The treaty was unprecedented in Barbary. Some of its highlights were: the provision for the abolition of all tribute, the release of all American prisoners, the payment of $10,000 to the United States as indemnity for the seizure of the *Edwin*, immediate restoration of all other American property currently in the dey's possession, and the stipulation that any future captives, in the event of open hostilities, would be treated as prisoners of war and not as slaves. Commodore Decatur and Consul General Shaler made practically no concessions and stood very firm on every point. Within three hours the Algerine minister and the Swedish consul returned with the prisoners and a signed treaty.

A few months later, on July 5, 1815, Commodore Stephen Decatur wrote to Secretary of the Navy Benjamin W. Crowninshield to inform him of the treaty: "It has been dictated at the mouths of our cannon, has been conceded to the losses which Algiers has sustained and to the dread of still greater evils apprehended. And I beg leave to express to you my opinion that the presence of a respectable naval force in this sea will be the only certain guarantee for its observance."

The treaty that Decatur and Shaler had obtained was by far the most liberal that any non-Muslim nation had ever extracted from any Barbary nation. It had been less than six weeks since Decatur's squadron had put out to sea from New York. The peace treaty was ratified on December 21, 1815, and signed by President Madison on December 26.

Commodore Decatur left Algiers on July 8 and sailed on to Tunis and Tripoli to settle matters there. Early in 1815, before the cessation of hostilities between Great Britain and the United States, both the bey of Tunis and the pasha of Tripoli had allowed the British to retake American prizes that had been lawfully captured and then brought into their respective ports. In both cases, this action was strictly against the treaty stipulations between their respective regencies and the United States. As a technical matter, Commodore Stephen Decatur had not been authorized to negotiate with either regency about these matters, and his decision to do so was entirely without previous sanction of the United States government.

The *Guerriere* anchored off Tunis on July 28, and Consul Noah came aboard to consult. Immediately, Commodore Decatur decided to communicate his demands to Bey Mahmud—Bey Hammuda had died of natural causes in 1814, and was succeeded by his brother 'Uthman, who in turn was assassinated on December 21, 1814, by his cousin Mahmud. Decatur demanded $46,000, which was deemed the value of the two American prizes that had been lost. Although Bey Mahmud initially refused, he quickly changed his mind and turned the money over to Consul Noah. Commodore Decatur's squadron then sailed for Tripoli on August 2, arriving at Tripoli on August 5. Here Stephen Decatur demanded $30,000 as indemnity for the loss of the American prizes. Pasha Yusuf Qaramanli had been tempted to refuse and declare war, but then word reached him of what had transpired in Tunis and Algiers. He yielded to the American demands, and the money was delivered to the American consul. The squadron sailed for Syracuse on August 9, 1815.

"I trust," a self-satisfied Commodore Stephen Decatur wrote home, "that the successful result of our small expedition, so honorable to our country, will induce other nations to follow the example; in which case the Barbary states will be compelled to abandon their piratical system."

Before Commodore Decatur sailed home, the *Guerriere* found herself alone en route from Cartagena to Malaga, Spain;

the rest of the squadron had sailed ahead to rendezvous with Bainbridge. Suddenly, she ran across seven Algerine warships standing to the northward, but heading in her direction. These approached the *Guerriere* in a line of battle, with the new flagship in the rear. Decatur thought it possible the Algerines had decided to break their new treaty. He ordered the beat to quarters and prepared his ship for action. He was heavily outnumbered and outgunned and could be easily overpowered.

The Algerine ships passed silently to leeward of the American frigate. Once the Algerine flagship was alongside the *Guerriere*, the Algerine captain hailed the American vessel from the gangway with a speaking trumpet. Breaking with protocol, the captain did not first identify his ship before demanding in the local Italian-based patois:

"Dove andante?" (Where are you bound?)

Decatur grabbed the speaking trumpet from the deck officer and shouted back:

"Dove me piace!" (Where I please!)

The *Guerriere* sailed on to Malaga without any further annoyance.

The United States of America had finally and decidedly ended all future trouble for American interests from the pirates of the Barbary States. Since her declaration of independence from Great Britain and the politics and practices of the Old World, she had been plunged by her Mediterranean commerce into a complicated and ignoble theater of religious hatred, geopolitical machinations, predatory mercantilist conspiracies, diplomatic extortion rackets, and piracy.

Barbary piracy was very much an Old World game, and one played for religious, political, and commercial gain. Yet even though the rules and the participants had long since established what passed for acceptable modes of conduct, the United States struggled to fight the Barbary terror and establish an independent path.

During the war with Tripoli, the United States began to test William Eaton's hypothesis that fighting back and protecting the national honor and the national interest with force was the best way to end Barbary piracy. Just at the moment of triumph, however, President Thomas Jefferson wavered and settled on the side of expediency. Jefferson's lack of resolve left American interests unguarded, and once again American maritime trade felt the Barbary terror. By 1816, however, the United States finally proved that William Eaton was right. This success ignited the imagination of the Old World powers to rise up against the Barbary pirates.

In late August 1816, a combined British and Dutch fleet under the command of Lord Exmouth (formerly Sir Edward Pellew) followed the example of Commodore Stephen Decatur, forcing a peace at the mouth of a cannon. This armada unleashed hell upon Algiers, destroying most of the coastal side of the city, as well as most of its navy and marina. The dey accepted all of Lord Exmouth's demands. More than eleven hundred Christian captives were released from slavery, and the dey agreed to abolish Christian slavery in Algiers forever.

Barbary piracy did not actually end there, but the American success gave the nations of Europe an example to follow. The matter was forevermore settled when the French sent an invasion force on May 26, 1830; by July 5, the city and palace had fallen to the occupation forces; a week later the dey fled to Naples. The terror of Barbary was finally laid to rest.

Bibliography

As this book was written for a general audience rather than for academics, specialists, or naval and military scholars, I have refrained from using footnotes or otherwise littering the text with source citations and references. Academics and scholars, or those who are interested in further study of this subject, may want to know something of my sources.

There were ten specific interpretive works that were so central to my understanding of these events and of the period in which they took place that I wish to single them out for special attribution. These are (in alphabetical order): Gardner W. Allen's *Our Navy and the Barbary Corsairs*, Robert J. Allison's *The Crescent Obscured: The United States and the Muslim World, 1776–1815*, Seton Dearden's *A Nest of Corsairs: The Fighting Karamanlis of the Barbary Coast*, Sir Godfrey Fisher's *Barbary Legend: War, Trade, and Piracy in North Africa, 1415–1830*, Kola Folayan's *Tripoli During the Reign of Yusuf Pasha Qaramanli*, Ray W. Irwin's *The Diplomatic Relations of the United States with the Barbary Powers, 1776–1816*, Christopher McKee's *Edward Preble, a Naval Biography 1761–1807*, Charles Prentiss's *The Life of the late Gen. William Eaton*, Lord Francis Rennell Rodd's *General William Eaton: The Failure of an Idea*, and Louis B. Wright and Julia H. McLeod's *The First Americans in North Africa: William Eaton's Struggle for a Vigorous Policy Against the Barbary Pirates: 1799–1805*. Each of these works was, in one form or another, crucial to my understanding of the story and helped guide my thinking through the various primary sources and archival material. Indeed, these books have informed virtually every page of my book.

A more complete listing of the archives, manuscripts, articles, and books I have consulted and found helpful in the research of this book includes:

Archives and Documentary Sources

American State Papers: Foreign Relations, volumes 1 and 2 (Washington: Gales and Seaton, 1832).

A Century of Lawmaking for a New Nation: U.S. Congressional Documents and Debates 1774–1873. This is a digital text database and searchable online collection from the various published congressional records housed in and maintained by the Library of Congress (http://memory.loc.gov/ammem/amlaw/lawhome.html).

A Compilation of the Messages and Papers of the Presidents, 1798–1902, edited by James D. Richardson, in ten volumes (Washington: Bureau of National Literature and Art, 1904).

Continental Congress & Constitutional Convention Broadsides Collection. This is a digital online collection from the Rare Book and Special Collections Division of the Library of Congress (http://lcweb2.loc.gov/ammem/bdsds/bdsdhome. html).

The Emerging Nation: A Documentary History of the Foreign Relations of the United States Under the Articles of Confederation, 1780–1789, edited by Mary A. Giunta (Washington: National Historical Publications and Records Commission, 1996).

Journals of the Continental Congress, 1774–1789, in 34 volumes (Washington, D.C.: U.S. Government Printing Office, 1904–1937).

Les Archives nationales de Tunisie (http://www.archives.nat.tn/) houses correspondence and papers relating to the consuls, commerce, and diplomatic relations with foreign nations (including the United States).

Naval Documents Related to the United States Wars with the Barbary Powers, in six volumes, compiled by the U.S. Navy's Office of Naval Records and Library (Washington, D.C.: U.S. Government Printing Office, 1939–1944).

The Revolutionary Diplomatic Correspondence of the United States, 1776–1783, edited by Francis Wharton (Washington, D.C.: U.S. Government Printing Office, 1889).

Treaties and Other International Acts of the United States of America 1776–1818, edited by Hunter Miller, in two volumes (Washington, D.C.: U.S. Government Printing Office, 1931).

Treaties with the Barbary Powers: 1786–1836, from "The Avalon Project: Documents in Law, History, and Diplomacy," Yale Law School (http://www.yale.edu/lawweb/avalon/diplomacy/barbary/barmenu.htm).

U.S. National Archives at College Park (http://www. archives.gov/) houses the Department of State records and consular dispatches from U.S. agents in Tangier, Algiers, Tunis, and Tripoli.

Manuscripts and Private Papers

The Adams-Jefferson Letters: The Complete Correspondence Between Thomas Jefferson and Abigail and John Adams, edited by Lester J. Cappon. Chapel Hill: University of North Carolina Press, 1988.

Correspondence and Documents Relative to the Attempt to Negotiate for the Release of American Captives at Algiers. Compiled by Mordecai Noah. Washington, 1816; Early American Imprints. Second series. No. 38474 (microform).

The Diplomatic Journal and Letter Book of James Leander Cathcart, 1788–1796. Proceedings of the American Antiquarian Society, October 1954.

The George Washington Papers, 1741–1799. Manuscript Division, Library of Congress (available in its entirety online as a digital, searchable text resource: http://memory.loc.gov/ammem/gwhtml/gwhome.html).

The Hull-Eaton Correspondence During the Expedition Against Tripoli, 1804–1805, edited by Charles Henry Lincoln. Worcester, Mass: American Antiquarian Society, 1911.

The James Barron Papers, Manuscripts Collection, Special Collections Division, Earl Gregg Swem Library, College of William and Mary.

The James Leander Cathcart Papers. Manuscript Division, Library of Congress.

The James Leander Cathcart Papers (1785–1806). Manuscript Division, Special Collections, the New York Public Library.

A Journal of the Captivity and Sufferings of John Foss, excerpted at length in Paul Baepler, ed., *White Slaves, African Masters: An*

Anthology of American Barbary Captivity Narratives. Chicago: University of Chicago Press, 1999.

Letterbook of James Simpson, 1793–1797. Miscellaneous Manuscripts collection, Manuscript Division, Library of Congress.

Letters of the Members of the Continental Congress, eight volumes, edited by Edmund C. Burnett. Gloucester, Mass.: P. Smith, 1963.

The Papers of Edward Preble. Manuscript Division, Library of Congress.

The Papers of Richard Dale. Manuscript Division, Library of Congress.

The Papers of Tobias Lear, 1790–1815. Manuscript Division, Library of Congress.

The Republic of Letters: The Correspondence between Thomas Jefferson and James Madison, 1776–1826, three volumes, edited by James Morton Smith. New York: Norton, 1995.

The Samuel Barron Papers, Manuscripts Collection, Special Collections Division, Earl Gregg Swem Library, College of William and Mary.

Sufferings in Africa: Captain [James] Riley's Narrative. An Authentic Narrative of the Loss of the American Brig Commerce, Wrecked on the Western Coast of Africa, in the Month of August, 1815, with an Account of the Sufferings of her Surviving Officers and Crew who were Enslaved by the Wandering Arabs on the Great African Desert, or Zahahrah. New York: Clarkson N. Potter, Inc., 1965 (1817).

The Thomas Jefferson Papers. Manuscript Division, Library of Congress (available in its entirety online as a digital, searchable text resource: http://memory.loc.gov/ammem/mtjhtml/mtjhome. html).

The William Eaton Papers. Manuscript Department, the Hunting Library.

Articles and Periodicals

Baker, Kevin. "The Shores of Tripoli." *The American Heritage* (Feb./Mar. 2002): 17–18.

Bartlett, Harley H. "American Captivities in Barbary." *Michigan Alumnus Quarterly Review* 61 (Spring 1955): 238–54.

Blum, Hester. "Pirated Tars, Piratical Texts: Barbary Captivity and American Sea Narratives." *Early American Studies* 1 (Fall 2003): 133–58.

Brown Wells, Sherrill. "Long-Time Friends: Early U.S.-Moroccan Relations, 1777–87." *Department of State Bulletin* 87, no. 2126 (September 1987).

Cantor, Milton. "A Connecticut Yankee in a Barbary Court: Joel Barlow's Algerian Letters to His Wife." *William and Mary Quarterly* 3rd ser., vol. 19, no. 1 (January 1962): 86–109.

Caplan, Dennis. "John Adams, Thomas Jefferson, and the Barbary Pirates: An Illustration of Relevant Costs for Decision Making." *Issues in Accounting Education* 18, no. 3 (2003): 265–74.

Carr, James A. "John Adams and the Barbary Problem: The Myth and the Record." *American Neptune* 26 (October 1966): 231–57.

Fishbein, Rand H. "Echoes from the Barbary Coast: History of U.S. Military Actions against Pirates." *The National Interest* 66 (Winter 2001/2002): 47–51.

Folayan, Kola. "Tripoli and the War with the U.S.A., 1801–5." *Journal of African History* 13, no. 2 (1972): 261–70.

_____. "The Tripolitan War: A Reconsideration of the Causes." *Africa; rivista trimestrale di studi e documentazione* Anno, XXVII (N.I., Marzo 1972): 615–26.

Fuchs, Barbara. "Faithless Empires: Pirates, Renegadoes, and the English Nation." *English Literary History* 67, no. 1 (2000): 45–69.

Gawalt, Gerard W. "America and the Barbary Pirates: An International Battle Against an Unconventional Foe." Special Presentations, Thomas Jefferson Papers (online), American Memory Project, Library of Congress (http://memory.loc.gov/ammem/mtjhtml/mtjprece.html).

Grimsted, David. "Early America Confronts Arabian Deys and Nights." *Reviews in American History* 24, no. 2 (1996): 226–31.

Harding, Nicholas B. "North African Piracy, the Hanoverian Carrying Trade, and the British State, 1728–1828." *The Historical Journal* 43, no. 1 (2000): 25–47.

Hitchens, Christopher. "To the Shores Of Tripoli: Muslim foes. Kidnappings. How the Barbary Wars foreshadowed things to come." *Time*, July 5, 2004: 56–61.

Hunt, Livingston. "Bainbridge under the Turkish Flag." *United States Naval Institute Proceedings* 52 (June 1926): 1147–62.

Irwin, Ray. "The Mission of Soliman Mellimelli: Tunisian Ambassador to the United States 1805–1807." *Americana Illustrated* (N.Y.) 26, no. 4 (October 1932): 465–71.

————. "Protégés of the United States and Consequences of the War with Tripoli 1801–1807." *Americana Illustrated* (N.Y.) 29, no. 3 (July 1935): 345–63.

Jewett, Thomas. "Terrorism in Early America: The U.S. Wages War Against the Barbary States to End International Blackmail and Terrorism." *The Early America Review* 4, no. 1 (Winter-Spring 2002) (online: http://www.earlyamerica.com/review/2002_winter_spring/terrorism.htm).

Kortepeter, Carl M. "The United States Encounters the Middle East: The North African Emirates and the U.S. Navy (1783–1830)." *Revue d'Histoire Maghrebine* (Tunisia) 10 (December 1983): 301–13.

Leiby, Richard. "Terrorists by Another Name: The Barbary Pirates." *Washington Post*, October 15, 2001.

Lord, Lewis. "Pirates!: On the Shores of Tripoli, America Becomes a World Power." *U.S. News & World Report*, March 4, 2002: 48–50.

Lydon, James G. "Thomas Jefferson and the Mathurins." *Catholic Historical Review* 49 (1963): 192–202.

Macleod, Julia H. "Jefferson and the Navy: A Defense." *The Huntington Library Quarterly* 7 (February 1945): 153–84.

Magruder, John H. "The Marine Corps Officers' Mameluke Sword." *Marine Corps Gazette* 38, no. 11 (1954) (http://www.geocities.com/Heartland/6350/mameluke.htm).

Martin, Tyrone G. "Trouble on Kaliusa Reef." *Naval History* 17, no. 5 (October 2003): 30–32.

Paine, Lincoln P. "War Is Better Than Tribute." *Naval History* 15, no. 3 (June 2001): 20–25.

Rodgers, Robert S. "Closing Events of the War with Tripoli 1804–1805." *United States Naval Institute Proceedings* 34, no. 3 (September 1908): 889–916.

Ross, Frank E. "The Mission of John Lamb to Algiers, 1785–1786." *Americana* 28 (July 1934): 287–94.

————. "The Mission of Joseph Donaldson, Jr. to Algiers, 1795–97." *Journal of Modern History* 7, no. 4 (1935): 422–33.

Smith, Gaddis. "The U.S. vs. International Terrorists: A Chapter from Our Past." *American Heritage* 28, no. 5 (1977): 37–43.

Wilson, Gary E. "The First American Hostages in Moslem Nations, 1784–1789." *American Neptune* 41 (July 1981): 208–23.

Windler, Christian. "Diplomatic History as a Field for Cultural Analysis: Muslim-Christian Relations in Tunis, 1700–1840." *The Historical Journal* 44 (2001): 79–106.

Wright, L. B., and J. H. Macleod. "Mellimelli." *Virginia Quarterly Review* 20 (1944): 555–65.

_____. "William Eaton's Relations with Aaron Burr." *Mississippi Valley Historical Review* 31 (March 1945): 523–36.

Books

Abun-Nasr, Jamil M. *A History of the Maghrib in the Islamic Period*. Cambridge, U.K.: Cambridge University Press, 1987.

Adams, William H. *The Paris Years of Thomas Jefferson*. New Haven, Conn.: Yale University Press, 1997.

Allen, Gardner W. *Our Navy and the Barbary Corsairs*. Hamden, Conn.: Archon Books, 1965 (1905).

Allison, Robert J. *The Crescent Obscured: The United States and Muslim World, 1776–1815*. Chicago: University of Chicago Press, 1995.

Anderson, Roger C. *Naval Wars in the Levant, 1559–1853*. Princeton, N.J.: Princeton University Press, 1952, pp. 393–426.

Arberry, A. J. *The Koran Interpreted: A Translation*. London: Oxford University Press, 1964.

Baepler, Paul. *White Slaves, African Masters: An Anthology of American Barbary Captivity Narratives*. Chicago: University of Chicago Press, 1999.

Baker, Thomas. *Piracy and Diplomacy in Seventeenth-Century North Africa*. Madison, N.J.: Fairleigh Dickinson University Press, 1989.

Bamford, Paul Walden. *The Barbary Pirates: Victims and the Scourge of Christendom*. James Ford Bell lectures, 0448-2220; no. 10. Minneapolis: The Associates of the James Ford Bell Library, University of Minnesota, 1972.

Barnby, H. G. *The Prisoners of Algiers: An Account of the Forgotten American-Algerian War, 1785–1797.* London: Oxford University Press, 1966.

Bemis, Samuel Flagg. *The Diplomacy of the American Revolution.* New York/London: D. Appleton-Century, 1935.

Bencherif, Osman. *The Image of Algeria in Anglo-American Writings, 1785–1962.* Lanham, Md.: University Press of America, 1997.

Binkley, Wilfred E. *American Political Parties: Their Natural History.* New York: Knopf, 1962.

Boot, Max. *The Savage Wars of Peace: Small Wars and the Rise of American Power.* New York: Basic Books, 2002.

Borden, Morton. *Parties and Politics in the Early Republic, 1789–1815.* New York: Crowell, 1967.

Boyd, Julian P. et al., eds. *The Papers of Thomas Jefferson.* Princeton, N.J.: Princeton University Press, 1955.

Brant, Irving. *James Madison: Secretary of State.* New York: Bobbs-Merrill, 1961.

Braudel, Fernand (trans. Miriam Kochan). *Capitalism and Material Life: 1400–1800.* New York: Harper and Row, 1973.

Braudel, Fernand (trans. Siân Reynolds). *The Mediterranean and the Mediterranean World in the Age of Philip II.* Berkeley: University of California Press, 1995.

Brighton, Ray. *The Checkered Career of Tobias Lear.* Portsmouth, NH: Portsmouth Marine Society, 1985.

Brown, L. Carl. *The Tunisia of Ahmad Bey, 1837–1855.* Princeton, N.J.: Princeton University Press, 1974.

Buhite, Russell D. *Lives at Risk: Hostages and Victims in American Foreign Policy.* Wilmington, Del.: SR Books, 1995.

Carr, Caleb. *The Lessons of Terror.* New York: Random House, 2002.

Carr, James A. *American Foreign Policy during the French Revolution–Napoleonic Period, 1789–1815: A Bibliography.* New York: Garland, 1994.

Case, Josephine Young. *Written in Sand.* Boston: Houghton Mifflin, 1945.

Castor, Henry. *The Tripolitan War, 1801–1805: America Meets the Menace of the Barbary Pirates.* New York: F. Watts, 1971.

Cathcart, James Leander. *The Captives. Eleven Years a Prisoner in Algiers*, compiled by his daughter, J. B. Newkirk. La Porte, Ind.: Herald, 1899.

_____. *The Diplomatic Journal and Letter Book of James Leander Cathcart, 1788–1796*. Worcester, Mass.: American Antiquarian Society, 1955.

Chapelle, Howard I. *The History of the American Sailing Navy: The Ships and Their Development*. New York: W. W. Norton, 1949.

Chidsey, Donald Barr. *The Wars in Barbary: Arab Piracy and the Birth of the United States Navy*. New York: Crown, 1971.

Churchill, Winston S. *A History of the English-Speaking Peoples*, four vols. New York: Barnes & Noble Books, 1993.

Coe, Samuel Gwynn. *The Mission of William Carmichael to Spain*. Baltimore: Johns Hopkins University Press, 1928.

Constable, Olivia Remie. *Iberia, Readings from Christian, Muslim and Jewish Sources*. Philadelphia: University of Pennsylvania Press, 1997.

Cook, Michael. *The Koran: A Very Short Introduction*. London: Oxford University Press, 2000.

Cooper, James Fenimore. *The History of the Navy of the United States of America*; with a new introduction by Edward L. Beach. Annapolis, Md.: Naval Institute Press, 2001.

Cordingly, David. *Under the Black Flag: The Romance and the Reality of Life Among the Pirates*. New York: Random House, 1996.

Crawford, Michael J., and William S. Dudley, eds. *The Early Republic and the Sea: Essays on the Naval and Maritime History of the Early United States*. Washington, D.C.: Brassey's, 2001.

Cunningham Jr., Noble E. *The Jeffersonian Republicans: The Formation of Party Organization, 1789–1801*. Chapel Hill: University of North Carolina Press, 1957.

Currey, E. Hamilton. *Sea Wolves of the Mediterranean: The Grand Period of the Moslem Corsairs*. New York: Dutton, 1910.

Davis, Robert C. *Christian Slaves, Muslim Masters: White Slavery in the Mediterranean, the Barbary Coast and Italy, 1500–1800*. New York: Palgrave Macmillan, 2003.

Dearborn, Henry A. *The Life of William Bainbridge, Esq. of the United States Navy.* Princeton, N.J.: Princeton University Press, 1931.

Dearden, Seton. *A Nest of Corsairs: The Fighting Karamanlis of the Barbary Coast.* London: John Murray, 1976.

de Kay, James T. *A Rage for Glory: The Life of Commodore Stephen Decatur, USN.* New York: Free Press, 2004.

Diouf, Sylviane. *Servants of Allah: African Muslims Enslaved in the Americas.* New York: New York University Press, 1998.

Dupuy, R. Ernest, and William Baumer. *The Little Wars of the United States.* New York: Hawthorn Books, 1968.

Durán, Khalid. *Children of Abraham: An Introduction to Islam for Jews.* New York: Ktav Publishing House, 2001.

Earle, Peter. *Corsairs of Malta and Barbary.* London: Sidgwick & Jackson, 1970.

Edwards, Samuel. *Barbary General: the Life of William H. Eaton.* Englewood Cliffs, N.J.: Prentice Hall, 1968.

Ellis, Joseph. *American Sphinx: The Character of Thomas Jefferson.* New York: Knopf, 1996.

Estes, Worth J. "A Naval Surgeon in the Barbary Wars: Dr. Peter St. Medard on New York, 1802–3." In *New Aspects of Naval History: Selected Papers from the Fifth Naval History Symposium*, ed. Department of History, U.S. Naval Academy. Baltimore: Nautical & Aviation Pub. Co., 1985, pp. 81–92.

Field Jr., James A. *From Gibraltar to the Middle East: America and the Mediterranean World, 1776–1882.* Chicago: Imprint Publications, 1991.

Fielding, Xan. *Corsair Country: The Diary of a Journey Along the Barbary Coast.* London: Travel Book Club, 1959.

Fisher, Allan G., and Humphrey J. Fisher. *Slavery and Muslim Society in Africa: The Institution in Saharan and Sudanic Africa and the Trans-Saharan Trade.* Garden City, N.Y.: Doubleday, 1971.

Fisher, Godfrey. *Barbary Legend: War, Trade, and Piracy in North Africa, 1415–1830.* Oxford, UK: Clarendon Press, 1957.

Folayan, Kola. *Tripoli During the Reign of Yusuf Pasha Qaramanli.* Ile-Ife, Nigeria: University of Ife Press, 1979.

Forester, C. S. *The Barbary Pirates.* New York: Random House, 1953.

Fowler, Jr., William M. *Jack Tars and Commodores: The American Navy, 1783–1815*. Boston: Houghton Mifflin, 1984.

Franklin, Benjamin. *The Autobiography of Benjamin Franklin*. Minneola, N.Y.: Dover, 1996.

Fuchs, Barbara. *Mimesis and Empire: The New World, Islam, and European Identities*. New York: Cambridge University Press, 2001.

Furlonge, Sir Geoffrey W. *The Lands of Barbary*. London: John Murray, 1966.

Gallagher, Charles F. *The United States and North Africa*. Cambridge, Mass.: Harvard University Press, 1963.

Gellner, Ernest. *Saints of the Atlas*. Chicago: University of Chicago Press, 1969.

Gibb, Sir H. A. R., and Harold Bowen. *Islamic Society and the West: A Study of the Impact of Western Civilization on Modern Moslem Culture in the Near East*. London: Oxford University Press, 1950.

Goldberg, Isaac. *Major Noah: American-Jewish Pioneer*. Philadelphia: The Jewish Publication Society of America, 1944 (1936).

Goldsborough, Charles W. *The U.S. Naval Chronicle*. Washington, D.C.: J. Wilson, 1824.

Grant, Bruce. *Isaac Hull, Captain of Old Ironsides: The Life and Fighting Times of Isaac Hull and the U.S. Frigate Constitution*. Chicago: Pellegrini and Cudahy, 1947.

Guttridge, Leonard F., and Jay D. Smith. *The Commodore: The U.S. Navy in the Age of Sail*. New York: Harper and Row, 1969.

Hall, Luella J. *The United States and Morocco: 1776–1956*. Metuchen, N.J.: Scarecrow Press, 1971.

Hallett, Robin. *Africa to 1785: A Modern History*. Ann Arbor: University of Michigan Press, 1970.

Hamlin, Benjamin. *Micah Leads His Marines: The Yankee Invasion of Tripoli in the Year 1805*. Dedham, Mass.: Transcript Press, 1937.

Hebb, David Delison. *Piracy and the English Government, 1616–1642*. Aldershot, UK: Scholar Press, 1994.

Heers, Jacques (trans. Jonathan North). *The Barbary Corsairs: Warfare in the Mediterranean, 1480–1580*. London: Greenhill Books, 2003.

Hess, Andrew C. *The Forgotten Frontier: A History of the Sixteenth-Century Ibero-African Century*. Chicago: University of Chicago Press, 1978.

Hirschberg, H. Z. *A History of the Jews in North Africa, from the Ottoman Conquests to the Present Time*, vol. II. Leiden, Netherlands: Brill, 1981.

Hofstadter, Richard. *The Idea of a Party System: The Rise of Legitimate Opposition in the United States, 1780–1840*. Berkeley: University of California Press, 1969.

Humphreys, Frank Landon. *Life and Times of David Humphreys. Soldier-Statesman-Poet*. New York: G. P. Putnam's Sons, 1917.

Hunwick, John. "Islamic Law and Polemics over Race and Slavery in North and West Africa (16th–19th Century)." In Shaun E. Marmon, ed., *Slavery in the Islamic Middle East*. Princeton, N.J.: Markus Wener Publishers, 1999.

Irving, Anthony. *Decatur*. New York: Charles Scribner's Sons, 1931.

Irwin, Ray W. *The Diplomatic Relations of the United States with the Barbary Powers, 1776–1816*. Chapel Hill: University of North Carolina Press, 1931.

Johnston, Sir Harry H. *A History of the Colonization of Africa by Alien Races*. London: Frank Cass Publishers, 1981 (1930).

Julien, Charles-André (trans. John Petrie). *History of North Africa*. London, Routledge & Kegan Paul, 1970.

Kaplan, Lawrence S. *Thomas Jefferson: Westward the Course of Empire*. Wilmington, Del.: Scholarly Resources Books Inc., 1999.

Khadduri, Majid. *War and Peace in the Law of Islam*. New York: AMS Press, 1979.

King, Charles R., ed. *The Life and Correspondence of Rufus King*. New York: G. P. Putnam's Sons, 1894.

Kitzen, Michael L. S. *Tripoli and the United States at War: A History of American Relations with the Barbary States, 1785–1805*. Jefferson, N.C.: McFarland & Company, 1993.

Koedel, Barbara E. *Glory, at Last!: A Narrative of the Naval Career of Master Commandant Richard Somers, 1778–1804*. Somers Point, N.J.: Atlantic County Historical Society, 1993.

Kurtz, Stephen G. *The Presidency of John Adams.* Philadelphia: University of Pennsylvania Press, 1957.

Lane-Poole, Stanley. *The Story of the Barbary Corsairs.* New York: G. P. Putnam's Sons, 1902.

Laroui, Abdallah (trans. Ralph Manheim). *The History of the Maghrib: An Interpretive Essay.* Princeton, N.J.: Princeton University Press, 1977.

Lehman, John F. *Making War: The 200-Year-Old Battle Between the President and Congress over How America Goes to War.* New York: Charles Scribner's Sons, 1992.

_____. *On Seas of Glory: The Heroic Men, Great Ships, and Epic Battles of the American Navy.* New York: Free Press, 2001.

Lewis, Bernard. *Cultures in Conflict: Christians, Muslims, and Jews in the Age of Discovery.* Oxford, UK: Oxford University Press, 1995.

_____. *From Babel to Dragomans: Interpreting the Middle East.* Oxford, UK: Oxford University Press, 2004.

_____. *The Middle East: A Brief History of the Last 2,000 Years.* New York: Simon & Schuster, 1995.

_____. *The Political Language of Islam.* Chicago: University of Chicago Press, 1991.

_____. *Race and Slavery in the Middle East.* Oxford, UK: Oxford University Press, 1990.

Lewis, Charles. *The Romantic Decatur.* Philadelphia: University of Pennsylvania Press, 1937.

Lloyd, Christopher. *English Corsairs on the Barbary Coast.* London: Collins, 1981.

Long, David F. *Ready to Hazard: A Biography of Commodore William Bainbridge, 1774–1833.* Hanover, N.H.: University Press of New England, 1981.

Maalouf, Amin (trans. Jon Rothschild). *The Crusades Through Arab Eyes.* New York: Shocken Books, 1985.

Mackesy, Piers. *The War in the Mediterranean, 1803–1810.* Westport, Conn.: Greenwood Press, 1981.

Maclay, Edgar S., ed. *Journal of William Maclay, United States Senator from Pennsylvania, 1789–1791.* New York: D. A. Appleton and Company, 1890.

Mahan, Alfred Thayer. *Sea Power in Its Relations to the War of 1812*. London: Sampson, Low, Marston & Co., Ltd., 1905.

Mariner's Museum. *Aak to Zumbra, a Dictionary of the World's Watercraft*. Newport News, Va., The Mariner's Museum, 2000.

Martin, Tyrone G. *A Most Fortunate Ship: A Narrative History of "Old Ironsides."* Annapolis, Md.: Naval Institute Press, 2003.

_____. *"USS Constitution, 'Old Ironsides,'"* a collector's edition (pamphlet) from the editors of *Naval History Magazine*. Annapolis, Md.: Naval Institute Press, n.d.

Matar, Nabil. *Turks, Moors and Englishmen in the Age of Discovery*. New York: Columbia University Press, 1999.

McCullough, David. *John Adams*. New York: Touchstone, 2002.

McKee, Christopher. *A Gentlemanly and Honorable Profession*. Annapolis, Md.: Naval Institute Press, 1991.

_____. *Edward Preble, a Naval Biography 1761–1807*. Annapolis, Md.: Naval Institute Press, 1972.

Miller, Nathan. *Broadsides: The Age of Fighting Sail, 1775–1815*. New York: John Wiley, 2000.

Mitchell, David. *Pirates*. New York: Dial, 1976.

Moalla, Asma. *The Regency of Tunis and the Ottoman Porte, 1777–1814*. London: RoutledgeCurzon, 2004.

Molotosky, Irvin. *The Flag, the Poet and the Song: The Story of the Star-Spangled Banner*. New York: Dutton, 2001.

Morgan, Edmund S. *Benjamin Franklin*. New Haven, Conn.: Yale University Press, 2002.

Moorehead, Alan. *The Blue Nile*. New York: Perennial, 2000.

_____. *The White Nile*. New York: Perennial, 2000.

Nash Jr., Howard P. *The Forgotten Wars: The Role of the U.S. Navy in the Quasi-War with France and the Barbary Wars, 1798–1805*. South Brunswick, N.J.: A. S. Barnes, 1968.

Nickerson, Jane Soames. *A Short History of North Africa, from Pre-Roman Times to the Present: Libya, Tunisia, Algeria, Morocco*. New York: Biblo and Tannen, 1968 (1961).

Panzac, Daniel. *The Barbary Corsairs: The End of a Legend, 1800–1820*. Leiden-Boston: Brill, 2004.

Parker, Richard B. *Uncle Sam in Barbary: A Diplomatic History*. Gainesville, Fla.: University of Florida Press, 2004.

Paullin, Charles Oscar. *Commodore John Rodgers: Captain, Commodore, and Senior Officer of the American Navy, 1773–1838, a Biography.* Annapolis, Md.: U.S. Naval Institute, 1967 (1910).

_____. *Diplomatic Negotiations of American Naval Officers 1778–1883.* Baltimore: Johns Hopkins University Press, 1912.

Perkins, Roger. *Gunfire in Barbary: Admiral Lord Exmouth's Battle with the Corsairs of Algiers in 1816.* Havant, Hampshire, UK: Kenneth Mason, 1982.

Peters, Rudolph. *Islam and Colonialism: the Doctrine of Jihad in Modern History.* New York: Mouton, 1979.

_____. *Jihad in Classical and Modern Islam: A Reader.* Princeton, N.J.: Markus Wiener, 1996.

Peterson, Harold L. *The American Sword, 1775–1945.* Mineola, N.Y.: Dover, 2003.

Playfair, Sir Robert Lambert. *The Scourge of Christendom: Annals of British Relations with Algiers Prior to the French Conquest.* New York: Books for Libraries Press, 1972 (1884).

Prentiss, Charles. *The Life of the late Gen. William Eaton: several years an officer in the United States' army, consul at the regency of Tunis on the coast of Barbary, and commander of the Christian and other forces that marched from Egypt through the Desert of Barca, in 1805 principally collected from his correspondence and other manuscripts.* (Brookfield, Mass.: Printed by E. Merriam, 1813) Ann Arbor, Mich.: Books-on-Demand, University of Michigan, 2002.

Quataert, Donald. *The Ottoman Empire, 1700–1922.* Cambridge, UK: Cambridge University Press, 2000.

Rediker, Marcus. *Between the Devil and the Deep Blue Sea: Merchant Seamen, Pirates and the Anglo-American Maritime World, 1700–1750.* Cambridge, UK: Cambridge University Press, 1987.

Rennell Rodd, Francis. *General William Eaton: The Failure of an Idea.* London: Routledge, 1932.

Shaban, Fuad. *Islam and Arabs in Early American Thought: The Roots of Orientalism in America.* Durham, N.C.: Acorn Press, 1991.

Silverburg, Sanford R., and Bernard Reich. *U.S. Foreign Relations with the Middle East and North Africa: A Bibliography and Supplement.* Lanham, Md.: Scarecrow Press, 1999.

Simon, Jeffrey D. *The Terrorist Trap: America's Experience with Terrorism*. Bloomington: Indiana University Press, 2001.

Smelser, Marshall. *The Congress Founds the Navy*. Westport, Conn.: Greenwood Press, 1973.

Southworth, John Van Duyn. *Age of Sails: War at Sea*. New York: Twayne Publishers, 1968.

Spencer, William. *Algiers in the Age of the Corsairs*. Norman: University of Oklahoma Press, 1976.

Sundberg, Trudy J., and John K. Gott. *Valiant Virginian: Story of Presley Neville O'Bannon, 1776–1850, First Lieutenant U.S. Marine Corps, 1801–1807*. Bowie, Md.: Heritage Books, 1994.

Symonds, Craig L. *Navalists and Antinavalists: The Naval Policy Debate in the United States, 1785–1827*. Newark, N.J.: University of Delaware Press, 1980.

Thompson, Ann. *Barbary and Enlightenment: European attitudes towards the Maghreb in the 18th century*. Leiden/New York: Brill, 1987.

Todd, Charles B. *Life and letters of Joel Barlow, LL.D.: Poet, Statesman, Philosopher*. New York: Da Capo Press, 1970.

Tucker, Glenn. *Dawn Like Thunder: The Barbary Wars and the Birth of the U.S. Navy*. Indianapolis and New York: Bobbs-Merrill, 1963.

Van Alstyne, Richard W. *American Diplomacy in Action: A Series of Case Studies*. Stanford, Calif.: Stanford University Press, 1944, pp. 497–503.

_____. *American Diplomacy in Action*, rev. ed. Gloucester, Mass.: P. Smith, 1968 (1947).

Vivian, Herbert. *Tunisia and the Modern Barbary Pirates*. New York: Longmans, Green & Co., 1899.

Walters, Ray. *Albert Gallatin: Jeffersonian Financier and Diplomat*. New York: Macmillan, 1957.

Ward, Ralph T. *Pirates in History*. Baltimore: York Press, 1974.

Wheelan, Joseph. *Jefferson's War: America's First War on Terror, 1801–1805*. New York: Carroll & Graff, 2003.

Whipple, A. B. C. *To the Shores of Tripoli: The Birth of the U.S. Navy and Marines*. New York: Naval Institute Press, 2001.

Wilson, Peter Lamborn (a.k.a. Hakim Bey). *Pirate Utopias: Moorish Corsairs & European Renagadoes*. New York: Autonomedia, 1995.

Wolfe, John B. *The Barbary Coast: Algiers Under the Turks 1500–1830*. New York: W. W. Norton & Co., 1979.

Woodress, James. *A Yankee's Odyssey: The Life of Joel Barlow*. Philadelphia: Lippincott, 1958.

Wright, Louis B., and Julia H. McLeod. *The First Americans in North Africa: William Eaton's Struggle for a Vigorous Policy Against the Barbary Pirates: 1799–1805*. Princeton, N.J.: Princeton University Press, 1945.

Young, James Sterling. *The Washington Community, 1800–1828*. New York: Harcourt Brace Jovanovich, 1966.

Photo Credits

Photos courtesy of the following: Archives Nationales, Republic of Tunis, p. 133; *The Captives*, compiled by Jane B. (Cathcart) Newkirk, 1899, p. 141 (bottom); Henry E. Huntington Library and Art Gallery, p. 135 (bottom); Library of Congress, pp. 141 (top), 142 (bottom), 144; Mariner's Museum, p. 138 (bottom); Naval Historical Center, pp. 134, 135 (top), 136, 137, 138 (top), 139, 140, 142 (top), 143 (top and middle); Naval Historical Foundation, p. 143 (bottom).

Index

Page numbers in *italics* refer to illustrations.